ADVANCE PRAISE

"This is an exciting and original book that presents a clear overview of the Barcelona Disputation of 1263. Although the Disputation has been studied repeatedly from a variety of angles, this book succeeds in providing a fresh and insightful view of the event by combining a summary of the known facts with a richly illustrated graphic dramatization. This visual apparatus makes the historical background come alive for students and readers, and the pedagogic apparatus of final discussion questions and suggestions makes this tool useful for classroom use as well as individual study. The translations of original sources are also highly useful. This presentation and format is wholly unique and as a result, this book makes an important new contribution to the study of the Disputation and to thirteenth-century Christian–Jewish interaction. It is clearly the work of an author in full command of the historical material who is also able to envision and implement a wholly original way to present it to students."

RYAN SZPIECH *University of Michigan*

"As a hybrid graphic history and academic work, Nina Caputo's *Debating Truth* not only offers an attractive and engaging book for classroom use but opens up welcome perspectives on the Barcelona Disputation. The graphic form forces the reader to contemplate the many gaps left in Nahmanides' account and in the historical record more generally."

JONATHAN DECTER *Brandeis University*

"The Barcelona Disputation is an ideal topic for Oxford's new series of graphic histories. A self-contained drama with important lessons and implications for broader society, it spotlights much of what was best and worst in medieval life, in presenting this episode in the life of Nahmanides. Nina Caputo, today's leading scholar of the great rabbi's life and work, is the perfect guide to the events of that dramatic confrontation in Barcelona."

CLIFFORD BACKMAN *Boston University*

DEBATING TRUTH

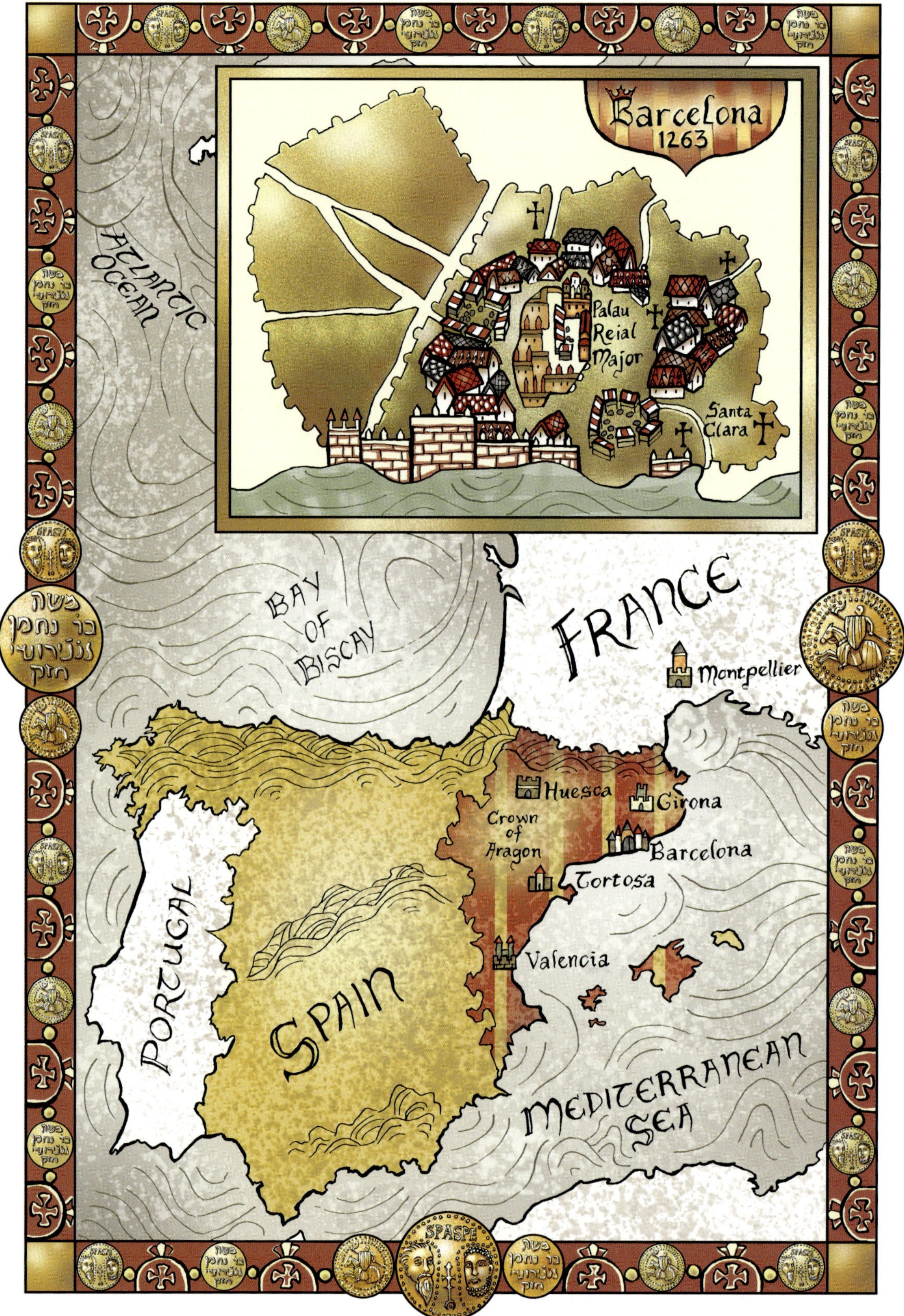
Barcelona
1263
Palau
Reial
Major
Santa
Clara
Atlantic
Ocean
Bay
of
Biscay
France
Montpellier
Huesca
Girona
Crown
of
Aragon
Barcelona
Tortosa
Valencia
Portugal
Spain
Mediterranean
Sea
SPASPE

DEBATING TRUTH

THE BARCELONA DISPUTATION OF 1263

A GRAPHIC HISTORY

NINA CAPUTO

LIZ CLARKE

New York Oxford
OXFORD UNIVERSITY PRESS

Oxford University Press is a department of the University of Oxford. It furthers the University's objective of excellence in research, scholarship, and education by publishing worldwide. Oxford is a registered trade mark of Oxford University Press in the UK and certain other countries.

Published in the United States of America by Oxford University Press
198 Madison Avenue, New York, NY 10016, United States of America.

For titles covered by Section 112 of the US Higher Education Opportunity Act, please visit www.oup.com/us/he for the latest information about pricing and alternate formats.

Library of Congress Cataloging-in-Publication Data

Names: Caputo, Nina, 1966- author. | Clarke, Liz, author.
Title: Debating truth : the Barcelona disputation of 1263 : a graphic history / Nina Caputo, Liz Clarke.
Description: First edition. | New York : Oxford University Press, [2016] | Includes bibliographical references.
Identifiers: LCCN 2016003454 | ISBN 9780190226367
Subjects: LCSH: Barcelona Disputation, Barcelona, Spain, 1263. | Na?hmanides, approximately 1195-approximately 1270. ?Vikua?h ha-Ramban. | Judaism—History—Medieval and early modern period, 425-1789. | Christianity and other religions—Judaism. | Judaism—Relations—Christianity. | Jews—Spain—History. | Spain—Ethnic relations.
Classification: LCC BM590 .C37 2016 | DDC 296.3/96—dc23
LC record available at http://lccn.loc.gov/2016003454

9 8 7 6 5 4 3 2 1

Printed by R.R. Donnelley, United States of America

CONTENTS

MAPS AND FIGURES

MAPS

FIGURES

PREFACE

In the summer of 1263, Nahmanides (Rabbi Moses ben Nahman, ca. 1195–1270), who was among the leading rabbis of his time, traveled from his home in Girona to Barcelona at the behest of King James I of Aragon (1213–1276) to debate with a Dominican friar named Paul about specific claims concerning the Messiah in Judaism and Christianity. Friar Paul had converted from Judaism to Christianity as an adult, so he brought with him some knowledge of rabbinic texts, which he used to challenge the faith of Jews in Provence and northern Spain. His strategy was entirely innovative. Using passages from the Talmud, a foundation of Jewish life in the diaspora, he claimed that Jewish leaders recognized that Jesus was the Messiah. The Barcelona disputation was an officially sanctioned opportunity for Friar Paul to perform this kind of argument. It was conducted in a public forum at the royal palace before an audience of Jewish and Christian dignitaries. The two disputants, each thoroughly convinced of the indisputable truth of his own religious faith and theological interpretations, argued for their positions before a panel of judges headed by James I himself.

The stakes for all parties were high. Though the details of the arguments articulated during this disputation were surely obscure and esoteric to most ordinary Jews and Christians of the day, large crowds from both communities attended to witness the spectacle. At a practical level, any policy decisions based on the outcome of the debate could have had profound real-life consequences for everyday Jewish–Christian relations. The friars expected that their argument—that the rabbis of the Talmud believed that Jesus was the Messiah—would render Nahmanides and the Jewish community defenseless against claims of Christian truth. Conversion would thus be a likely result. Arguing in this forum opened the remote possibility that, if the king were convinced by the friars' arguments, he could issue a royal ordinance compelling the Jews to convert or submit to extensive Christian oversight.

For Nahmanides' part, a successful defense of Judaism and of a Jewish interpretation of the Talmud at any cost was paramount. His posture in the disputation was defensive. But it is important not to forget that Nahmanides was a Jew performing as a Jewish theologian in the restricted setting of a Christian royal court, speaking the language of the dominant society and debating matters of theology. Though he argued from a defensive position, the king and the friars permitted him—indeed, expected him—to defend his faith vigorously.

Two medieval accounts of the Barcelona disputation remain today. The first is an anonymous précis written in Latin and preserved in two copies in the royal archives; the second is a much longer firsthand account written in Hebrew by Nahmanides. Not surprisingly, the two disputation accounts agree on the substance of the debate but diverge when it comes to the nature of the exchange. The Latin version presents Nahmanides as a mute and ineffectual opponent who was unprepared and unable to respond to Friar Paul's thoroughly innovative polemical use of rabbinic sources as proof. The Hebrew account, on the other hand, is a highly literary, dramatic, and detailed text written in dialogue form that professes to reproduce the debate accurately and faithfully as it unfolded. In this version, the friars appear incompetent.

The immediate outcome of the disputation was relatively anticlimactic: Nahmanides returned home to Girona and resumed his life as usual. And there is no evidence that Friar Paul's arguments moved other members of the Jewish community to embrace Christianity. In the weeks immediately following the disputation, King James authorized the Dominicans to compel Jews to attend sermons based on the argument Friar Paul advanced during the disputation. However, the king quickly emended his earlier order, making Jewish attendance voluntary. The disputation precipitated an active interest in Jewish texts and learning on the part of the Crown and the church.

Nahmanides' disputation account became the occasion for controversy in 1265. The same Dominicans who orchestrated the disputation in Barcelona brought a complaint against Nahmanides, charging that he falsified the truth and blasphemed in a written account of the disputation that he had given to the bishop of Girona. According to the Christian records, Nahmanides claimed he wrote his account at the behest of the bishop of Girona (it is unlikely that the version he delivered to the bishop was written in Hebrew, but no manuscript copies of the Catalan document are known to survive). An ecclesiastical tribunal assembled at the instigation of the friars found Nahmanides guilty of blasphemy. As punishment, King James declared that Nahmanides should be exiled from the Crown of Aragon for two years. Hoping for a more final judgment, however, the friars rejected this solution and turned to Pope Clement IV for support. Clement implored the king to levy a more stringent punishment, but no final order of exile remains in the royal archive. It is thus quite possible that the king never enforced the exile. Nevertheless, we know that Nahmanides departed for the Holy Land some time thereafter, where he joined a small but elite cohort of European rabbis who founded rabbinic academies there.

The disputation certainly had clear consequences for Nahmanides, but what is the broader significance of this event? The Barcelona disputation appears on many syllabuses for undergraduate "Jewish History" or "Introduction to Judaism" courses. Typically it serves to demonstrate the slow but steady erosion of Jewish privileges and autonomy leading to the mass attacks on Jewish communities in 1391 and the expulsion of Jews from Spain in the late fifteenth century. Therefore, it tracks as an important *Jewish* event, but it has not been presented as an event that sheds light on medieval Aragonese society and culture as a whole. King James I committed significant energies to expanding his political dominion into the Muslim-held territories of al-Andalus and governing (and especially taxing) conquered populations. He also coordinated efforts to expand Aragonese trade across the Mediterranean and within Europe, maintaining relatively smooth relations with the papacy and the lay clergy, and supporting newly founded mendicant orders. As a rule, he protected Jewish and Muslim religious autonomy as long as it did not interfere with royal ordinance or taxation. It is in this broad political and religious context that this graphic history places the Barcelona disputation.

Disputation, a process of proving arguments through sustained and rational debate, had a significant impact in many areas of medieval life. The emerging professional classes of theologians, lawyers, physicians, record keepers, and bureaucratic technocrats who were trained in the relatively recently established universities earned their credentials through verbal and/or written disputation. In its most rarified form, among theologians and philosophers, scholasticism produced a class of intellectual elites who claimed possession both of the truth and of the only trustworthy means of demonstrating the truth; an inability to master or mobilize these skills, they believed, reflected a moral deficiency. This mode of disciplined thinking and argumentation also filtered into other layers of European society. The church charged members of the mendicant orders of Dominican and Franciscan friars with a grass-roots program meant to eradicate heresy, most especially the Albigensian heresy that gained strength in the late-twelfth and early-thirteenth centuries around Provence. Mendicant friars actively promoted a pure form of Christian orthodoxy by preaching to laypeople in marketplaces throughout Christendom. Trained in scholastic methodology, many friars inflected their sermons with the assumption that logical argument necessarily led to correct and irrefutable truths.

Christian–Jewish theological disputation literature dates back to the second century, but the turn to rational argument as the preferred basis for demonstrating truth added a new urgency and immediacy to the debate. Beginning at the end of the eleventh century, examples of rational *contra judaeos* disputation literature proliferated. There is good reason to believe that Jews and Christians discussed and debated theological differences on an individual basis. However, public disputations in which kings played an instrumental role and leaders from the Jewish community were obliged to defend Jewish texts and practices stand out as a departure from the relatively nonconfrontational literary genre. The first of these disputations took place in Paris in 1240 (as a direct consequence of this event, wagon-loads of Talmud volumes were publicly incinerated in 1242); the Barcelona disputation was the second, and a third was held in Paris in 1271. A final disputation was staged in Tortosa over the course of several months from 1413 to 1414. While the outcomes and consequences varied from one disputation to the next, only the Tortosa disputation completely and irreparably devastated the Jewish communities involved.

By the thirteenth century, Judaism and Jews played only a minor political, cultural, military, and social role in Western Christian society, both locally and globally. Why, then, did the church, when it was arguably at the height of its political power, concern itself with engaging Jews and Judaism in a theological debate? The fact that Christianity developed on the scriptural foundation of Judaism made the fact of theologically engaged Jews an issue of concern. In an early (fifth century) consideration of this problem, Augustine of Hippo provided the theological and legal justification for the preservation and tolerance of active Jewish communities within Christendom. As they were perceived to be in possession of the original covenant and witnesses to the arrival of Jesus Christ, he argued, Jews should be preserved in a humiliated state as a living testament to the fact that Christianity has displaced Judaism and the Jews' outdated rituals and interpretation of scripture. In contrast, while Islam and Muslims represented a formidable military and political adversary, the relatively recent birth of Islam and its distinctive sacred scripture made it theologically less threatening. The church chose to combat Islam with military rather than intellectual and theological weapons, and there is no evidence that Christians staged comparable public disputations with Muslims.[1]

The thirteenth century marked a watershed in the way Christian elites managed and imagined the composition of "Christendom," or the world in which Christianity reigned both politically and theologically.

1 For a discussion of thirteenth-century Franciscan and Dominican missionizing campaigns among Muslims, see J. V. Tolan, *Saracens: Islam in the Medieval European Imagination* (New York: Columbia University Press, 2002), 214–55, especially 234–42.

Initial Crusade victories at the end of the eleventh century helped solidify a notion that Christendom by all rights extended beyond the territories of immediate papal authority to include areas that properly *should* be in the orbit of Christian authority—most especially Jerusalem and al-Andalus, Muslim-controlled Iberia. Pope Urban II's sermon at the Council of Clermont in 1095 signaled, both rhetorically and practically, the start of an active battle involving all Christians to protect and expand Christianization. The famous military campaigns against Muslims in Iberia and Jerusalem found an intellectual counterpart on the continent in preaching campaigns and the composition of theological and polemical works aimed at defining and protecting orthodoxy while identifying, labeling, and destroying heresy of all sorts—including other religions.

The graphic history that follows tells the story of the Barcelona disputation from Nahmanides' perspective. Because his account of the disputation sparked the controversy that followed, most dialogue presented here follows a very close paraphrase of the Hebrew version available to us today. Nahmanides' account concludes at the end of the disputation. We know from other sources that the Jewish communities of the Crown of Aragon and Nahmanides individually faced additional consequences following this theological debate. The much shorter representation of the disputation from the perspective of the friars is a close paraphrase of the Latin document that records this event. We turn to a body of royal and papal documents to round out the conclusion of this story.

A note on names and sources: Because nearly all of the figures who appear in this book were and are known by multiple names depending on which source one is reading, when it was written, and in which language, I have Anglicized the personal names in the book. Thus, Jaime appears as James, Pere as Peter, Moshe as Moses, etc. Unless otherwise noted, all biblical references use the numbering of chapters and verses standard to the Hebrew Bible, JPS edition and all citations of the Talmud refer to the Babylonian Talmud.

ACKNOWLEDGMENTS

The idea to write this book came to me while I was on fellowship at the Oxford Centre for Hebrew and Jewish Studies, when my colleague Ron Schechter produced an advance copy of his graphic history, *Mendoza the Jew*. Inspired by the myriad possibilities available in the genre, I showered him with questions about the publication process, his collaboration with the artist, and his editorial and organizational decisions. Ron offered to put me in touch with Charles Cavaliere, his editor at Oxford University Press, and the creative process began unfolding very quickly. I owe an enormous debt of gratitude to many, many people for helping me and encouraging me in the production of this book. First to all of my colleagues in the Oxford Seminar in Advanced Jewish Studies, "On the Word of a Jew": Marco DiGiulio, Todd Endelman, Stefanie Fischer, Rachel Furst, Mitch Hart, Sara Lipton, David Rechter, Ron Schechter, and Josh Teplitsky. The intellectual energy and generosity that infused our meetings and off-hours discussions nurtured this project as well as others that are still in the works. (And the environs of Yarnton Manor and Oxford didn't hurt either.)

In social and more formal discussion, my colleagues and friends Sean Adams, Jeff Adler, Gil Anidjar, Juliana Barr, Michelle Campos, Bonnie Effros, Peter Gordon, Jessica Harland-Jacobs, Robert Kawashima, Dragan Kujundzic, Howard Louthan, Jon Sensbach, Andrea Sterk, Lori Weintrob, Brigitte Weltman-Aron, and Luise White all provided unflagging encouragement, for which I am very appreciative. Several students were also instrumental in helping with this project. Danielle Reid and Sarah Harms, in different ways, helped me learn to read rather than look at comics and graphic novels, which made it possible for me to recognize the potential of a graphic history. Luc Houle read through the essays and offered very astute and helpful suggestions. I'm also grateful to Rebecca Devlin, Alana Lord, Ralph Patrello, and Andrew Welton, who organized the 2015 Vagantes conference at UF, for inviting me to give a keynote lecture on this project. Writing that paper was incredibly useful in helping me work through central methodological and historiographic issues, as were the comments and questions from participants in the conference.

My colleague Jeff Needell was kind enough to offer characteristically sharp and thoughtful comments on the graphic and an early draft of the essays. Jennifer Rea, author of another graphic history in this series, shared pointers for pacing and structuring the narrative.

I feel incredibly lucky that Charles Cavaliere was the editor to whom I was directed. There is no question that an editor who can entertain the potential of a graphic history based on a medieval theological debate is a rare animal indeed. He was amazingly helpful, patient, and supportive throughout. And I'm also very thankful that Charles introduced me to Liz Clarke, who has illustrated all of the graphic histories in the Oxford series. Liz did a magnificent job. She created the perfect atmosphere and mood in her drawings. Throughout her creative work she always asked the right questions and each of her recommendations was inspired. In addition, Anna Lankina, Kat Klos, and Justin Mansfield were kind enough to provide their expert help in my translation of the letter from Pope Clement IV to King James I, and Jonathan Gnoza corrected and refined my translations of other Latin sources. Julieta Cardenas and Marianne Paul at OUP expertly shepherded this project through production. The reviewers of the proposal—Thomas Barton, University of San Diego; Leigh Ann Craig, Virginia Commonwealth University; Jennifer Kolpacoff Deane, University of Minnesota, Morris; Steven Epstein, University of Kansas; Moira Fitzgibbons, Marist College; Laura S. Lieber, Duke University; Phil Lieberman, Vanderbilt University; Richard Tristano, St. Mary's University of Minnesota; and one anonymous reviewer—posed challenging and important questions that proved instrumental as Liz and I crafted the volume. Jonathan Decter, Ryan Szpiech, and Clifford Backman reviewed the manuscript for the press (and were generous enough to reveal their identities and share their marginal notes with me). I could not have asked for better or more suitable readers. Their comments and suggestions were enormously helpful and this book is certainly better as a result.

My thanks to Kara and Adam, and Ivon and Deborah, for what seem to be less frequent but richer times together. Finally, and again, thanks to Mitch for everything, and more.

DEBATING TRUTH

PART I
THE GRAPHIC HISTORY

CHAPTER 1

"OUR LORD KING ORDERED ME TO DEBATE FRIAR PAUL . . ."

IN 1267, NAHMANIDES
(RABBI MOSES BEN NAHMAN, 1195-1270)
ARRIVED IN ACRE
IN THE LATIN KINGDOM OF JERUSALEM.
AMONG THE MOST IMPORTANT RABBIS OF HIS TIME, NAHMANIDES' BIBLICAL COMMENTARIES CIRCULATED WIDELY AND RABBIS FROM AROUND THE JEWISH WORLD CONSULTED HIM FOR INTERPRETATIONS OF JEWISH LAW. HE WAS ALSO A RESPECTED LEADER WHO INTERMEDIATED BETWEEN THE JEWISH COMMUNITY AND KING JAMES I, THE CONQUEROR OF ARAGON.
AS THE PORT OF ACRE CAME INTO VIEW, HE REFLECTED UPON EVENTS IN THE RECENT PAST AND THE CIRCUMSTANCES THAT COMPLETELY ALTERED HIS LIFE.
Barcelona
MEDITERRANEAN SEA
Acre
our lord the king ordered me to debate with Friar
IN JULY 1263 NAHMANIDES HAD TRAVELED TO THE **PALAU REIAL MAJOR** IN BARCELONA TO PARTICIPATE IN A PUBLIC THEOLOGICAL DEBATE WITH FRIAR PAUL CHRISTIANI, A JEWISH CONVERT TO CHRISTIANITY. SOME TIME AFTER HE RETURNED HOME AND RESUMED HIS NORMAL ACTIVITIES, THE BISHOP OF GIRONA ASKED HIM TO COMPILE A DOCUMENT RECOUNTING HIS RECOLLECTION OF THE DEBATE.

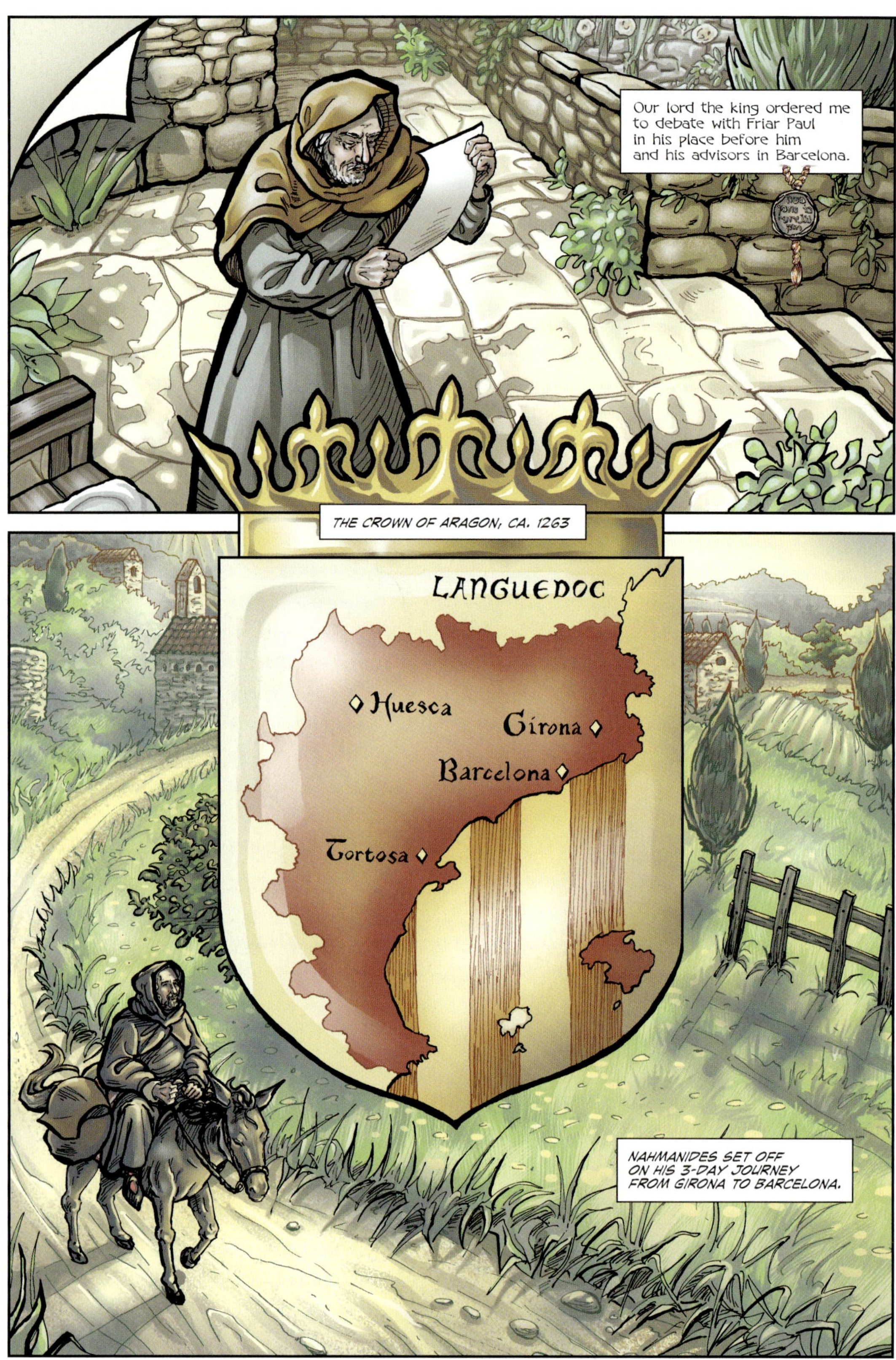
Our lord the king ordered me to debate with Friar Paul in his place before him and his advisors in Barcelona.
THE CROWN OF ARAGON, CA. 1263
LANGUEDOC
Huesca
Girona
Barcelona
Tortosa
NAHMANIDES SET OFF ON HIS 3-DAY JOURNEY FROM GIRONA TO BARCELONA.

BARCELONA

THE PALAU REIAL MAJOR.
KING JAMES I, THE CONQUEROR OF ARAGON, REIGNED FROM 1213, WHEN HE TOOK THE THRONE AT AGE 5, UNTIL JULY 1276, WHEN HE DIED IN VALENCIA FROM A BATTLE WOUND.
FRIAR PAUL CONVERTED TO CHRISTIANITY AND JOINED THE DOMINICAN ORDER IN THE 1230S.
RAMON DE PEÑAFORTE (1186-1275) SERVED AS ARCHBISHOP OF TARRAGONA AND LATER AS GENERAL OF THE DOMINICAN ORDER.

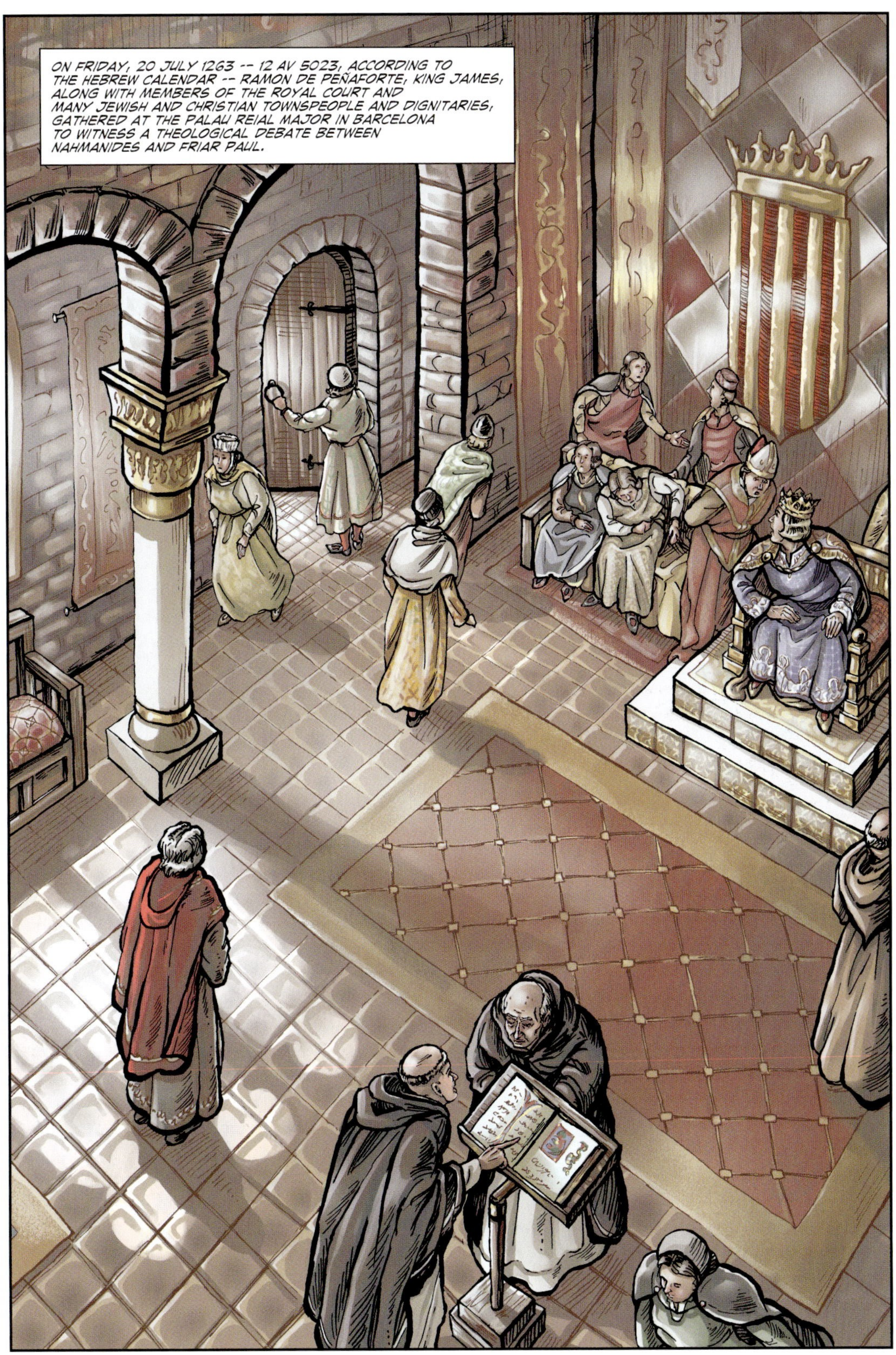
ON FRIDAY, 20 JULY 1263 -- 12 AV 5023, ACCORDING TO THE HEBREW CALENDAR -- RAMON DE PEÑAFORTE, KING JAMES, ALONG WITH MEMBERS OF THE ROYAL COURT AND MANY JEWISH AND CHRISTIAN TOWNSPEOPLE AND DIGNITARIES, GATHERED AT THE PALAU REIAL MAJOR IN BARCELONA TO WITNESS A THEOLOGICAL DEBATE BETWEEN NAHMANIDES AND FRIAR PAUL.

I will do
as you command,
my lord king, if you give me
permission to speak
as I wish.
I request
the permission of the king
and of Friar Ramon de Peñaforte
and his associates
who are here.

Only if
you do not speak
contemptuously.

I do not want to
subject myself to
your judgment on this;
I must speak as I please
during the disputation
just as you may say
what you wish.
As for me,
I have sufficient wisdom
to speak discreetly.
But I must speak
as I wish.

Disputations
between the gentiles and the Jews
have focused on many matters of tradition
on which principles of belief
do not rely.
However,
I do not want to
debate in this exalted court
anything but matters on which
our theological differences
hinge.

You have spoken well.
Now, we have agreed to open with the matter of whether the Messiah has already come, as the Christians believe, or if he will come in the future, as the Jews believe.
After that, we will discuss the question of whether the Messiah is substantially divine or fully human, born of a man and a woman.
And after that, we will address the question of whether the Jews or the Christians observe the true law.
Then Friar Paul said that he would argue, based on our Talmud, that the Messiah announced by the prophets had already arrived.

Before we debate this question, I ask that he explain to me how this is possible.

I heard that he previously went about Provence and other places saying such things to the Jews, and I am very surprised.

He will want to suggest that the sages of the Talmud believed that Jesus was the Messiah and that he was fundamentally human *and* truly divine, as the Christians believe.

Is it not a known fact that in truth Jesus lived during the time of the Second Temple and Jesus was born and died before the destruction of the Temple?

The sages of the Talmud, such as Rabbi Akiva,* lived after the destruction of the Temple.

*2ND-CENTURY TEACHER AND EXEGETE.

MONTPELLIER

As did the people who taught the Mishnah of Rabbi Judah ha-Nasi and Rabbi Nathan. And, Rav Ashi,* who assembled and recorded the Talmud, lived some 400 years *after* the destruction.
If these wise men believed in the messianic nature of Jesus how did they stand by the religion and traditions of the Jews, for they remained Jews throughout their days and died as Jews.
*THREE RABBIS WHO EDITED AND REDACTED THE MISHNAH AND TALMUD BETWEEN THE 2ND AND 5TH CENTURIES.

And why didn't they and their students turn to the religion of Jesus as Friar Paul did, since he understood from their words that the faith of the Christians was correct -- God forbid -- and apostatized on account of their words?
The rabbis taught us the faith of Moses and Judaism. All our actions today are a product of the Talmud.

The whole Talmud is intended to teach us the traditions of the Torah and the Commandments and how our forefathers in the time of the Temple conducted themselves according to the words of the prophets and Moses (on him may there be peace).

These long words are intended to put a stop to the disputation. Nevertheless, you must hear what I am saying.

This is clear evidence that he will not speak words of substance.
However, I will listen to them because you, our lord King, wish so.

It says in Genesis: '*the staff shall not pass from the tribe of Judah ... until Shiloh has come,*'* and Shiloh is the Messiah. Thus, Jacob says that Judah will always have power until the Messiah comes.
Today, since you have neither a single tribe nor a ruler's staff, the Messiah, who is from the tribe of Judah, has already come, and he holds rule of government.

*GENESIS 49:10 -- JACOB'S BLESSING OF JUDAH AS HE OFFERS BLESSINGS TO HIS 12 SONS.

The prophet did not mean to say that there would be *no* break in the rule of Judah during any time; rather, that it would not *end* and completely depart from Judah. This verse means that at every time that there is kingship for Israel, it will reside with Judah.

During the seventy years of exile in Babel there was no royal government in Judah or in Israel.*
And during the time of the Second Temple there was no king in Judah for 380 years until the destruction of the Second Temple.
*587-538 B.C.E.
During that time, the priests from the family of the Hashmonians* and their servants ruled.
Certainly now, as the nation is in *galut* (exile), outside of its homeland, there is no king.
*THE HIGH PRIESTLY FAMILY THAT GOVERNED JUDEA DURING THE 2ND CENTURY B.C.E.

During those times, even though you had no kings, you had a legitimate government.
The Talmud explains that '*the staff shall not pass from Judah*' refers to the leaders during the Babylonian exile who ruled harshly, '*and the scepter from between his feet*' refers to the disciples of Rabbi Hillel, who taught Torah to the multitudes.*
*SANHEDRIN 5 A

But today you do not have legitimate ordination of rabbis in accordance with the Talmud, so that form of government has also ceased.
Thus, no one among you can properly be called 'Rabbi'! The title you apply to yourselves today, *Maestri*, is mistaken and your use of that title is fraudulent!

This topic is outside the defined lines of the disputation!
And what you say is not truthful. The title *maestri* is equivalent to *rav*, not *rabbi*. Rav is a title of honor that does not require official ordination!
But, I acknowledge that I'm neither a *maestri* nor a 'good student.'

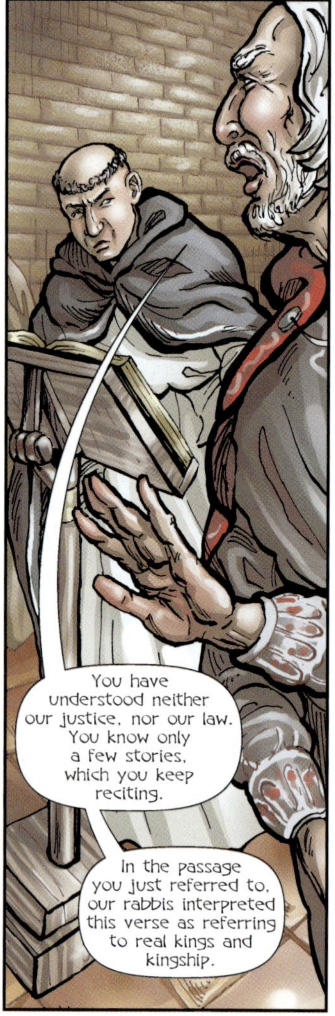
You have understood neither our justice, nor our law. You know only a few stories, which you keep reciting.
In the passage you just referred to, our rabbis interpreted this verse as referring to real kings and kingship.

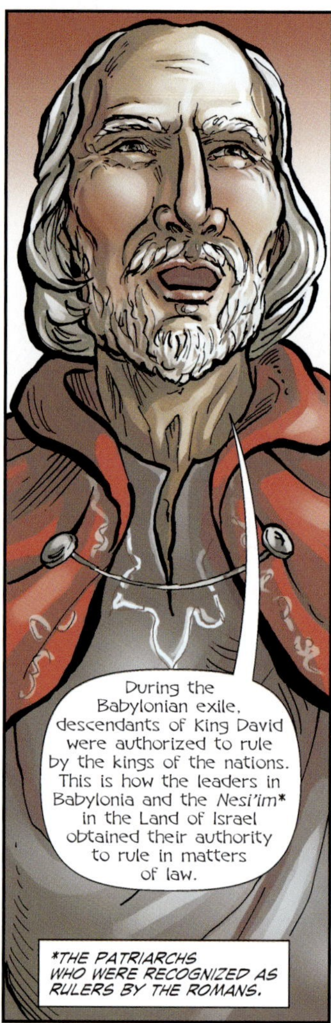
During the Babylonian exile, descendants of King David were authorized to rule by the kings of the nations. This is how the leaders in Babylonia and the *Nesi'im** in the Land of Israel obtained their authority to rule in matters of law.
*THE PATRIARCHS WHO WERE RECOGNIZED AS RULERS BY THE ROMANS.

This continued for more than 400 years after Jesus. But the issue here is who will rule when there *is* a kingdom. The prophet said it would be Judah.
Kingship was suspended at the time of the Babylonian exile and again during the Second Temple, so Judah had no power then.

Yes, the scripture says that the scepter will not depart permanently, but it can be suspended -- vagare, in Latin.
See, Friar Peter understands the law as I did!
No! I do not subscribe to your argument. The Babylonian exile was relatively short -- 70 years. There were many who remembered the Temple. But now you have waited more than one thousand years! This is complete removal of kingship.
Now you change your mind!
The prophet does not distinguish between a speedy return and a slow return. Also, Jacob, our father, promised Judah that he would rule over all of Israel, not just his tribe. It is written: '*Judah, your brothers will praise you.*'*
*GENESIS 49:8
And in Chronicles: '*Judah prevailed over his brothers and from him came the one who would rule as prince.*'* Thus, kingship over all of Israel was interrupted when Solomon died.
*I CHRON. 5:2
The prophet did not promise Judah that his people would never be sent into exile, only that his tribe would be king of Israel for all time.

In Midrash Lamentations the rabbis said that the Messiah already came!
'A man was plowing and his cow lowed...'
'An Arab passer-by said to him: "Bar Yehudai, Yehudai, untie your cow, untie your plow, untie your plowshare, for the Temple has been destroyed."'
'He untied his cow, untied his plow, and untied his plowshare.'
'The cow lowed a second time. The Arab said to him, "Tie up your cow, tie up your plow, tie up your plowshare, for your Messiah was born."'

I do not believe in that *aggadah* at all, although it is proof of my words.
Here is proof that he denies the authority of their books!

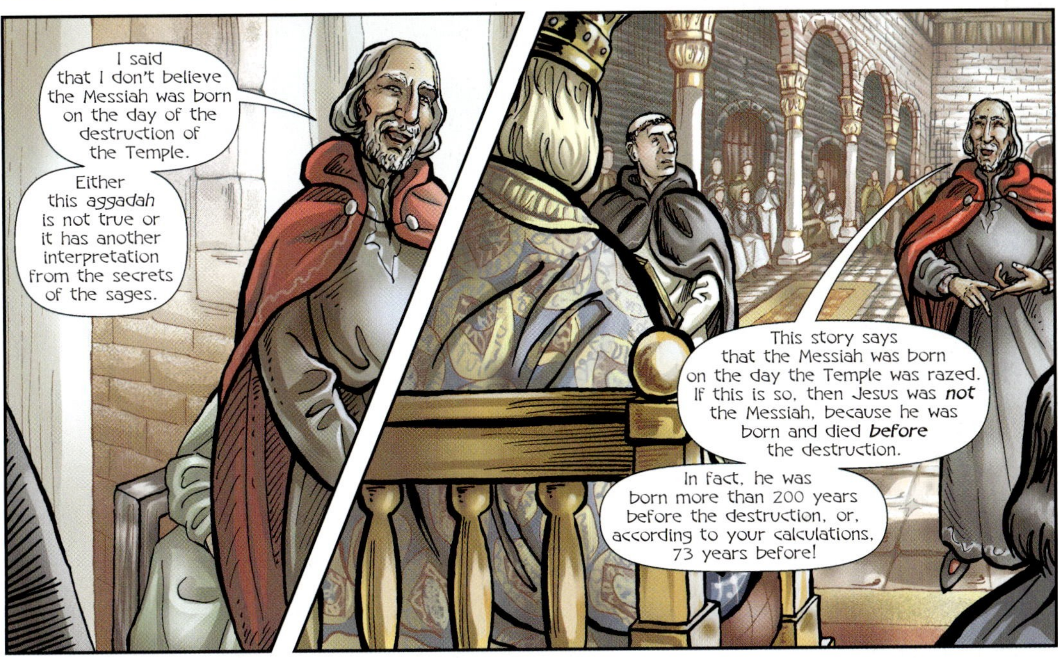
I said that I don't believe the Messiah was born on the day of the destruction of the Temple.
Either this *aggadah* is not true or it has another interpretation from the secrets of the sages.
This story says that the Messiah was born on the day the Temple was razed. If this is so, then Jesus was ***not*** the Messiah, because he was born and died ***before*** the destruction.
In fact, he was born more than 200 years before the destruction, or, according to your calculations, 73 years before!

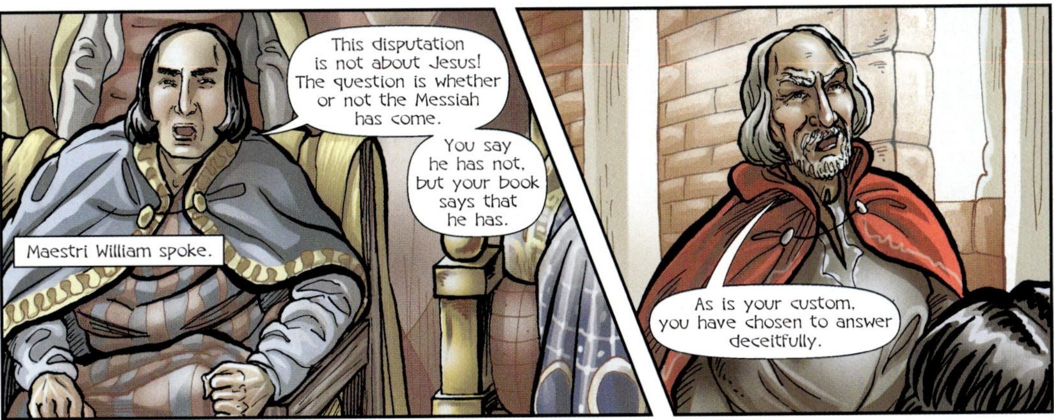
Maestri William spoke.
This disputation is not about Jesus! The question is whether or not the Messiah has come.
You say he has not, but your book says that he has.
As is your custom, you have chosen to answer deceitfully.

The sages did not say that the Messiah **came** on that day, but that he was born. Moses was not born as Israel's leader; he became a redeemer when he came to Pharaoh as was God's command and said: *'so says the Lord: send forth my people...'**
When the Messiah comes and says to the Pope according to God's command: *'send forth my people,'* then he will have come. As of today, he has not come and we have no Messiah.
*EXODUS 7:26
There is a section from Isaiah* that talks about the death of the Messiah and how he fell into the hands of his tormentors. This happened to Jesus. Do you agree that this refers to Jesus?
According to the true meaning, this too refers to Israel. The prophet Isaiah refers to Israel as God's servant.
*52:13-53:12
I will prove with the words of your sages that this verse **does** refer to the Messiah!
It is true that our rabbis (may they be blessed) interpret it as being about the Messiah, but they never said that he would die at the hands of his enemies. Thus, you will never find a statement in the Talmud or the *aggadot* that the Messiah ben David would be killed.
I will explain to you the portion in Isaiah 52, if you wish, with a clear and good interpretation that shows there was no mention that the Messiah would be killed, as yours was.
According to the Talmud: *'Rabbi Joshua ben Levi asked Elijiah when the messiah would come. Elijiah answered: "Ask the Messiah himself." Rabbi Joshua said: "Where is he?" "At the entrance to Rome tending to the sick." Rabbi Joshua walked there and found him.'**
If so, he's already come and he's in Rome and he's Jesus!
*SANHEDRIN 98 A

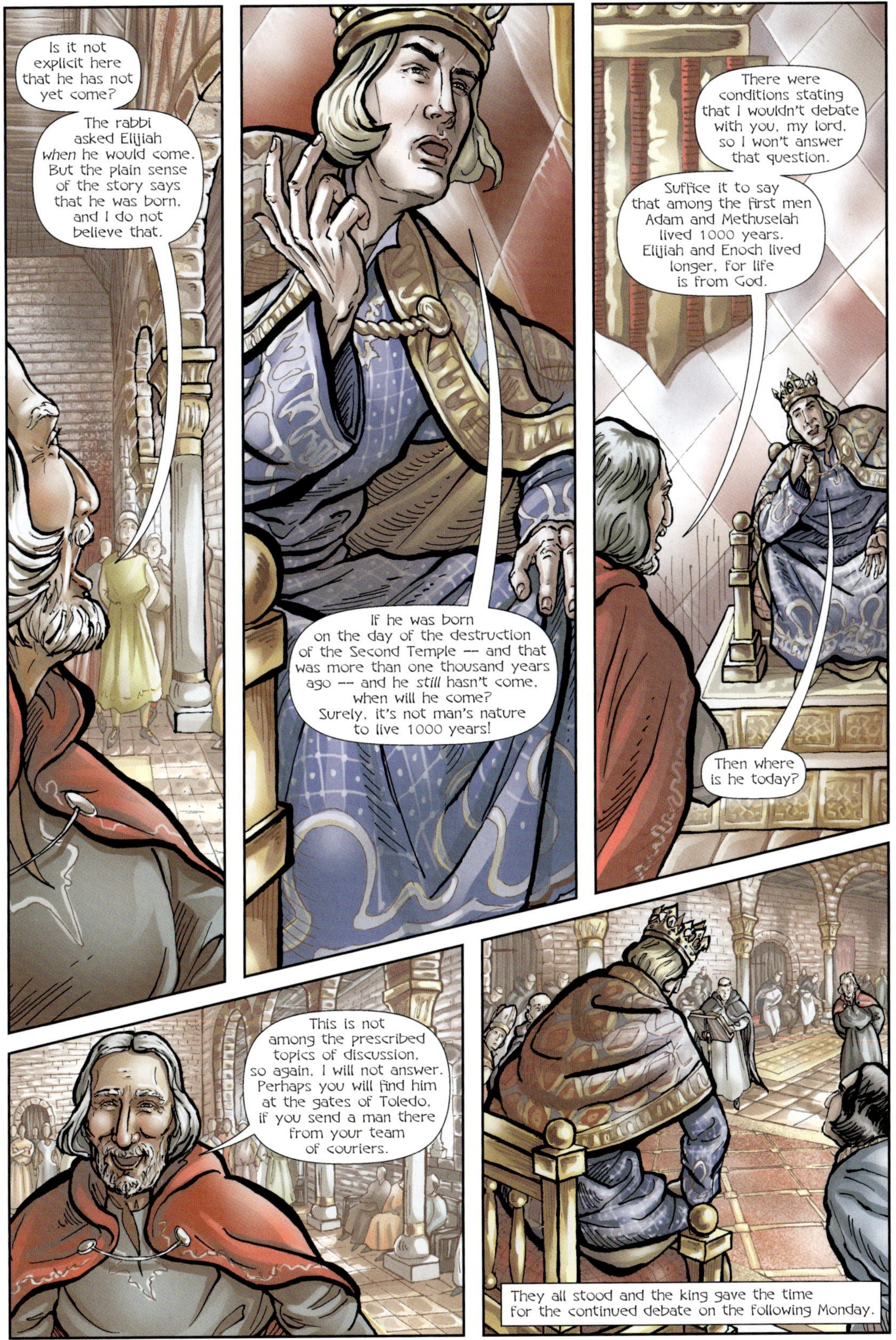
Is it not explicit here that he has not yet come?
The rabbi asked Elijiah *when* he would come. But the plain sense of the story says that he was born, and I do not believe that.
If he was born on the day of the destruction of the Second Temple -- and that was more than one thousand years ago -- and he *still* hasn't come, when will he come? Surely, it's not man's nature to live 1000 years!
There were conditions stating that I wouldn't debate with you, my lord, so I won't answer that question.
Suffice it to say that among the first men Adam and Methuselah lived 1000 years. Elijiah and Enoch lived longer, for life is from God.
Then where is he today?
This is not among the prescribed topics of discussion, so again, I will not answer. Perhaps you will find him at the gates of Toledo, if you send a man there from your team of couriers.
They all stood and the king gave the time for the continued debate on the following Monday.

CHAPTER 2

"WE HAVE THREE TYPES OF BOOKS . . ."

On that day the king went to the cloisters in the city and gathered there all of the people of the city, gentiles and Jews. And the bishop and all of the priests and the Franciscan masters and preachers...
My lord, please hear me.

He is the prosecutor so he should speak first.
Please permit me to explain my views on the Messiah, then he will be able to respond.

Friar Paul asked me if the Messiah had already come; I said he had not. He brought a book of homilies that says the Messiah was born on the day the Temple was destroyed.

I replied that I did not believe that, but that it was proof of my argument.
Now I will explain to you why I said I did not believe that.
We have three types of books. The first is *biblia* and all of us believe it in its entirety.

The second is called the Talmud, and it explains all the 613 commandments of the Torah.
Finally, we have the Midrash or *sermones*. It is as if the bishop gave a sermon and someone wrote it down. One may believe the content of Midrash or not.

So, we do have sages who wrote that the Messiah would not be born until the time of the end is near, and that he'll lead us from exile.
Thus, I don't believe that he was born on the day of the destruction.

We call the book Friar Paul refers to *Sefer Aggadah*, which means *Razionamiento* -- really a book of sayings, like what one friend tells to another.

But I accept the simple meaning of this story as you wish, because it shows clearly that Jesus is not the Messiah. As I said, he was not born on that day.

You, my lord king, raised a better question than the friars did. Men usually don't live 1000 years. Adam lived 930 years. Scripture explains that he died for his sins. Perhaps he'd have lived longer or forever had he not sinned.
Jews and Christians agree that sin, punishment, and death will end with the Messiah.

If so, then the Messiah will live thousands of years, maybe forever.
You also asked where the Messiah is located. The answer is in the scripture: Adam lived in the Garden of Eden, but was exiled for his sin. Thus, the Messiah, who is free of sin, is there. So says the *Sefer Aggadah*.

Have you not said that according to that *aggadah* he is in Rome?
I didn't say that he is permanently in Rome, but that he was seen there on a certain day, which he was.
The reason for this is stated in the *aggadot*, but I don't wish to reveal it before so many people.
I did not want to reveal that in the *aggadah* it says that the Messiah will remain in Rome until he will destroy it.
I privately communicated this to the king.
Do you agree that the sin of Adam will be cancelled when the Messiah comes?
Yes, we do!
But not in the same way you think. Everyone entered hell because of Adam's sin. In the days of Jesus, the Messiah, the punishment was lifted and he freed them from there.

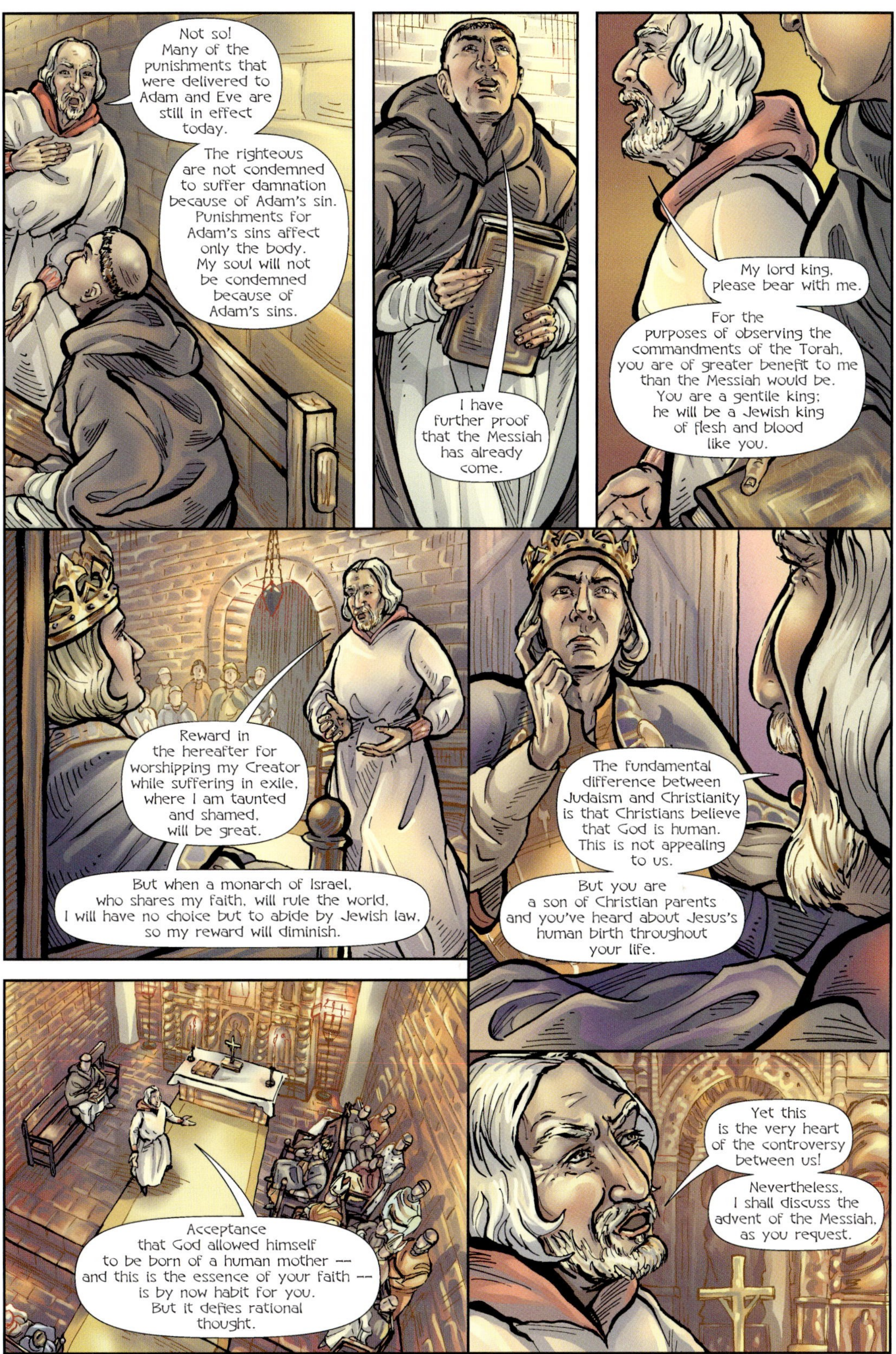
Not so!
Many of the punishments that were delivered to Adam and Eve are still in effect today.
The righteous are not condemned to suffer damnation because of Adam's sin. Punishments for Adam's sins affect only the body. My soul will not be condemned because of Adam's sins.
I have further proof that the Messiah has already come.
My lord king, please bear with me.
For the purposes of observing the commandments of the Torah, you are of greater benefit to me than the Messiah would be. You are a gentile king; he will be a Jewish king of flesh and blood like you.
Reward in the hereafter for worshipping my Creator while suffering in exile, where I am taunted and shamed, will be great.
But when a monarch of Israel, who shares my faith, will rule the world, I will have no choice but to abide by Jewish law, so my reward will diminish.
The fundamental difference between Judaism and Christianity is that Christians believe that God is human. This is not appealing to us.
But you are a son of Christian parents and you've heard about Jesus's human birth throughout your life.
Acceptance that God allowed himself to be born of a human mother -- and this is the essence of your faith -- is by now habit for you. But it defies rational thought.
Yet this is the very heart of the controversy between us!
Nevertheless, I shall discuss the advent of the Messiah, as you request.

Do you believe that he has already come?
No. I believe and know that he has not yet come.
Other than Jesus, nobody has claimed that title. And the prophet said that the Messiah: 'will have dominion from sea to sea ... unto the ends of the earth.'* But Jesus had no dominion.
*PSALMS 72:8

If he was persecuted during his life and in hiding, how could he help Israel? In the end, he was not even able to help himself.

Before Rome accepted Jesus as the Messiah, the city ruled over most of the world, but after they accepted his religion, they lost many kingdoms. Now the worshippers of Muhammad have more power than Christians.

The prophet said: 'they will beat their swords into plowshares, and their spears into pruning hooks; nation shall not lift up sword against nation, neither shall they learn war any more.'*
From the time of Jesus until now, the entire world has been full of violence and robbery.
*ISAIAH 2:4

Indeed, Christians spill more blood than the rest of the nations, and they also lead immoral lives.

How difficult would it be for you, my lord king, and for your knights if they would 'also ... not learn war any more'*!
Despite your belief that Jesus eliminated war, you still carry weapons and ride on armored horses.
*ISAIAH 2:4

He constantly gives such longwinded speeches! I have a question to ask...

Be quiet. He is the one who's asking the questions.

Your sages said that the Messiah would be revered above the angels.

This could not be anyone other than Jesus, because he is your Messiah and he is divine by nature, and he did what the *aggadah* said he would.*

*YALKUT ISAIAH, 52:13 -- A MEDIEVAL COMPILATION OF **AGGADOT.**

That *aggadah* shows that the Messiah will do more than the angels. He will command the pope and all the kings in the name of the Lord to liberate the people. He will bring great signs and miracles and he will not fear them.

Also, he will remain in Rome until he destroys it.

I will further explain this passage if you so desire.

Another *aggadah* says that the Messiah prays that God will forgive Israel for their transgressions and that he received their afflictions. Thus, the agony of the Messiah is the assassination of Jesus, which he knowingly took upon himself.

He has no shame! Jesus did none of those things.
This *aggadah* teaches that the Messiah is human, not divine. He does not possess the ability to give life.
These afflictions are nothing more than his sorrow as he observes his people in exile as he has been so delayed.

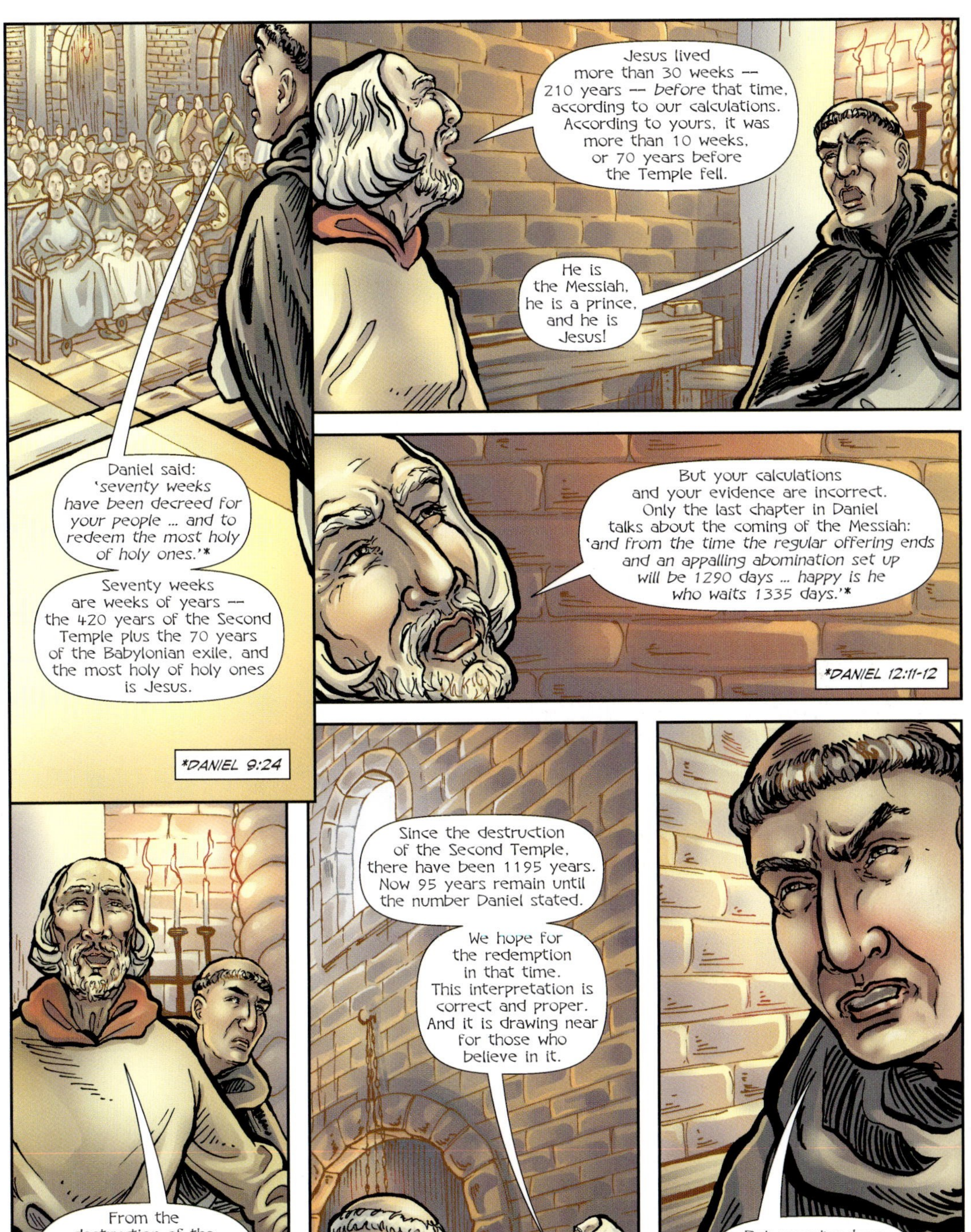
Jesus lived more than 30 weeks -- 210 years -- *before* that time, according to our calculations. According to yours, it was more than 10 weeks, or 70 years before the Temple fell.
He is the Messiah, he is a prince, and he is Jesus!
Daniel said: '*seventy weeks have been decreed for your people ... and to redeem the most holy of holy ones.*'*
Seventy weeks are weeks of years -- the 420 years of the Second Temple plus the 70 years of the Babylonian exile, and the most holy of holy ones is Jesus.
*DANIEL 9:24
But your calculations and your evidence are incorrect. Only the last chapter in Daniel talks about the coming of the Messiah: '*and from the time the regular offering ends and an appalling abomination set up will be 1290 days ... happy is he who waits 1335 days.*'*
*DANIEL 12:11-12
From the destruction of the Temple, there will be 1290 years, because the days are really years. The Messiah will come within 1290 days and destroy those who worship a false god.
After 45 days, he will gather Israel into their land.
Since the destruction of the Second Temple, there have been 1195 years. Now 95 years remain until the number Daniel stated.
We hope for the redemption in that time. This interpretation is correct and proper. And it is drawing near for those who believe in it.
But your teachers in the *aggadah* explained that these days are like the 45 days when Moses was hidden after he was revealed as the redeemer.* So they are referring to real days, not years.
*YALKUT HOSEA, 518

There is no Jew in the world who would not agree that the meaning of *yom* is a real day. He's changing the meaning of the words to suit his whim!

He shouted to the king, so they brought a Jew, the first they found, and asked him.

What does *yom* mean in your language?
Day.
My lord, this Jew is suitable to be a judge for Friar Paul, but not for me because in the scripture '*yom*' indicates time more generally, and days refer to years.

The angel commanded that Daniel: '*Shut the words and seal the book until the time of the end.*'*
But I am discussing matters of great weight with one who can neither understand nor believe, so it is appropriate that he be judged by a fool.
*DANIEL 12:4

Jerome does interpret the word 'days' in this verse as 'days of the people' or epochs.
You can see from his words that the days in this case are not meant literally. Thus they required interpretation. The 'days of the people' are years, because people say that many days have passed since a certain event, and that refers to many years.

Their sages say that the Messiah entered the Garden of Eden. The aggadah says: 'Why did Messiah enter the Garden of Eden? Because he saw his ancestors there worshipping idols, and he parted from their path and served God, the Holy One, and God reserved him for the Garden of Eden.'*
*DEREKH ERETZ ZUTA
This says that he was the descendant of idolatrous parents, but was certainly a real man. God rewarded Jesus when he decried idolatry.
In the aggadah it states: 'fourteen living people entered the Garden of Eden to search for Serah, daughter of Asher and Bathyah, daughter of Pharaoh.'
If Jesus were the Messiah, he would not be residing among women in the Garden of Eden.
It is as I said: The Messiah resides in the Garden of Eden, in the home of the first man before he sinned. So says the aggadah.

On the fifth day of the week,
our lord the king set his royal palace
as the location for the disputation,
saying it should be held
without too much pomp.
We sat near the entrance
to the palace.

Friar Paul opened with
meaningless words of no interest.
Afterwards he began anew.
I will bring proof
from their great sage,
who has been without equal
for 400 years.
His name is Maestri Moses
of Egypt,* and he says that
the Messiah will die and
that his son and grandson
will rule after him.
*MAIMONIDES, OR
RABBI MOSES BEN MAIMON,
CA. 1138-1204

He does not say,
as you did, that the Messiah
would die as all men do.
And he asked that
someone bring him
the Book of Judges.*
*THE FINAL BOOK IN MAIMONIDES'
GREAT WORK, MISHNEH TORAH

Rabbi Moses
ben Maimon makes no such
statement in that book,
though I agree that there are
those among our sages who
say as much.
The book of aggadah
says that the Messiah was born
on the day of the Destruction and
that he will live forever.

It is the opinion of those who interpret scripture literally that he would be born at the cusp of the time of redemption, and would live for many years and then die in honor and his son would inherit his crown.

I already said that this is what I believe.
The only difference between this world and the days of the Messiah is our political servitude.

They brought Friar Paul the book he requested. He searched in it but didn't find the desired passage.

I took the book from his hand and read to them...
Listen to the words of the book that he brings: 'the future messiah king will arise within Israel, build the temple, and gather the banished of Israel.'*
He writes lies!
*MISHNEH TORAH, BOOK OF JUDGES, PARAGRAPH 39

A moment ago
he was the greatest sage,
now he's a liar?
It is not proper
to show disrespect
for scholars!

Maimonides
has not lied.
What he said is verified
in the Torah and
prophets.
The Messiah will gather
the twelve tribes of Israel;
Jesus gathered no one...

The Messiah
will rebuild the
Temple in Jerusalem.
Since it still stood
during Jesus's lifetime,
he did not
do that.

The Torah says:
'*when all of these things
have come upon you,
the blessing and the curse ...
and the eternal, your God
will put all these curses
upon your enemies
and on them who hate you
and persecuted you.*'*
*DEUT. 30:1 AND 7
I explained to them
that '*your enemies*'
refers to the Christians,
and that '*they hate you*'
refers to the Arabs,
the two nations that
persecute us.
They did not answer,
but rose to leave.

CHAPTER 3

"JESUS NEVER WALKED WITH THE RIGHTEOUS IN THE GARDEN OF EDEN . . ."

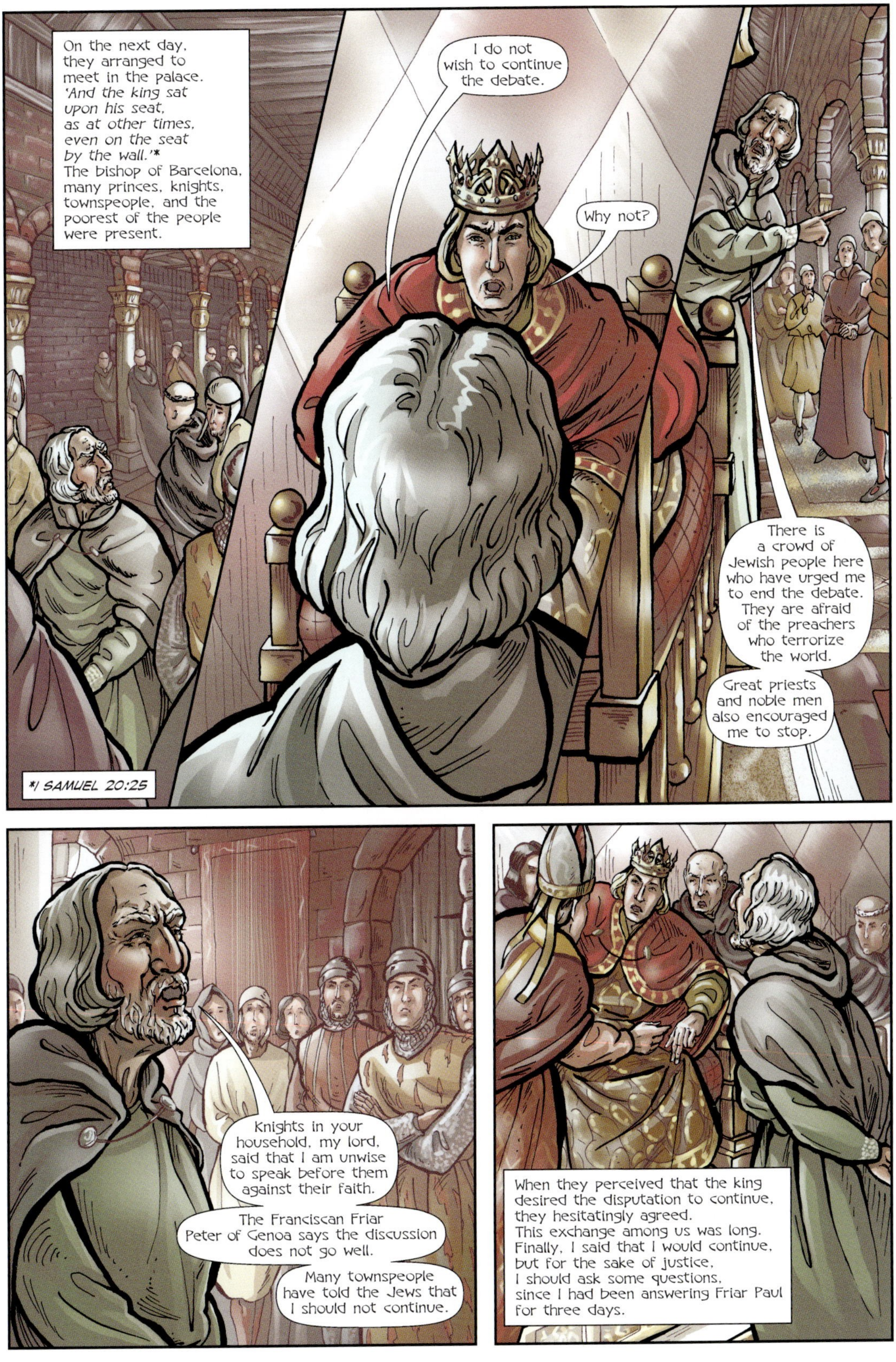

On the next day, they arranged to meet in the palace. *'And the king sat upon his seat, as at other times, even on the seat by the wall.'** The bishop of Barcelona, many princes, knights, townspeople, and the poorest of the people were present.

I do not wish to continue the debate.

Why not?

There is a crowd of Jewish people here who have urged me to end the debate. They are afraid of the preachers who terrorize the world.

Great priests and noble men also encouraged me to stop.

*I SAMUEL 20:25

Knights in your household, my lord, said that I am unwise to speak before them against their faith.
The Franciscan Friar Peter of Genoa says the discussion does not go well.
Many townspeople have told the Jews that I should not continue.

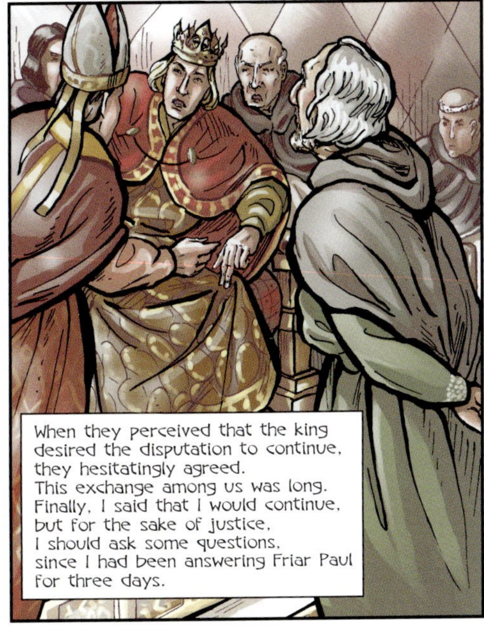

When they perceived that the king desired the disputation to continue, they hesitatingly agreed. This exchange among us was long. Finally, I said that I would continue, but for the sake of justice, I should ask some questions, since I had been answering Friar Paul for three days.

Regardless, you must answer his questions.
Do you believe that the Messiah described by the prophets will be truly human or divine?
At the start, we agreed that we would first speak about whether the Messiah had already come, and then whether he is God himself.
You have not demonstrated that he has come, as I refuted each of your vain proofs.
I will bring conclusive proof, if you will hear me. After it has been clarified that Jesus is not the Messiah, there will be no reason to debate whether the Messiah who will come will be human.
The wise judges agreed that justice was with me on that matter.
Still you must answer!
It is true that when the Messiah comes, he will be fully human, the son of a man and a woman from their coupling, like me.
He will be from the line of David and, it is written: '*and there shall come forth from the stem of Jesse.*'*
*ISAIAH 11:1

If he were the spirit of God, he would not be *'of the stem of Jesse.'*

And even if he did take shelter in the womb of a woman who was the seed of David, he did not inherit his kingdom. David always had male heirs.

The psalmist says: *'The Lord says to my lord, Sit at my right hand.'** Who would call David 'my lord'? Only God! And how can a mere man sit at the right hand of God?

It's a good question. If the Messiah was wholly man from the seed of David, David would not call him 'my lord.'

If I had a son or grandson, even if he ruled the world, I would not call him 'my lord.' I would want him to call me 'my lord' and kiss my hand!

*PSALMS 110:1

Are you the wise Jew who discovered this new interpretation and converted as a result?
Did you tell the king to gather Jewish scholars to debate this point? Do you think we've never heard this? There is not a priest or a child who does not ask this question of Jews. It is a very old question indeed!
You must answer him!

Now, hear me! King David wrote the psalms so that they would be sung at the altar of God. He did not sing them himself, for he was forbidden to according to the law of the Torah.

But, he gave the psalms to the Levites.* Thus, King David wrote the Psalms in language that befit the Levites.
If it said 'God spoke to me,' the Levites would have been lying. But they could say: 'God spoke to my lord' -- meaning, David -- 'sit at my right hand.'
*I CHRONICLES 16:7
'Sitting' means that the Lord, (may he be blessed), will protect David from enemies throughout his days -- 'for he raised his spear against 800 and killed them at one time.'*
Are there any among your knights here today who could do so with his own strength?
*II SAMUEL 23:8
Again he reverted to his previous line of argument and brought evidence from the Midrash.
It is written: 'And I will walk among you.'*
They devised a parable. This can be compared to a king who went out for a walk with his laborer in an orchard, but the laborer avoided him. The king asked: 'why do you hide, I am like you.'
*LEVITICUS 26:12
Now Friar Paul concluded his reading.
In the same manner, the Holy one, may he be blessed, will walk in the Garden of Eden among the righteous, who will be afraid of Him. He will say: 'why are you afraid? I am like you. I will be your God and you shall be My people.'*
*LEVITICUS 26:12
Since God said 'I am like you' it shows that he turned into a man, like them.

The Midrash he cited is proof against him!

This Midrash is a parable. The meaning is that the righteous of this world cannot understand the truth of prophecy and they cannot see what is called the Divine Glory.

In the future, the souls of the righteous will be cleansed and they will be able to recognize the Divine Glory.

This episode refers to the future and will occur in the Garden of Eden. But Jesus never walked with the righteous in the Garden of Eden. Instead, he was a fugitive from his enemies throughout his lifetime!

The king then rose, and they all followed.

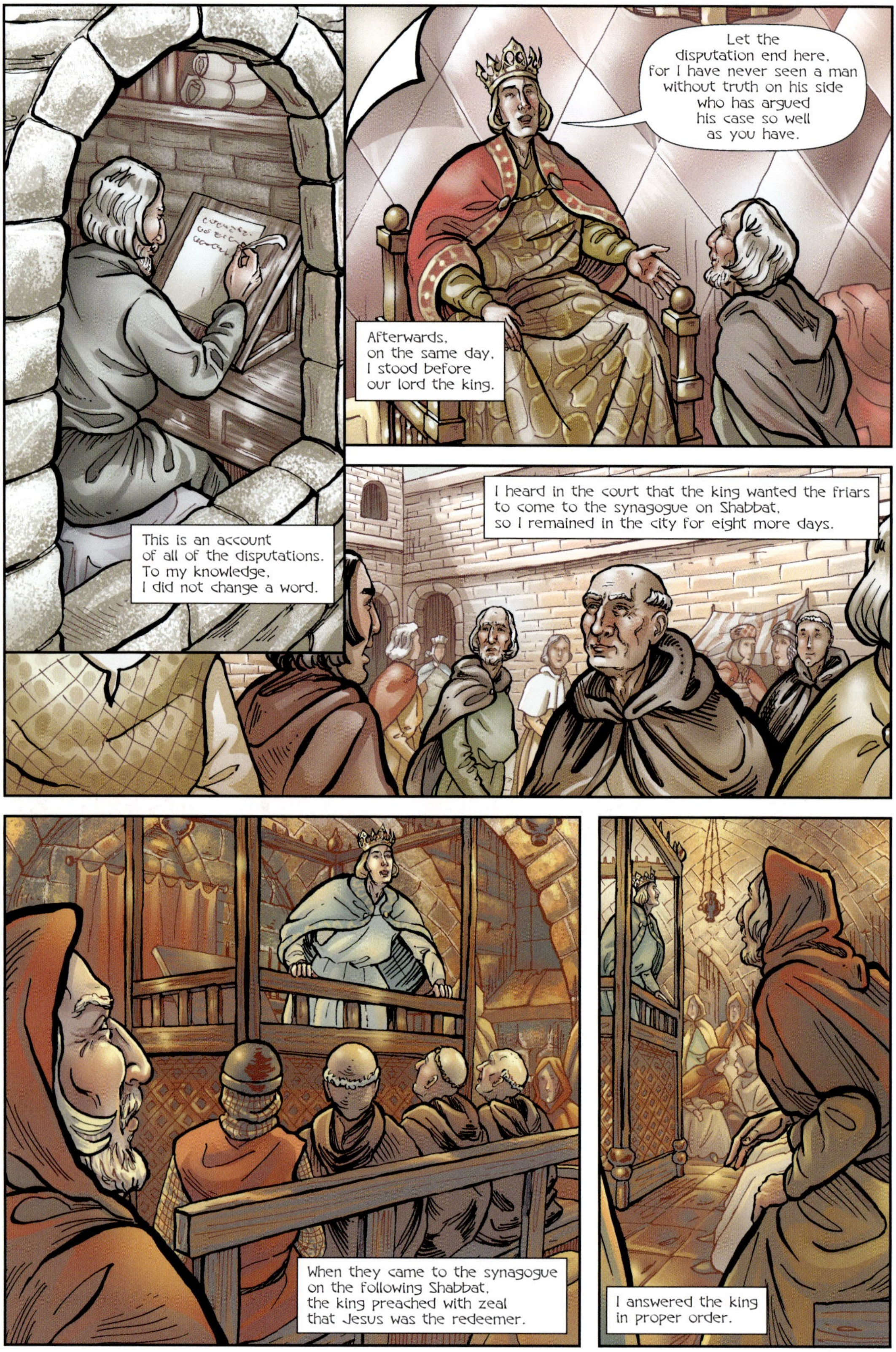

This is an account
of all of the disputations.
To my knowledge,
I did not change a word.

Afterwards,
on the same day,
I stood before
our lord the king.

Let the
disputation end here,
for I have never seen a man
without truth on his side
who has argued
his case so well
as you have.

I heard in the court that the king wanted the friars
to come to the synagogue on Shabbat,
so I remained in the city for eight more days.

When they came to the synagogue
on the following Shabbat,
the king preached with zeal
that Jesus was the redeemer.

I answered the king
in proper order.

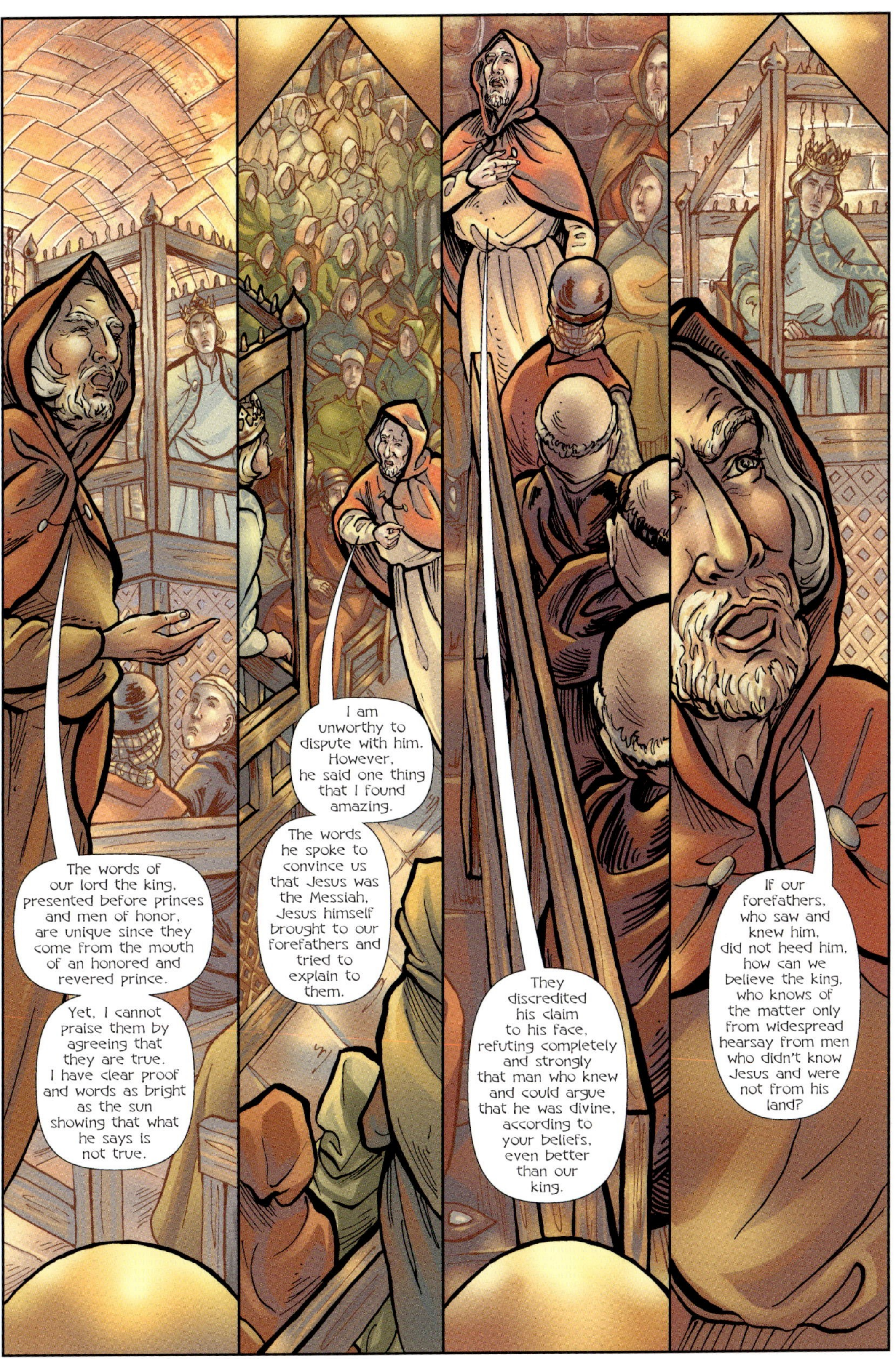
The words of our lord the king, presented before princes and men of honor, are unique since they come from the mouth of an honored and revered prince.
Yet, I cannot praise them by agreeing that they are true. I have clear proof and words as bright as the sun showing that what he says is not true.
I am unworthy to dispute with him. However, he said one thing that I found amazing.
The words he spoke to convince us that Jesus was the Messiah, Jesus himself brought to our forefathers and tried to explain to them.
They discredited his claim to his face, refuting completely and strongly that man who knew and could argue that he was divine, according to your beliefs, even better than our king.
If our forefathers, who saw and knew him, did not heed him, how can we believe the king, who knows of the matter only from widespread hearsay from men who didn't know Jesus and were not from his land?

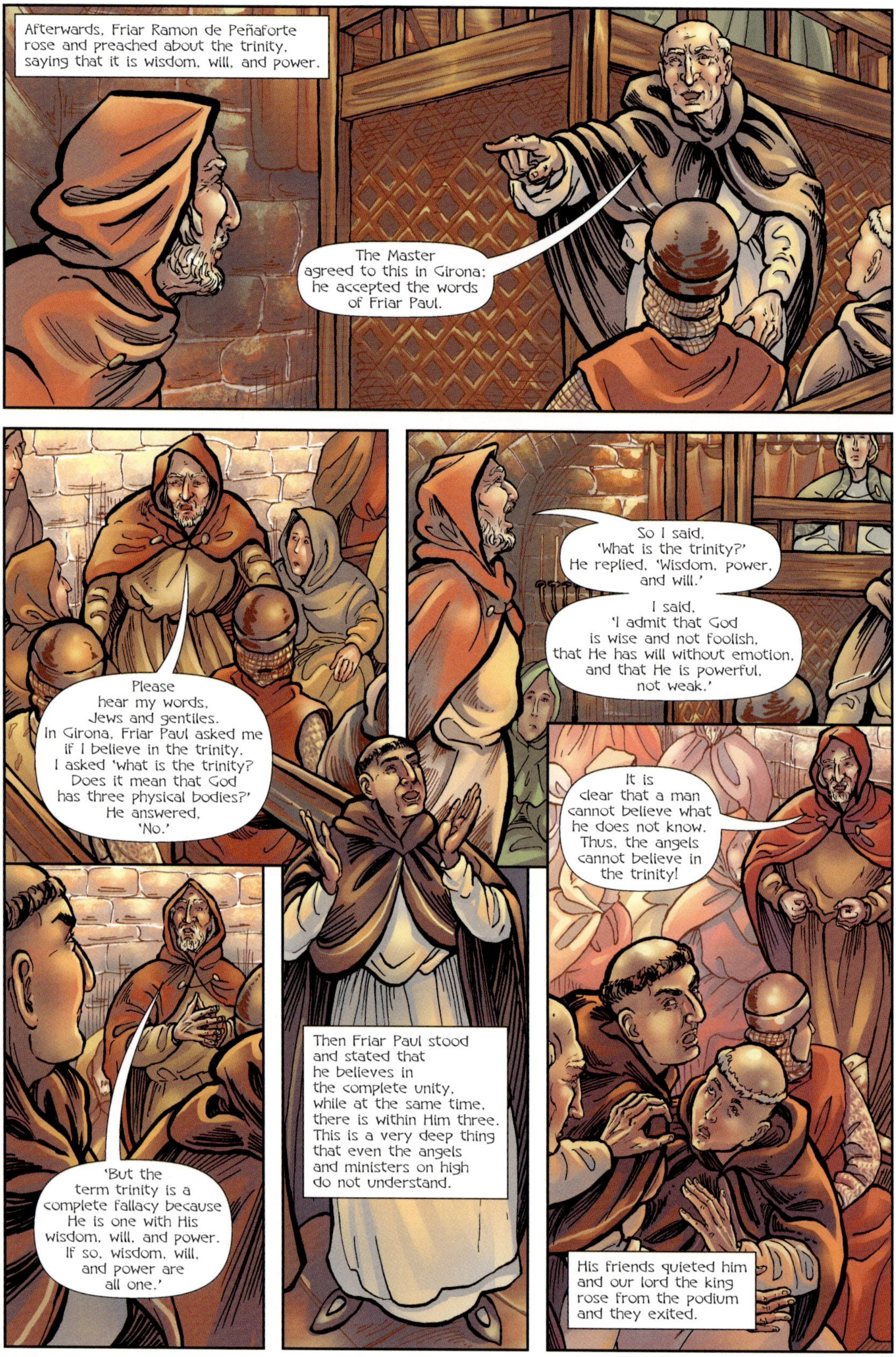

Afterwards, Friar Ramon de Peñaforte rose and preached about the trinity, saying that it is wisdom, will, and power.

The Master agreed to this in Girona; he accepted the words of Friar Paul.

Please hear my words, Jews and gentiles. In Girona, Friar Paul asked me if I believe in the trinity. I asked 'what is the trinity? Does it mean that God has three physical bodies?' He answered, 'No.'

So I said, 'What is the trinity?' He replied, 'Wisdom, power, and will.'

I said, 'I admit that God is wise and not foolish, that He has will without emotion, and that He is powerful, not weak.'

'But the term trinity is a complete fallacy because He is one with His wisdom, will, and power. If so, wisdom, will, and power are all one.'
Then Friar Paul stood and stated that he believes in the complete unity, while at the same time, there is within Him three. This is a very deep thing that even the angels and ministers on high do not understand.
It is clear that a man cannot believe what he does not know. Thus, the angels cannot believe in the trinity!
His friends quieted him and our lord the king rose from the podium and they exited.

On the following day I stood before our lord king. He gave me 300 *dinarim*. I left with great love. May God make me worthy of life in the World to Come. Amen.
Return to your city, your life, and to peace.
KING JAMES BORROWED THE SAME AMOUNT IN JULY 1263 FROM A LOCAL JEWISH MERCHANT TO MAKE A GIFT TO 'THE RABBI OF GIRONA.'

CHAPTER 4

"MOSES, CALLED MASTER, HAVING BEEN SUMMONED BY THE LORD KING . . ."

NAHMANIDES RETURNED TO GIRONA AND THE FRIARS SOUGHT ADDITIONAL ROYAL SPONSORSHIP TO CONTINUE THEIR PREACHING CAMPAIGN.
26 August, 1263
James I summons Saracens and Jews to attend sermons of the preaching monks, under penalty of a fine.
THE DOMINICANS ALSO CONTINUED TO PURSUE AN ACTIVE INVESTIGATION AND REGULATION OF JEWISH BOOKS, A PROGRAM KING JAMES ENDORSED ON A LIMITED BASIS.
28 August, 1263
James I orders that all of his officers see to it that all books known by the title of *soffrim*,* whose author is a certain Jew by the name of Moses son of Maimon, an Egyptian from Cairo, and containing blasphemies related to Jesus Christ, be burnt publicly. The king orders those Jews who own copies of this book to hand them over to his agents.
*THIS ALMOST CERTAINLY REFERS TO MAIMONIDES' **SEFER SHOFETIM**.

AS FRIARS CIRCULATED WORD OF THEIR GREAT SUCCESS, ROYAL EMISSARIES DELIVERED SUMMONS TO JEWISH AND MUSLIM COMMUNITIES.
29 AUGUST, 1263
JAMES I INFORMS ALL JEWS THAT HE SENDS FRIAR PAUL CHRISTIANI TO SHOW THEM THE WAY OF SALVATION. HE WILL COME TO THEIR SYNAGOGUES, THEIR HOMES, OR OTHER PLACES, TO PREACH TO THEM ABOUT THE HOLY SCRIPTURE...

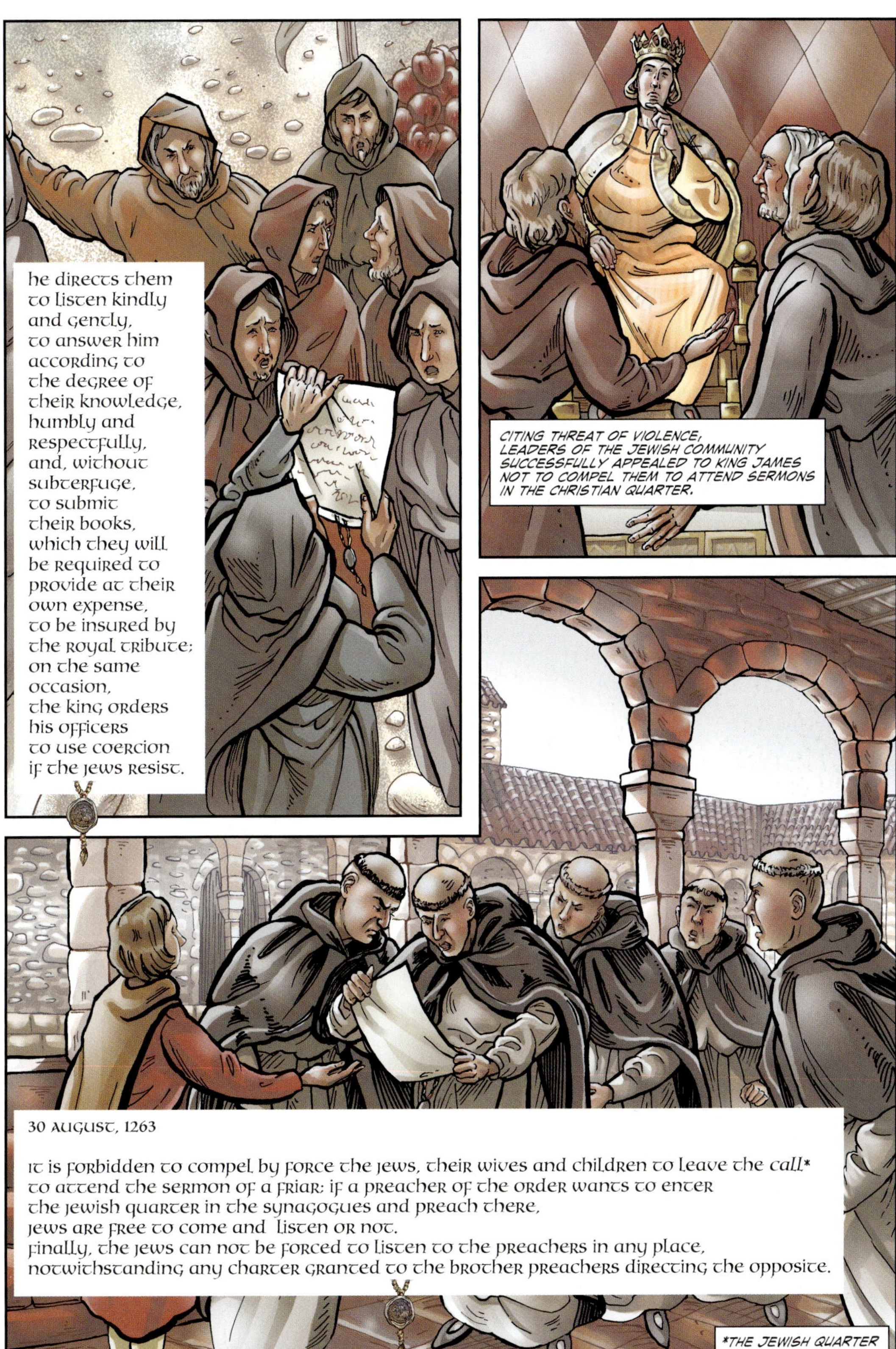
he directs them
to listen kindly
and gently,
to answer him
according to
the degree of
their knowledge,
humbly and
respectfully,
and, without
subterfuge,
to submit
their books,
which they will
be required to
provide at their
own expense,
to be insured by
the royal tribute;
on the same
occasion,
the king orders
his officers
to use coercion
if the jews resist.
CITING THREAT OF VIOLENCE, LEADERS OF THE JEWISH COMMUNITY SUCCESSFULLY APPEALED TO KING JAMES NOT TO COMPEL THEM TO ATTEND SERMONS IN THE CHRISTIAN QUARTER.
30 AUGUST, 1263
it is forbidden to compel by force the jews, their wives and children to leave the *call** to attend the sermon of a friar: if a preacher of the order wants to enter the jewish quarter in the synagogues and preach there, jews are free to come and listen or not. finally, the jews can not be forced to listen to the preachers in any place, notwithstanding any charter granted to the brother preachers directing the opposite.
*THE JEWISH QUARTER

THOUGH ROYALLY SANCTIONED REGULATION OF JEWISH BOOKS BY THE FRIARS WAS DISRUPTIVE AND DISTRESSING, MOST ASPECTS OF LIFE IN THE JEWISH QUARTERS LARGELY REMAINED LITTLE CHANGED FOLLOWING THE DISPUTATION.

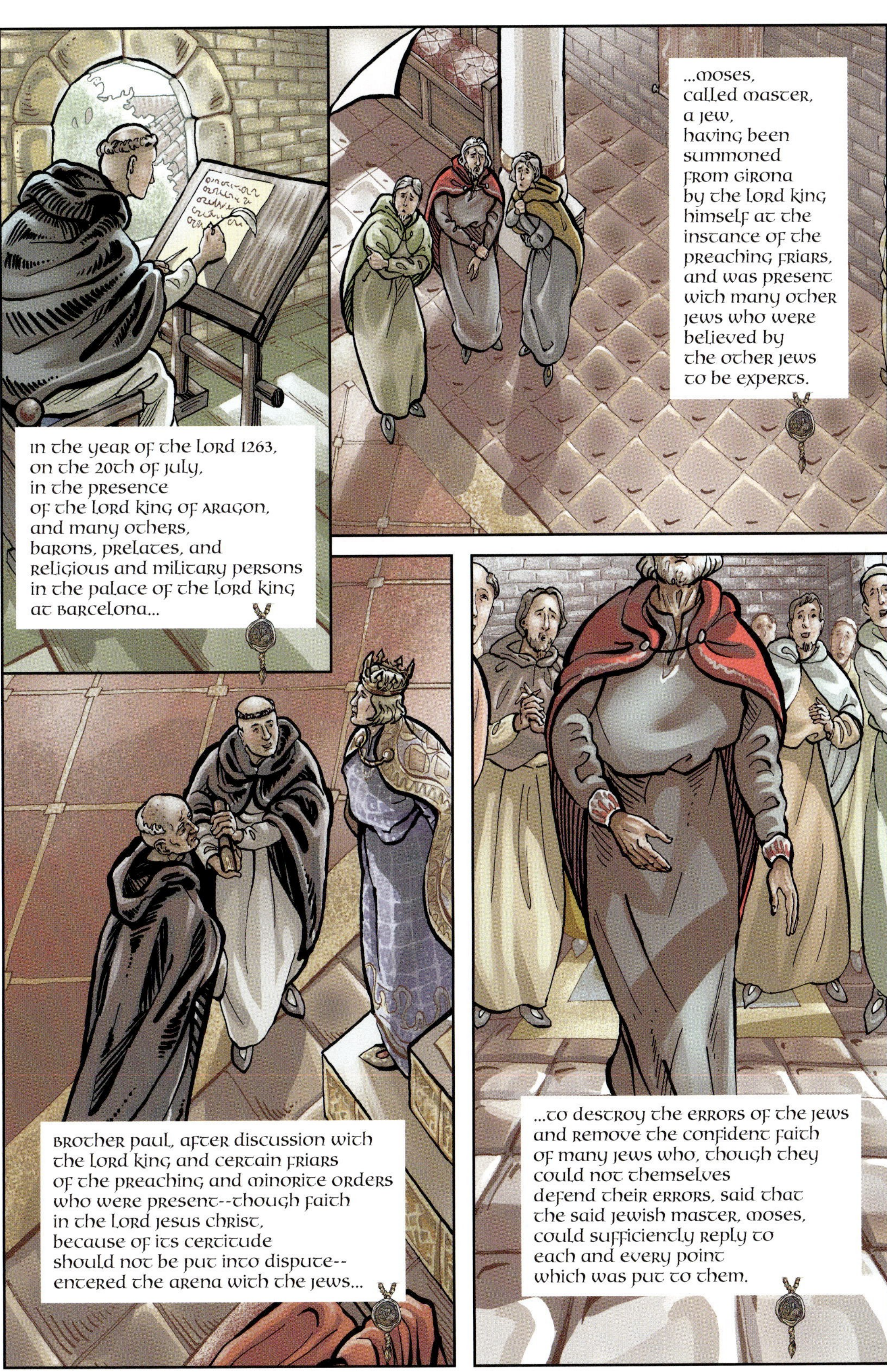
in the year of the Lord 1263,
on the 20th of July,
in the presence
of the Lord king of Aragon,
and many others,
barons, prelates, and
religious and military persons
in the palace of the Lord king
at Barcelona...
...Moses,
called master,
a Jew,
having been
summoned
from Girona
by the Lord king
himself at the
instance of the
preaching friars,
and was present
with many other
Jews who were
believed by
the other Jews
to be experts.
Brother Paul, after discussion with
the Lord king and certain friars
of the preaching and minorite orders
who were present--though faith
in the Lord Jesus Christ,
because of its certitude
should not be put into dispute--
entered the arena with the Jews...
...to destroy the errors of the Jews
and remove the confident faith
of many Jews who, though they
could not themselves
defend their errors, said that
the said Jewish master, Moses,
could sufficiently reply to
each and every point
which was put to them.

Friar Paul proposed to the Jewish master that he would prove, with the help of God, through writings accepted and authoritative among the Jews, the following things in order:

that the Messiah whom the Jews expect has already come; further, that the Messiah himself, as had been prophesied, must be both God and man; further, that he suffered and died for the salvation of mankind; further, that legal or ceremonial matter ceased and had to cease after the coming of the said Messiah.

When the said Moses had been asked whether he wished to reply to these arguments, he firmly asserted, 'yes,' and said that he would remain, if necessary, for this reason, in Barcelona for a day or a week or a month or even a year.

Yes.

When it was proved to him that he ought not to be called 'master,' because no Jew ought to be called by this name since the time of the passion of Christ, he conceded that it was true for the last 800 years.

When previously confronted by Brother Paul in Girona about Christian belief in the Holy Trinity, Moses had conceded that if Christians believed what they said then it was a valid belief.
When this was repeated before the king, he did not deny it, but was silent, and by his silence, assented.

The said Jew was asked whether the messiah had come; he answered 'NO.'
NO.

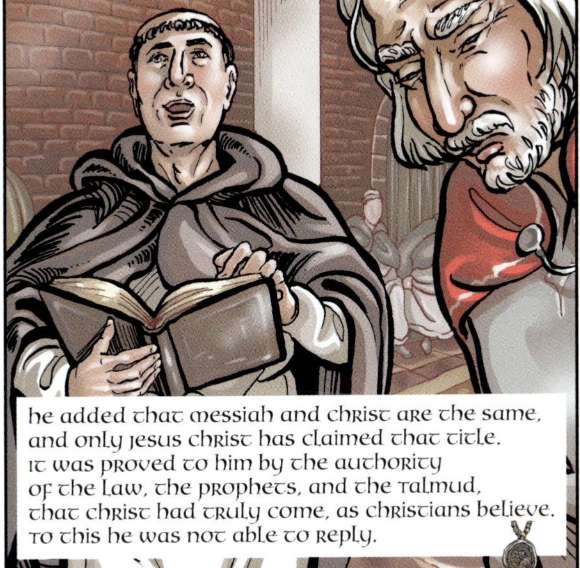

He added that messiah and Christ are the same, and only Jesus Christ has claimed that title. It was proved to him by the authority of the Law, the Prophets, and the Talmud, that Christ had truly come, as Christians believe. To this he was not able to reply.

Defeated by irrefutable proofs, he conceded that Christ, the messiah, was born 1000 years ago in Bethlehem and later appeared in Rome. And when asked where that messiah is, whom the Jews declared to have been born and to have appeared at Rome, he said that he did not know.

However, afterwards he said that he had been born, but had not yet come, because the messiah is said to have come only when he assumes dominion over the Jews and frees them and the Jews follow him.

Friar Paul quoted the Talmud, which says that the messiah will come to them if they listen to his voice and do not harden their hearts. Psalm 95:7 says: 'Today if you listen to his voice.' To say the messiah was born is the same as he has come. Moses was unable to reply.

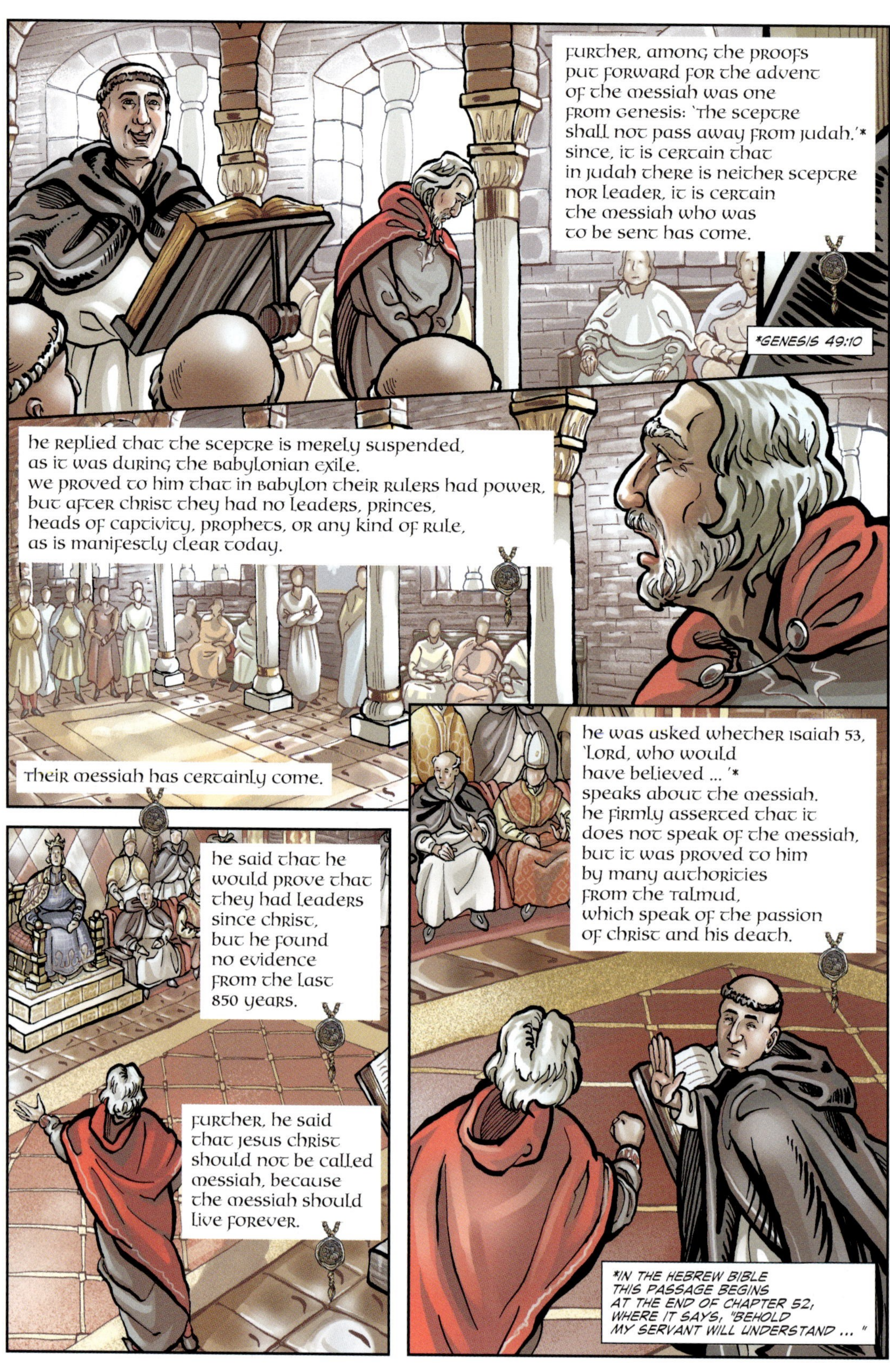
Further, among the proofs
put forward for the advent
of the messiah was one
from Genesis: 'The sceptre
shall not pass away from Judah.'*
Since, it is certain that
in Judah there is neither sceptre
nor leader, it is certain
the messiah who was
to be sent has come.
*GENESIS 49:10
He replied that the sceptre is merely suspended,
as it was during the Babylonian exile.
We proved to him that in Babylon their rulers had power,
but after Christ they had no leaders, princes,
heads of captivity, prophets, or any kind of rule,
as is manifestly clear today.
Their messiah has certainly come.
He said that he
would prove that
they had leaders
since Christ,
but he found
no evidence
from the last
850 years.
Further, he said
that Jesus Christ
should not be called
messiah, because
the messiah should
live forever.
He was asked whether Isaiah 53,
'Lord, who would
have believed ...'*
speaks about the messiah.
He firmly asserted that it
does not speak of the messiah,
but it was proved to him
by many authorities
from the Talmud,
which speak of the passion
of Christ and his death.
*IN THE HEBREW BIBLE
THIS PASSAGE BEGINS
AT THE END OF CHAPTER 52,
WHERE IT SAYS, "BEHOLD
MY SERVANT WILL UNDERSTAND ... "

Further, since he could not
explain the authorities,
he said publicly that
he did not believe in
the proofs cited,
though they were in ancient,
authoritative books of the Jews,
because, as he said,
they were sermons,
in which their teachers often lied
to encourage the people.

Thus, he dismissed the teachers
and the scriptures of the Jews.
Further, he denied all, or nearly all,
the things which he had previously admitted
and which had been proved to him,
and then, having been refuted again
through authorities and defeated,
he was compelled to admit them again.

Further, since he could not reply
and had been defeated many times,
and both Jews and Christians
were treating him with scorn,
he said obstinately in front of everyone
that he would not reply at all,
because the Jews had told him not to.

Also, some Christians,
namely Brother P. of Girona
and some respectable citizens
had sent to him to advise him
not to reply at all.
This lie was publicly refuted
by the said Brother P.
and the respectable citizens.
Clearly he was trying to escape
from the disputation by lies.

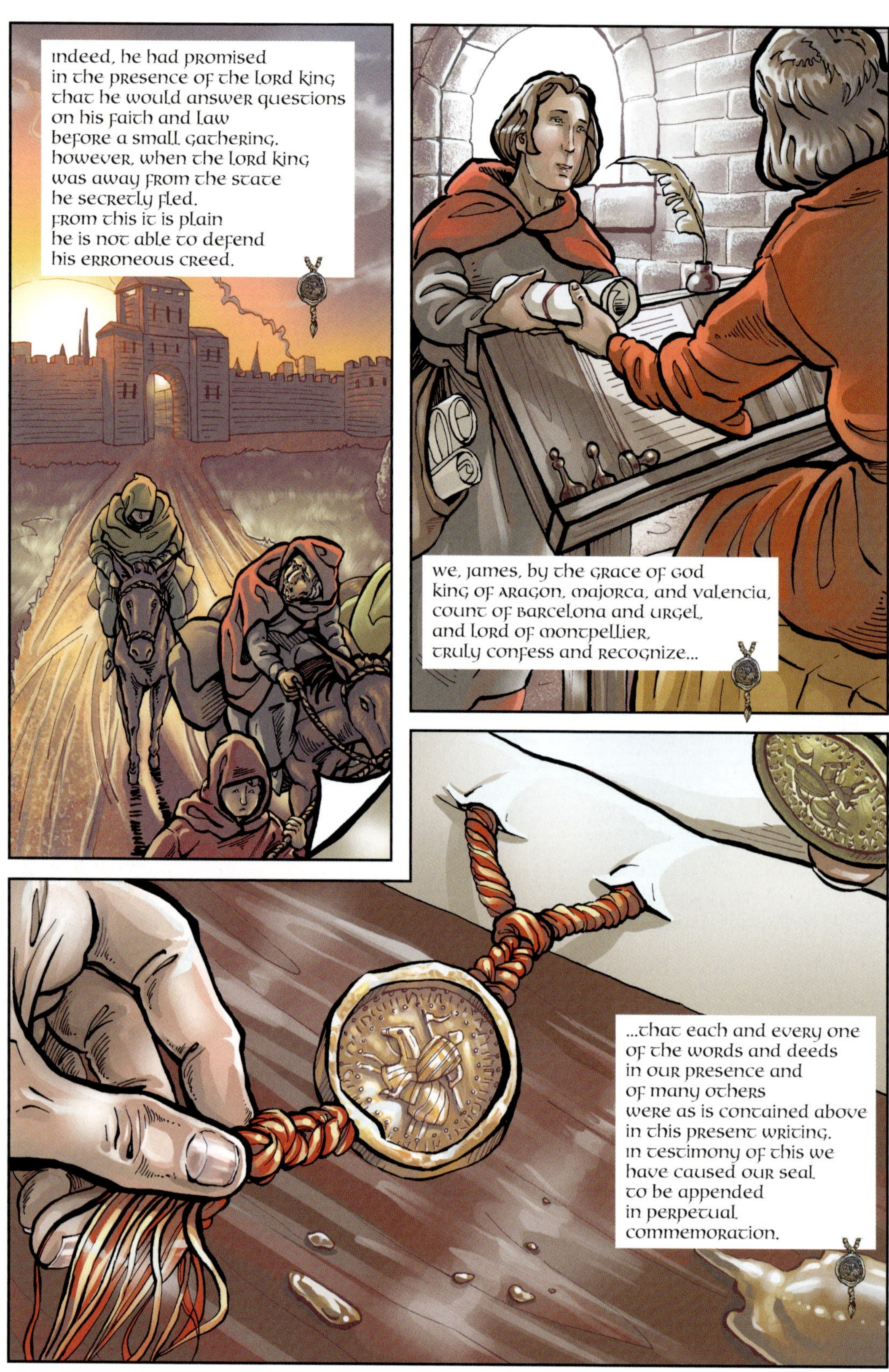
indeed, he had promised
in the presence of the lord king
that he would answer questions
on his faith and law
before a small gathering.
however, when the lord king
was away from the state
he secretly fled.
from this it is plain
he is not able to defend
his erroneous creed.
we, james, by the grace of god
king of aragon, majorca, and valencia,
count of barcelona and urgel,
and lord of montpellier,
truly confess and recognize...
...that each and every one
of the words and deeds
in our presence and
of many others
were as is contained above
in this present writing.
in testimony of this we
have caused our seal
to be appended
in perpetual
commemoration.

IN 1264, FOLLOWING STRONG JEWISH APPEALS, KING JAMES MODIFIED THE PROVISIONS GOVERNING CENSORSHIP OF JEWISH BOOKS.
CHRISTIAN AUTHORITIES WOULD HENCEFORTH IDENTIFY OFFENSIVE PASSAGES IN JEWISH BOOKS.
LEADERS COULD APPEAL INITIAL DECISIONS BEFORE A FIVE-MAN TRIBUNAL, BUT FAILED APPEAL COULD LEAD TO FINES AND BOOK BURNINGS.

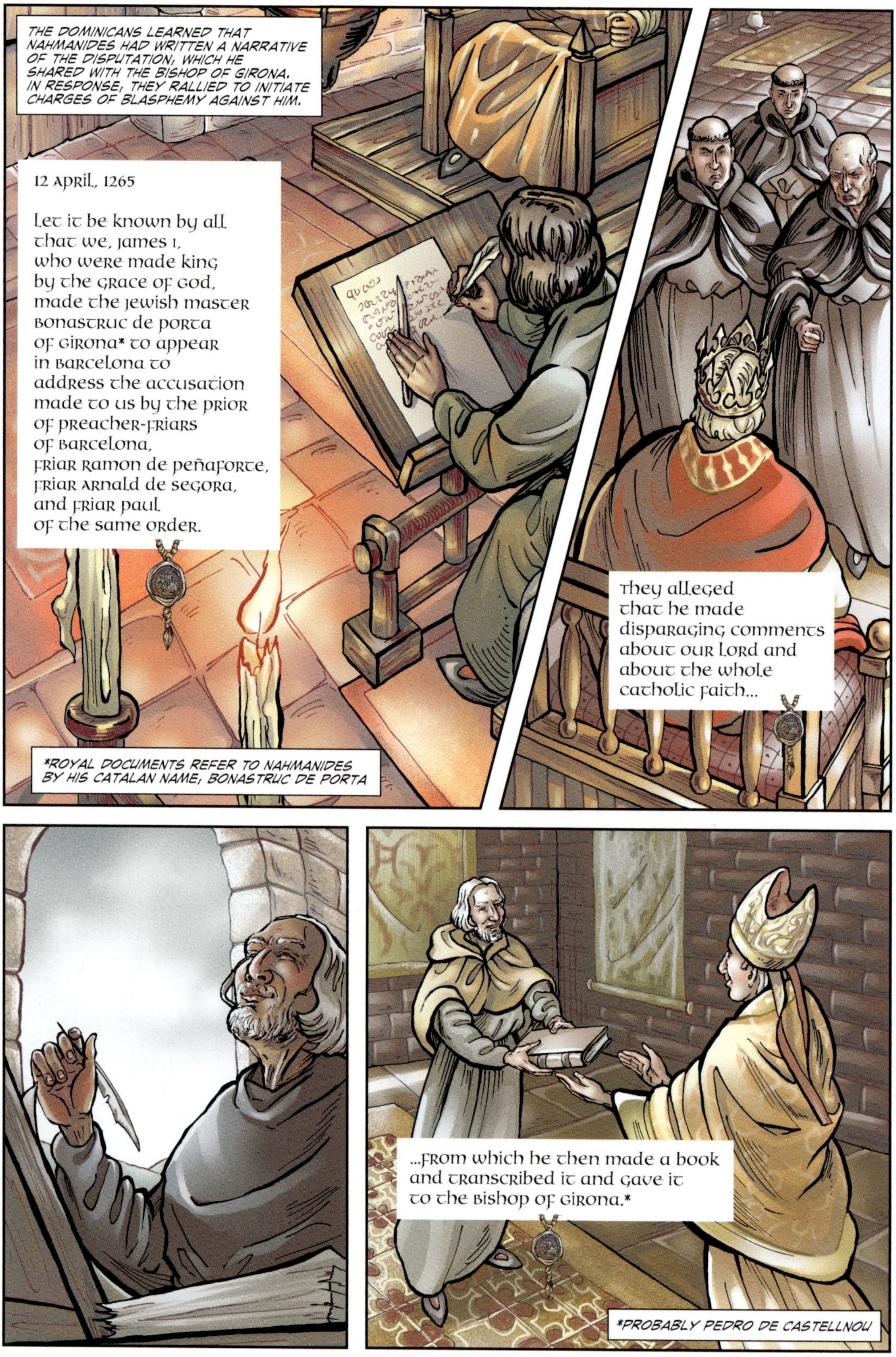

THE DOMINICANS LEARNED THAT NAHMANIDES HAD WRITTEN A NARRATIVE OF THE DISPUTATION, WHICH HE SHARED WITH THE BISHOP OF GIRONA. IN RESPONSE, THEY RALLIED TO INITIATE CHARGES OF BLASPHEMY AGAINST HIM.

12 April, 1265

Let it be known by all that we, James I, who were made king by the grace of God, made the Jewish master Bonastruc de Porta of Girona* to appear in Barcelona to address the accusation made to us by the prior of preacher-friars of Barcelona, friar Ramon de Peñaforte, friar Arnald de Segora, and friar Paul of the same order.

*ROYAL DOCUMENTS REFER TO NAHMANIDES BY HIS CATALAN NAME, BONASTRUC DE PORTA

They alleged that he made disparaging comments about our Lord and about the whole catholic faith...

...from which he then made a book and transcribed it and gave it to the Bishop of Girona.*
*PROBABLY PEDRO DE CASTELLNOU

In our presence with a venerable group
composed of various clerics and jurists...

...he responded that
he had spoken those
incriminating words
during the disputation
with Friar Paul
that took place
in our presence
at the royal palace.

he said that at the opening of the disputation,
we granted him permission of free speech
[to say] anything he might wish in this disputation.

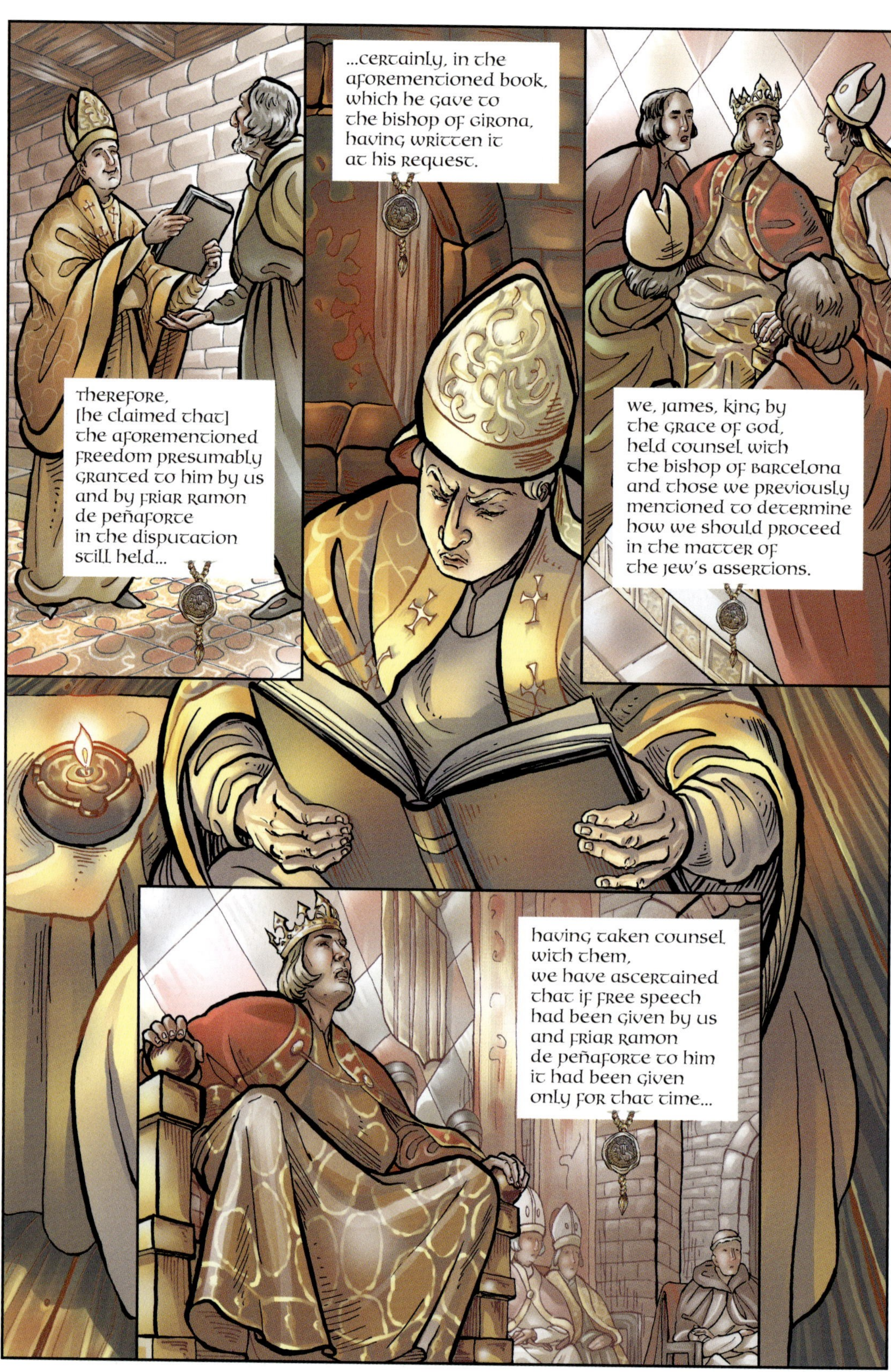
Therefore,
[he claimed that]
the aforementioned
freedom presumably
granted to him by us
and by friar Ramon
de Peñaforte
in the disputation
still held...
...certainly, in the
aforementioned book,
which he gave to
the bishop of Girona,
having written it
at his request.
We, James, king by
the grace of God,
held counsel with
the bishop of Barcelona
and those we previously
mentioned to determine
how we should proceed
in the matter of
the Jew's assertions.
Having taken counsel
with them,
we have ascertained
that if free speech
had been given by us
and friar Ramon
de Peñaforte to him
it had been given
only for that time...

we wanted, by way of sentencing,
to banish that jew from our land
for a period of two years
and make him burn the books
that were written concerning
the aforementioned words.

The preaching friars said that they would not be willing to accept this sentence under any circumstances.
After which, we, James, king by the grace of God, concede to you, master Bonastruc de Porto the Jew, that henceforth you need not respond to any of the preceding charges at any time unless it is in our presence.

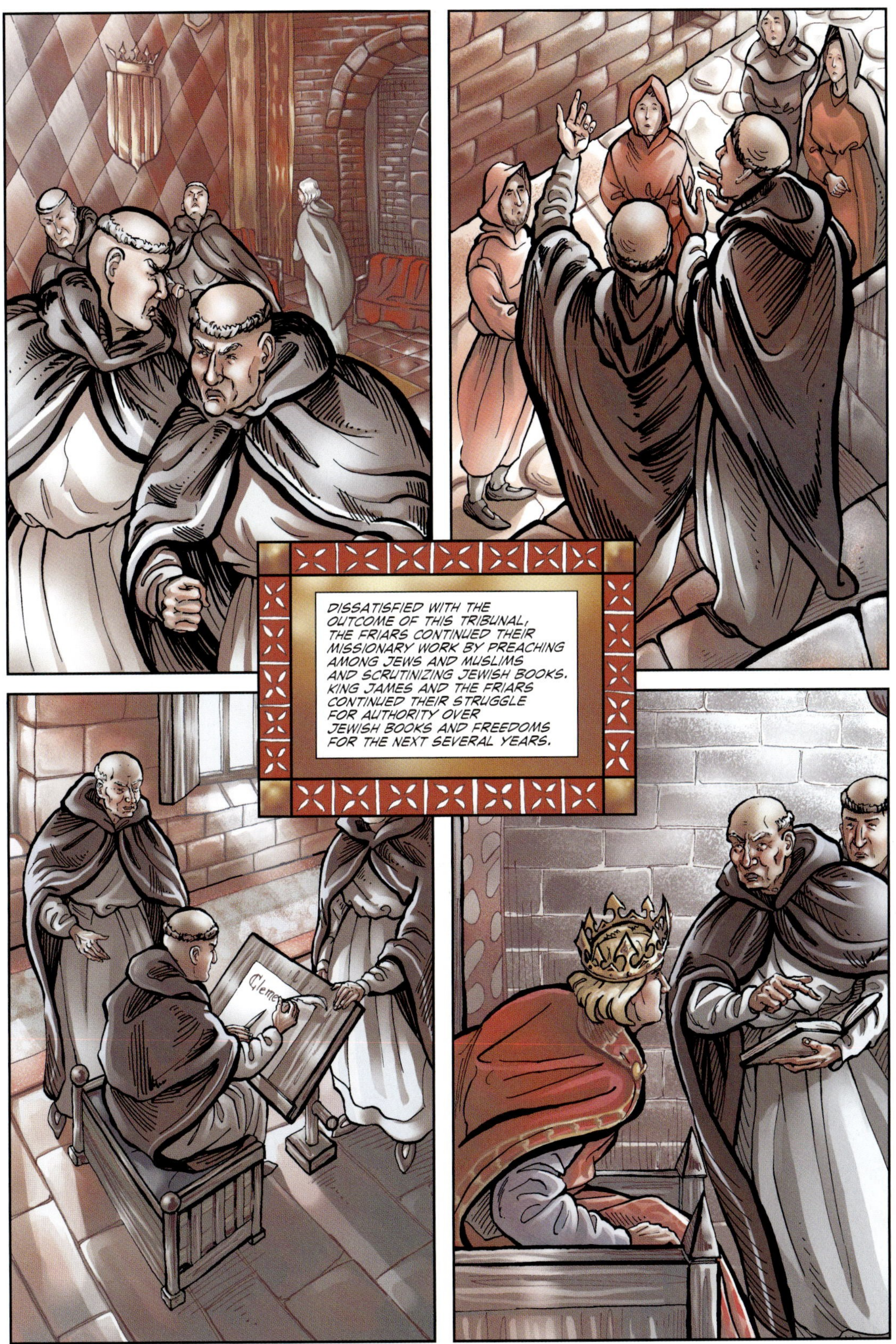
DISSATISFIED WITH THE OUTCOME OF THIS TRIBUNAL, THE FRIARS CONTINUED THEIR MISSIONARY WORK BY PREACHING AMONG JEWS AND MUSLIMS AND SCRUTINIZING JEWISH BOOKS. KING JAMES AND THE FRIARS CONTINUED THEIR STRUGGLE FOR AUTHORITY OVER JEWISH BOOKS AND FREEDOMS FOR THE NEXT SEVERAL YEARS.

FRIAR PAUL, RAMON DE PEÑAFORTE, AND ARNALD DE SEGORA COMPLAINED TO THE RECENTLY APPOINTED POPE CLEMENT IV THAT THE PUNISHMENT NAHMANIDES RECEIVED AT THE KING'S ECCLESIASTIC TRIBUNAL WAS INSUFFICIENT GIVEN THE GRAVITY OF HIS BLASPHEMY.

ca. 1266
to the illustrious king of aragon.
mother church
celebrates feast days,
not undeservingly,
as she joyously commemorates
your magnificent deeds,
and redoubles her songs of delight
and happiness, in reviewing,
nearly every day of late,
with delight the fervor
of your zeal and the rewards
of your diligence,
that of so dear and devoted a son.

she exults and rejoices
in the commemoration
of your happy successes,
throughout which
she virtuously directed
the salvation of the
christian people
into your hands,
with the right hand
of the lord and
the courage given
to you by him,
against the saracens,
blasphemers of her name
and outrageous
persecutors of
the catholic faith...

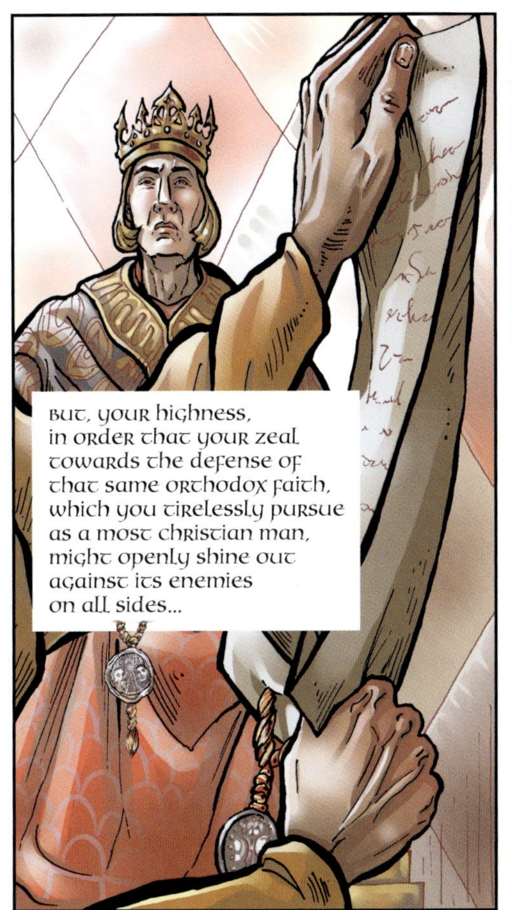
But, your highness,
in order that your zeal
towards the defense of
that same orthodox faith,
which you tirelessly pursue
as a most christian man,
might openly shine out
against its enemies
on all sides...

...let your favor be
most strong and public
in helping it against the jews,
who before all others
who persecute the faith
and blaspheme the name
of christianity...

...both blaspheme it
more bitterly and
persecute it more
villainously:
as for the rest,
do not admit jews to
any official positions,
and do not promote
them to one,
but inasmuch as
the privileges granted
to them by the
apostolic see permit,
humble and tame
their malice
by reining it in.

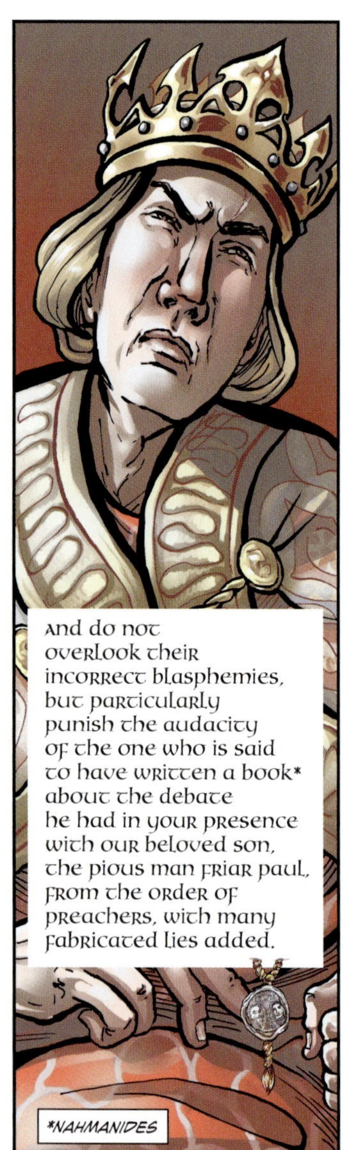
And do not overlook their incorrect blasphemies, but particularly punish the audacity of the one who is said to have written a book* about the debate he had in your presence with our beloved son, the pious man Friar Paul, from the order of preachers, with many fabricated lies added.
*NAHMANIDES

And to extend his error, he has reproduced many different copies with plans to send them to various regions.

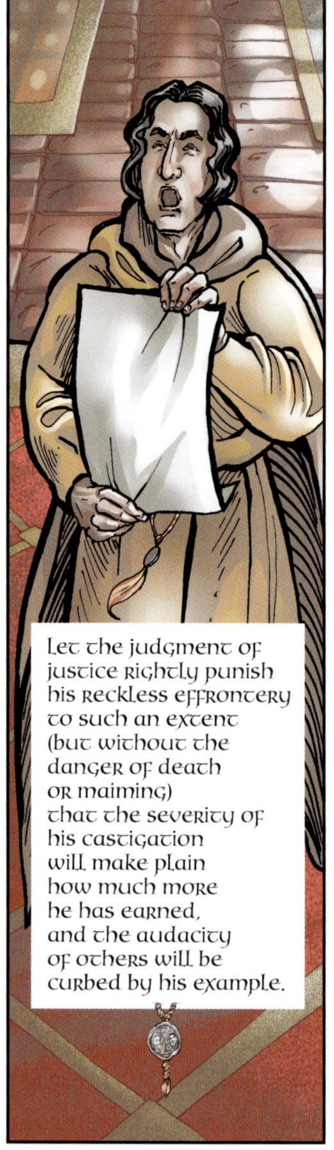
Let the judgment of justice rightly punish his reckless effrontery to such an extent (but without the danger of death or maiming) that the severity of his castigation will make plain how much more he has earned, and the audacity of others will be curbed by his example.

THE FRIARS FURTHER DEVELOPED THEIR PROGRAM OF USING STUDY OF RABBINIC SOURCES TO PREACH AGAINST JUDAISM.

CHAPTER 5

"I WRITE THIS LETTER TO YOU FROM JERUSALEM . . ."

POPE CLEMENT IV DISPATCHED THIS INFORMATION TO KING JAMES AND TO VARIOUS BISHOPS IN THE REGION.
NAHMANIDES AND THE JEWISH COMMUNITY ALSO RECEIVED WORD OF POPE CLEMENT'S CONTINUED INTEREST IN NAHMANIDES' INTERPRETATION OF THE DISPUTATION.
LIKELY CONCERNED THAT THE POPE'S INTEREST IN HIS ACTIONS COULD PLACE HIMSELF AND THE COMMUNITY AT LARGE IN PERIL, NAHMANIDES BEGAN CONTEMPLATING THE POSSIBILITY OF LEAVING THE CROWN OF ARAGON.

SINCE POPE CLEMENT
DISPATCHED HIS LETTER
CONDEMNING NAHMANIDES
TO BISHOPS THROUGHOUT THE REGION
AND THE DOMINICANS WERE PERSISTENT
IN THEIR PREACHING EFFORTS
ALL OVER FRANCE,
HE WOULD NOT HAVE
ESCAPED SCRUTINY THERE.

IN THE 1260S A GROUP OF FRENCH RABBIS
EMIGRATED TO THE LATIN KINGDOM IN ACRE,
WHERE THEY ESTABLISHED AN ACADEMY.

RABBI YEHIEL OF PARIS,
WHO DEFENDED THE TALMUD
IN A DISPUTATION STAGED
BY PAPAL INQUISITION
TWO DECADES EARLIER,
WAS AMONG THE ÉMIGRÉS,
THOUGH HE PERISHED ON THE WAY.

NAHMANIDES DECIDED TO TRAVEL TO THE HOLY LAND.

DEPARTING FROM THE PORT IN BARCELONA.

NAHMANIDES FOUND HIS WAY TO THE JEWISH SETTLEMENT IN ACRE...
...WHERE HE WAS WARMLY WELCOMED.

NAHMANIDES QUICKLY ESTABLISHED HIS PLACE IN AMONG THE JEWISH SCHOLARS OF ACRE.
HE FORMED HIS OWN RABBINIC ACADEMY, WHERE HE TAUGHT HIS INTERPRETATION OF THE TALMUD AND TORAH...
...COMPOSED COMMENTARIES ON THE BIBLE AND TALMUD...
...AND WROTE AND DELIVERED SERMONS.

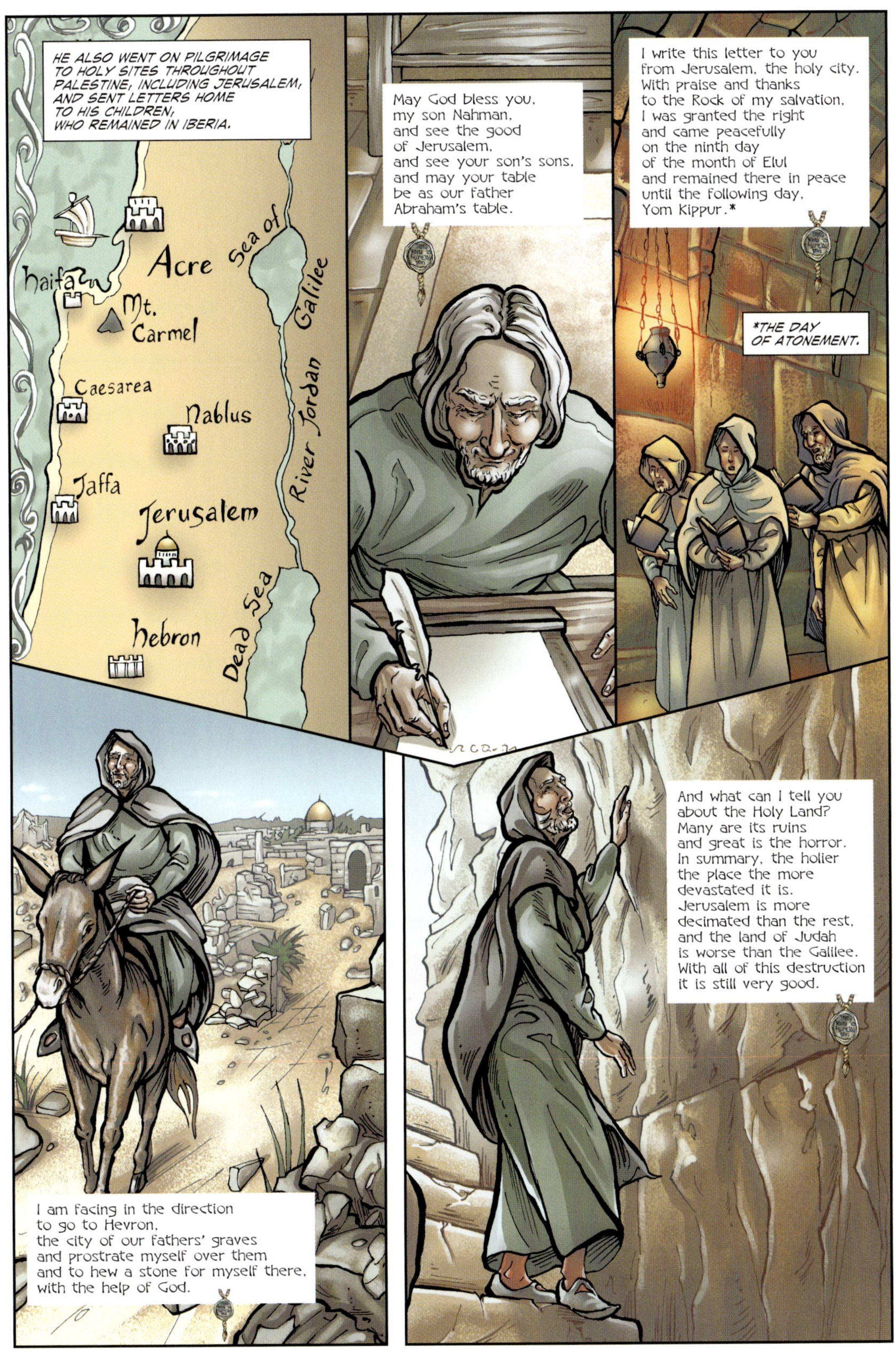
HE ALSO WENT ON PILGRIMAGE TO HOLY SITES THROUGHOUT PALESTINE, INCLUDING JERUSALEM, AND SENT LETTERS HOME TO HIS CHILDREN, WHO REMAINED IN IBERIA.
Acre
Sea of Galilee
Haifa
Mt. Carmel
Caesarea
Nablus
River Jordan
Jaffa
Jerusalem
Dead Sea
Hebron
May God bless you, my son Nahman, and see the good of Jerusalem, and see your son's sons, and may your table be as our father Abraham's table.
I write this letter to you from Jerusalem, the holy city. With praise and thanks to the Rock of my salvation, I was granted the right and came peacefully on the ninth day of the month of Elul and remained there in peace until the following day, Yom Kippur.*
*THE DAY OF ATONEMENT.
I am facing in the direction to go to Hevron, the city of our fathers' graves and prostrate myself over them and to hew a stone for myself there, with the help of God.
And what can I tell you about the Holy Land? Many are its ruins and great is the horror. In summary, the holier the place the more devastated it is. Jerusalem is more decimated than the rest, and the land of Judah is worse than the Galilee. With all of this destruction it is still very good.

There is a settlement of nearly two thousand; among them are about three hundred Christians, those who escaped the Sultan's sword. But there are none from Israel among them, for they fled from there when the Tartars came, (though) some of them were killed by their swords.
Just two brothers remain, dyers who buy their dyes from the government. With them in their home they (Jews) gather until there is a *minyan** for prayers and for Shabbat (services).
*QUORUM OF TEN NEEDED FOR PRAYER.
Now we have encouraged them and we found a desolated house built with marble columns and a beautiful dome. We took the house for a synagogue. Because the city is lawless all who want to claim ruins claims them. We made donations for repairs on the house, and they are already under way.
They sent to the city of Shehem to bring from there the Torah scrolls that were taken from Jerusalem when the Tartars came. Thus they will establish a synagogue there and they will pray.
For many people frequently come to Jerusalem, men and women, from Damascus and Aleppo and all the other districts of the land to see the Temple and to weep over it.

He who is worthy to see Jerusalem in ruins, may He deem us worthy to see it also in a complete and restored state, when the glory and spirit (of God) will return.

You, my son, and your brothers, and the entire house (i.e. family) of your father, may you be deemed worthy of Jerusalem in good and in consolation of Zion.
Your worrying and forgetful father, who is seeing and rejoicing.
Moses ben Rav Nahman

NAHMANIDES REMAINED IN PALESTINE, MOST LIKELY IN ACRE, UNTIL HIS DEATH IN 1270; THE PRECISE DATE OF HIS DEATH IS UNKNOWN. ONE OF HIS FORMER STUDENTS IDENTIFIED ACRE AS THE LOCATION OF HIS GRAVE.

ACRE REMAINED A CENTER OF JEWISH LEARNING UNTIL MAY 1291, WHEN THE CITY FELL TO THE EGYPTIAN ARMY UNDER SULTAN AL-ASHRAF.
MANY CHRISTIAN AND JEWISH RESIDENTS OF THE CITY PERISHED.
THE BULK OF THE JEWISH LEARNING PRODUCED IN PALESTINE DURING THE 13TH CENTURY WAS DESTROYED WITH THE CITY AND ITS INHABITANTS.
ONE OF THE FEW REFUGEES WHO ESCAPED MAY HAVE PRESERVED A SMALL COLLECTION OF WRITINGS PRODUCED IN THE VIBRANT ACADEMIES OF ACRE. THIS MAY BE WHY THE SERMON NAHMANIDES DELIVERED FOR ROSH HA-SHANNAH* WAS KNOWN TO EUROPEAN JEWISH COMMUNITIES.
*THE NEW YEAR

PART II
THE PRIMARY SOURCES

The following section presents translations of the primary sources that formed the core of this graphic history. Nahmanides' Hebrew disputation account (Document I) will be immediately recognizable to readers who read the graphic history first. Written as a dialogue explicitly meant to mimic a living exchange, it lends itself to dramatization. Most of the graphic history either quotes the Hebrew account directly or closely paraphrases it, adapting the text to capture its sense while preserving the narrative flow.[1] In contrast to the Hebrew account, the Latin account (Document II), is terse and businesslike. The style, form, and voice reflect the author's very deliberate effort to produce a précis of arguments, rather than an animated discussion. Documents III to VI are letters from the royal archives, written during the final week of August 1263 and concerning active Dominican missionizing among Jews. Two of these letters secure the friars' authority to compel Jews to attend public sermons and censor Jewish books within the Crown of Aragon. Representing an abrupt turn, the other two chip away at the king's previous guarantees. An additional pair of documents deals with the accusations of blasphemy the friars leveled against Nahmanides and his subsequent expulsion from his lifelong home. The first of these (Document VII) is a general statement from the king describing the investigative tribunal and its outcome, and the second is a response from Pope Clement IV, showing his dissatisfaction with the outcome. Though we have no evidence attesting to Nahmanides' responses to these charges or the order of expulsion, poems and letters written by him from Palestine provide evidence that he made his way there sometime after the disputation. Document IX is a letter from Nahmanides to his son, Nahman, describing his experiences in the Holy Land. Finally, selected canons from the Fourth Lateran Council of 1215 provide an introduction to the overarching ideological framework for purifying Christendom. The first and

1 Although Nahmanides' account of the Barcelona disputation has been rendered into English before, copyright restrictions made it impossible to reproduce either of the two standard translations. I therefore chose to translate the text anew in the interest of collecting all of the central documents together in this volume. It is my hope that this translation offers an accessible and fluid rendition. Bibliographic information about previous translations can be found in the *Sources for Additional Reading* at the end of this book.

third canons provide a statement of Christian dogma formulated in philosophical terms and a broad characterization of heresy. The final four canons of the Council specifically address the treatment of Jews and Muslims.

DOCUMENT I

Nahmanides' Hebrew Account of the Barcelona Disputation

Unlike the graphic portion of this book, the text reproduced here includes an introductory story that provides a rationale for preserving Friar Paul's arguments for posterity.[2]

1) Jesus of Nazareth had five students, Matai, Nakai, Neitzar, Bunai, and Todah. When Matai was brought forward he asked, "should Matai be killed? It is written 'when (*matie*) will I come and see the face of God' (Psalms 42:3)?" They responded, "no, Matai should be killed, as it is written 'when (*matie*) will he die and perish' (Psalms 41:6)?" When Nakai was brought forward he said, "should Nakai die? For it is written 'the innocent (*naki*) and righteous shall not kill you' (Exodus 23:7)." They said to him, "this is not so, Nakai should be killed, as it is written 'in secret places he slays the innocent (*naki*).'" When Neitzar came forward he said, "shall he be killed? It is written 'and a shoot (*netzar*) will grow from his roots' (Isaiah 11:1)." They responded, "this is not so, Neitzar will be killed, as it is written 'and you are cast out of your grave like a despised offshoot (*netzar*)' (Isaiah 14:19)." When Bunai came forward, he said, "shall he be killed? For the scripture says, 'Israel is my son, my firstborn' (Exodus 4:22)." They said, "no, Bunai will be killed, it is written 'behold, I kill your son (*benkha*), your firstborn' (Exodus 4:23)." When Todah came forward, he said, "shall Todah be killed? For the scripture says, 'a song of thanksgiving (*todah*)' (Psalms 100:1)." They said to him, "this is not so, Todah will be killed, as it is written, 'whoever offers a sacrifice of thanksgiving (*todah*) honors me' (Psalms 50:23)" (Babylonian Talmud, *Sanhedrin* 43a).[3] Rabbi Solomon

2 Translated from Hayim Dov Chavel, "Vikuah ha-Ramban," in *Kitvei Rabbenu Moshe ben Nahman*, 2 vols. (Jerusalem: Mosad ha-Rav Kook, 1964), 1:302–20. I have reproduced the paragraph numbers printed in the critical edition of the Hebrew document for ease of navigation. All biblical quotes included in this text are based on the numbering of the Hebrew Bible, JPS edition.

3 Thus far, Nahmanides is reproducing a passage from the Babylonian Talmud in which members of a rabbinical court weigh evidence in the cases of treachery and heresy against five disciples of Jesus: Matai, Nakai, Neitzar, Bunai, and Todah (the first two correspond to Matthew and Luke, respectively, though the other three have no known historical parallels). The Talmudic passage makes its point through wordplay based on the names of the accused. In each case, the court offers scriptural precedents defending a lenient sentence of acquittal; and in each case the panel of judges finds in favor of biblical prooftexts that support the strictest legal penalty possible—execution. Nahmanides seems to be comparing Friar Paul to the disciples represented in this tale.

[ben Isaac][4] wrote that they [the apostles] were close to the government, and thus they [the Rabbis] needed to answer all of their vain arguments. It is for this purpose that I record the arguments with which I responded to the delusion[s] of Friar Paul, who publicly disgraced his education before our lord, the king, and his wise men and counselors.

2) Our lord the king commanded me to debate with Friar Paul[5] before him and his council in his palace in Barcelona. I answered and said: "I will do as you command, my lord king, if you give me permission to speak as I please. And I request in this matter the permission of the king and of Friar Ramon de Peñaforte[6] and his colleagues who are here."

3) Friar Ramon (de Peñaforte) replied: "Only if you do not speak contemptuously."

4) I replied to them: "I do not want to subject myself to your judgment on this; I must speak as I please during the disputation just as you may say what you wish. As for me, I have [sufficient] wisdom to speak discreetly. But I must speak as I wish." They all granted me freedom to speak freely.

5) Then I answered and said: "Disputations between the gentiles and the Jews have focused on many matters of tradition on which principles of belief do not rely. However, I do not want to debate in this exalted court anything but matters on which the entire controversy hinges."

6) All of them answered, saying: "You have spoken well. Now, we have agreed to open with the matter of whether the Messiah has already come, as the Christians believe, or if he will come in the future, as the Jews believe. After that, we will discuss the question of whether the Messiah is substantially divine or fully human, born of a man and a woman. And after that, we will address the question of whether the Jews or the Christians observe the true law."

7) Then Friar Paul said that he would argue, based on our Talmud, that the Messiah announced by the prophets had already arrived.

8) I replied: "Before we dispute this question, I request that he instruct me and explain to me how this is possible. I heard that he previously went about Provence and many other places saying such things to the Jews, and I am very surprised. He will answer me, wanting to suggest that the sages of the Talmud believed that Jesus was the Messiah and that he was

4 Rashi (1040–1105) was among the most influential teachers of and commenters on the Hebrew Bible, Talmud, and contemporary Jewish practice of the middle ages. Compilations of his legal decisions began circulating throughout Europe in the twelfth century.

5 Nahmanides transliterates his name as Pul in Hebrew. Most English scholarship refers to the friar as Friar Paul, Paulo, or Pablo Christiani. All of the names in this translation have been Anglicized for consistency.

6 The Hebrew is written out in two words: Peña Forte.

fundamentally human *and* truly divine, as the Christians believe. Is it not a known fact that in truth the case of Jesus took place [during the time of] the Second Temple and Jesus was born and died before the destruction of the Temple? The sages of the Talmud, such as Rabbi Akiva and his circle, lived after the destruction [of the Temple]. And the same people who taught the Mishnah of Rabbi [Judah ha-Nasi] and Rabbi Nathan lived many years after the destruction. Indeed, Rav Ashi, who assembled and recorded the Talmud, lived some 400 years after the destruction.[7] If these wise men believed in the messianic nature of Jesus, and [believed] that he was a true [Messiah] and that his faith and religion were true, and if these words from which Friar Paul argues were written as he says, how then did the [rabbis] stand by the religion of the Jews and their traditions, for they were Jews and remained in the faith of the Jews throughout their days and died as Jews. They and their sons and their students who heard all of their words from their mouths lived and died as Jews, just as we do today. (And why would they along with their students, who accepted the Torah from their mouths, not have apostatized and turned to the religion of Jesus as Friar Paul did, since he understood from their words that the faith of the Christians was correct—God forbid—and apostatized on account of their words.) And it was [the rabbis] who taught us the faith of Moses and Judaism, since all our actions today are a product of the Talmud and what we saw that the sages of the Talmud did, who were our leaders from the day of [the Talmud's] composition until today. For is not the whole Talmud [intended] to teach us the traditions of the Torah and the Commandments and how our fathers [in the time of the Temple] conducted themselves according to the words of the prophets and Moses, (may there be peace on him)? If they believed in Jesus and his faith, how could they not have done as Friar Paul has done, who understands their words even more than they do themselves?"

9) Friar Paul answered (and said [to me]): "These long words are intended to put a stop to the disputation. Nevertheless, you must hear what I am saying."

10) I said to them: "This is clear evidence that he will not speak words of substance. [However,] I will listen to them because you, our lord king, wish so."

11) He began, saying: "Here, it says in the Scriptures *the staff shall not pass from the tribe of Judah . . . until Shiloh has come* (Genesis 49:10), and [Shiloh] is the Messiah. If so, then the prophet[8] says that Judah will always

---

7 Three rabbis who edited and redacted the Mishnah and Talmud between the second and fifth centuries.

8 Jacob, speaking in Genesis 49:10.

have power until the Messiah who comes from him. Thus, today, since you have neither a single tribe nor a ruler's staff, the Messiah, who is from his [Judah's] descendants has already come, and he holds rule of government."

12) I answered and said: "It was not the intention of the prophet to say that there would be no break in the rule of Judah at all during any time; rather, he said that it would not end and completely depart from him [Judah]. The implication [of this verse] is that at every time that there is kingship for Israel, it will reside with Judah. And if their kingship shall cease due to sin, it will return to Judah. The proof of my words is that for a long period of time[9] before Jesus, kingship had been removed from Judah and not from Israel, and for a long time it was also removed from both Israel and Judah. Surely, during the seventy years of exile in Babel there was no royal government in Judah or in Israel at all. And during the [time of the] Second Temple there was no king in Judah, only Zerubavel[10] and his sons for a [small] number of years, and they remained after that for 380 years until the destruction [of the Second Temple], when the priests from the family of the Hashmonians and their servants ruled. And certainly now, as the nation is in exile (*galut*), when there is no nation [in the homeland] there is no king."

13) Friar Paul answered: "During all of those same times, even though you had no kings, you did have a [legitimate] government. So they explained in the Talmud:[11] *the staff shall not pass from Judah*, [refers to] the leaders during the Babylonian exile who ruled the nation with a scepter (harshly),[12] and *and the scepter from between his feet*, this refers to the sons and disciples of Rabbi Hillel, who taught Torah to the multitudes.[13] But today you do not have a recognized ordination in accordance with the Talmud, so also that form of government has ceased for you.[14] Thus, there is no one among

9 Literally, "many days." The language in this statement foreshadows a later point in the disputation about under what circumstances it is acceptable to interpret the word *yom*—day—as year. See pages 105–106, paragraphs 62–68.

10 Referenced in Ezra, Nehemiah, and Zechariah as builder of the Temple.

11 Sanhedrin 5a.

12 He is referring here to the Exilarchs, or the leaders of the Jewish communities in Babylon or current-day Iraq.

13 Rabbi Hillel was a teacher from the first century B.C.E. who advocated an egalitarian view of education based on personal and interpretive achievements rather than social standing.

14 According to the Bible, Moses appointed Joshua and 70 elders as recognized leaders and judges (Numbers 11:16–17, 24–25, and 27:22–23; Deuteronomy 34:9). Only an ordained scholar could adjudicate in matters of Jewish law. Tradition holds that an uninterrupted line of ordination or *semikhah* followed, whereby every judge or official leader received ordination from one who was already ordained. Most scholars agree that this practice ended in the fourth century.

you who can properly be called 'Rabbi.' The title you apply to yourselves today, *Maestri*, is mistaken and you fraudulently lead by that title."

14) I answered him with scorn: "This is outside of the [parameters defined for the] disputation, but you are not speaking the truth. [The title] 'Rabbi' is not the same as *Maestri*; rather, a 'Rav' is a *Maestri*, and one does not need ordination to be called Rav according to the Talmud. Nevertheless, I concede that I am neither a *Maestri* nor a *Talmid Tov*."[15] I said this by way of instruction. I then returned [to the matter at hand] and said to him: "I will show you that our rabbis of blessed memory did not mean to interpret the verse as referring to anything other than real kingship. However, you have understood neither our justice nor our law, you know only a few homilies (*haggadot*[16]) with which you have familiarized yourself. This matter that the sages mentioned is as follows: according to strict law, a solitary man of justice is exempt from paying [a fine][17] as long as he received permission from the *Nasi*,[18] and he was a king. They meant in the time of the *galut* (exile), seeing that there were descendants of [Davidic] royalty, the individuals to whom the kings of the nations[19] bestowed a degree of authority, such as the leaders of the Babylonian Exile[20] or the *Nesi'im* in the Land of Israel, they had the ability to grant permission [to rule] and ordination. And this continued among the Sages of the Talmud for more than four hundred years after Jesus. Moreover, it is not the opinion of the Sages of the Talmud that Judah would always control a staff and scepter, but rather the prophet assured Judah that when there is a kingdom, Judah would rule. Nevertheless, kingship was suspended for many years, as I mentioned, because during the time of the Babylonian Exile they had neither staff nor scepter. Also, during the Second Temple, when there was a kingship of priests and their servants, Judah held no staff except of government. There was neither an exilarch

15 *Talmid tov* means a good student, specifically one who internalizes the text and its interpretations and has the wherewithal to mobilize those interpretations.

16 This word can be spelled beginning with an *aleph* (transliterated as "a") or a *heh* (transliterated as "h"). In contemporary usage, *aggadah* is generally associated with the homilies or stories under discussion here, while *haggadah* is generally associated with the Passover liturgy. To avoid confusion, we have used the more common "*aggadah*" in most instances in the graphic. The spelling preferred by Nahmanides in the printed version of the text, however, is *haggadah*. In this more complete translation of the Hebrew disputation account, I have chosen to preserve the spellings Nahmanides used in the text.

17 In the case of a false or incorrect judgment. At issue here is the official recognition of the right to rule.

18 Prince.

19 Nahmanides uses the term *goyim*, which indicates gentile peoples and has pejorative overtones.

20 The Exilarchs; see footnote 12.

(*Rosh Galut*) nor a prince (*Nasi*), because leadership and the powers of the prince were held by the kings among the priests and their judges and ministers, and those who were pleasing in their eyes."

15) The Friar Peter of Genoa answered: "This is the truth; the scripture says that [the scepter] will not depart completely, but it can be suspended, *vagare* in the vernacular."

16) I responded to the king: "See, Friar Peter interprets the law as I did."

17) Friar Peter said: "I did not subscribe to the claim, because seventy years of Babylonian exile is a short period. There were many who remembered the first Temple, as is written in the Book of Ezra (3:12); and this may be called a suspension, *vagare* in the vernacular. But, now you have waited more than one thousand years. This is complete removal."

18) I said: "Now you have reconsidered, for is it not the case that removal happens to a thing that returns, and is it not so that, in the words of the prophet, there is no distinction between many [years] and few [years]? All the more so, since the periods of time I mentioned were long periods. Moreover, since Jacob, our father, may there be peace upon him, did not promise Judah that he would have the scepter and the right to rule over his tribe alone; rather, he gave him kingship over all of Israel, as it is written *Judah, your brothers will praise you* (Genesis 49:8). And it is also written, *Judah prevailed over his bothers and from him came the one who would rule as prince* (I Chronicles 5:2). Thus the kingdom of all the tribes of Israel was interrupted from the time that Solomon died, as it is written *there were none who followed the house of David, but only the tribe of Judah* (I Kings 12:20). If so, then it is a clear thing that the prophet says nothing other than it will not be a complete cessation [of rulership]. And the truth is that at the time of the exile it was called neither interruption nor cessation at all. Therefore, it was not due to Judah but rather due to part of the people, because the prophet did not specify to Judah that [his descendants] would never rule over Israel in exile, instead that he would be the king of Israel for all time."

19) Friar Paul responded and argued that in the Talmud they said that the Messiah already came. He brought an *haggadah* that is in *Midrash Lamentations*, which states: *a man was plowing, and his cow lowed, an Arab passer-by said to him, 'bar Yehudai, bar Yehudai, untie your cow, untie your plow, untie your plowshare, for your Temple has been destroyed.' He untied his cow, untied his plow, and untied his plowshare. [The cow] lowed a second time. [The Arab] said to him, 'tie up your cow, tie up your plow, tie up your plowshare, for your Messiah has been born.'*[21]

21 Midrash Lamentations, 1:51.

20) I replied, saying: "I do not believe in that homily at all, although it is proof for my words."

21) Then the same man shouted: "Here is proof that he denies [the authority of] their books!"

22) I said: "It is true that I do not believe that the Messiah was born on the day of the destruction [of the Temple], and this *haggadah* is either not true or it has an alternative interpretation from the secrets of the sages. However, I will accept the same literal meaning you cited, for this is proof for me. Thus, it says that on the day of the destruction after the Temple was razed, at that same time, the Messiah was born. If this is so, then Jesus was not the Messiah, as you have said, because he was born and died before the destruction. In truth, he was born more than two hundred years prior to the destruction. And according to your calculations, 73 years before." Thus, the man was silenced.

23) Maestri William, the king's judge, answered: "This disputation is not about Jesus. Rather, the question is whether or not the Messiah has come. You said that he has not come, and this book of yours says that he has."

24) I said to him: "You chose to answer with legal deceit. Nevertheless, I will answer you on this matter. The sages did not say that he came; they said that he was born. On the day that Moses our teacher (may he be blessed) was born he did not come, he was not yet a redeemer,[22] but when he came to Pharaoh as was God's command and said to him *so says the Lord: send forth my people* (Exodus 7:26), then he came [as Moses the prophet]. So too the Messiah, when he will come to the pope and say to him according to the command of God *send forth my people*, then he will have come. And know that as of today, he has not come [as the redeemer], and we do not yet have a messiah at all.[23] David the King was not king and was not anointed on the day of his birth, but when Samuel anointed him he became a messiah [an anointed one]. And on the day that Elijah will anoint the Messiah in accordance with God's command, he will be called Messiah. And after that day, he will come to the pope and redeem us and then it will be said that the redeemer has come."

25) The same man argued: "Here is a portion [from Isaiah], beginning with the verse *Behold, my servant will prosper* (52:13), that talks about the death of the Messiah and about how he came into the hand [of those who afflict him] and they gave him over to the wicked, as was the case with Jesus. Now, do you believe that this portion refers to Jesus?"

---

22 In other words, he did not make himself known as Israel's leader.

23 He is making the point that there are two types of messiah: one who is an anointed leader, like David, and one who will be sent as a redeemer.

26) I said to him: "According to the true meaning, it does not discuss him; rather, [it refers] to the nation of Israel generally, for this is how the prophets refer to them: *Israel my servant* (Isaiah 41:8), *Jacob my servant* (44:1)."[24]

27) Friar Paul said: "I will prove with the words of your sages that it *does* refer to the Messiah!"

28) I said to him: "And it is true that in the books of *haggadot* our rabbis, may their memories be for a blessing, interpret it as being about the Messiah, but they did not ever say that he would die at the hands of his enemies. Thus, you will never find in any book from among the books of Israel, not in the Talmud and not in the *haggadot*, that the Messiah ben David would be killed, or that he would be delivered to the hand of his enemies, or that he would be buried among the wicked.—And the Messiah that you established for yourselves was not even buried!—I will explain to you the portion [in Isaiah 52], if you wish, with a good and clear interpretation [showing] that there is no mention that he would be killed, as your Messiah was." But they did not want to hear.

29) He returned [to the previous topic] and said: "In the Talmud Rabbi Joshua ben Levi asked Elijah when the Messiah would come, and he answered: 'ask the Messiah himself.' [R. Joshua] said: 'And where is he?' [Elijah] said: 'At the entrance to Rome among the sick.' [R. Joshua] walked there and found him, and asked him, etc. [25] If this is so, then he already came, and he is in Rome, and he is Jesus (who rules over Rome)."

30) I replied to him: "Is it not explicit here that he has not come? Does he not ask Elijah *when* he would come? And he also asked in the same text when the honorable one would arrive. But, though the plain sense of this homily states that he was born, I do not believe that."

31) Then our lord the king answered: "If he was born on the day of the destruction of the Second Temple and that was more than one thousand years ago and he hasn't come again, when will he come, because it is not in man's nature to live one thousand years."

32) I said to him: "There were conditions [stating] that I would not debate with you, so I will not answer in the debate. Suffice it to say that among the first men there were already those, like Adam and Methuselah, who lived for one thousand years. And Elijah and Enoch lived longer than that, for life is from God."

33) He said: "Then where is he today?"

34) I said: "This is not among the prescribed topics of the disputation so I will not answer you. Perhaps you will find him at the gates of Toledo,

24 Also see Isaiah 44:21, 45:4, 48:20, 49:3.

25 Sanhedrin 98a.

if you send a man there from your team of couriers." I said this by way of a joke.

35) Then they stood and the king gave the time for the disputation on the following Monday.[26]

36) On that day the king went to the cloisters in the city and gathered there all of the people of the city, gentiles and Jews. And the bishop and all of the priests and the Franciscan masters and preachers, and that same man [Friar Paul] rose to speak.

37) I said to our lord the king: "My lord, please hear me." And he said to me: "He should begin and speak first, for he is the prosecutor."

38) I said: "Permit me to explain my views in the matter of the Messiah, then he will be able to respond to the matter with clarity."

39) I rose, saying: "*Hear me, all people* (Micah 1:2), Friar Paul asked me if the Messiah that the prophets talk about had already come, and I said he had not come. He brought a book of homilies (*Sefer Aggadah*) that says that he was born on the very day that the Temple was destroyed. And I said that I did not believe that, but that it was proof of my argument. Now I will explain to you why I said I did not believe that. [You should] know that we have three types of books. The first is the *biblia*[27] and all of us believe it in its entirety. The second is called the Talmud, and it explains the commandments of the Torah, for the Torah contains 613 commandments and not one of those is not explained in the Talmud. We accept it as an explanation of the commandments. Finally, we have a third body of literature that is called Midrash, that is to say, *sermones*.[28] It is as if the bishop were to stand and give a sermon, and one of the audience found it pleasing and wrote it down. If one believes the content of this literature, then all the better; if one does not believe it, then no harm is done. So, we do have sages who wrote that the Messiah would not be born until the time of the end is near, then he will come to bring us from the *galut* (exile). Thus, I do not believe in the statement in the book that the Messiah was born on the day of the destruction. Moreover, we call this book *Sefer Haggadah*, which means *Razionamiento*.[29] That is to say, it is simply sayings that one person tells his friend. But I accept the simple meaning of the *haggadah* according

26 23 July, 1263; 15 Av, 5923.

27 Here Nahmanides transliterates the vernacular term for "bible," rather than using the Hebrew term, *Torah*, which includes the five books of Moses, or Tanakh, referring to the full Hebrew Bible.

28 Sermons. Again, Nahmanides presents a transliteration of the vernacular to introduce this body of commentary.

29 Meaning story or tale in Italian.

to your wish, because it demonstrates with clarity that your Jesus is not the Messiah. As I told you, he was not born on that same day. But his affairs had already passed[30] a long time before. You, my lord king, raised and asked me a better and more difficult question than they did. For it is not customary that man should live one thousand years. Now, I will clarify for you the answer to your question. The first man lived seventy years less than one thousand years. The Scripture explains that he died because of his sins, and perhaps he would have lived longer, or even forever, had he not sinned. The gentiles and the Jews all concede that the sin and punishment of the first man will be cancelled in the days of the Messiah. Thus, after the Messiah comes [death] will cease for all of us, though for the Messiah himself, it will end completely. If this is the case, then it is evident that the Messiah will live for thousands and thousands of years or forever. And thus, the Psalmist states *He asks for life from you* (Psalms 21:5). It is now clarified."

40) "You have asked further, our lord king, where he [the Messiah] is located. The answer is in the Scripture, for the first man was located in the Garden of Eden, which is on earth. And when he sinned, it was said, *and the Lord God sent him from the Garden of Eden* (Genesis 3:23). If this is so, then he, who is free of the sins of man, resides there in the Garden of Eden. Indeed, so said the sages in the book of *haggadot* that I mentioned."

41) The king said: "Did you not say that the same *haggadah* places him in Rome?"

42) I said to him: "I did not say that he was located in Rome; I said that he was *seen* in Rome on that day, as Elijah told the same sage that he would find him there on the same day, and he was seen there. His appearance there was for a purpose, according to the mentioned *haggadot*, but I don't want to explain before this large group of people." And it was the case that I did not want to tell them what the *haggadah* says, that the messiah would remain in Rome until he destroyed it, just as we find in the case of Moses Rabbenu (may there be peace upon him), who was raised in the Pharaoh's home until he (Pharaoh) was punished by him (Moses), who drowned all of his nation in the sea. As it says about King Hiram of Tzur,[31] *so I made fire within you, and it has consumed you* (Ezekiel 28:18). And Isaiah (27:10) said: *there the calf will graze, there it will lie down and consume its branches*. And in *Perkei Hekhalot* it says, *until one man will say to his friend: 'here is Rome and all that is in it for*

30 That is, they have been completed.

31 Tyre.

a perutah'[32] *and he will say 'it is not desirable to me.'*"[33] All this I communicated directly to the king.

43) I asked and added: "Do you agree that the sins of Adam will be cancelled at the time of the Messiah?"

44) My lord the king and Friar Paul both answered: "Yes! But not as you think, as everyone entered Gehenna because of his very sin. However, in the days of the Messiah [the sin] was cancelled and Jesus removed them from there."

45) I answered and said: "They say in our country:[34] he who wants to deceive has witnesses who are far away. Many punishments are recorded for Adam and Eve: *cursed be the ground because of you . . . it will sprout thorns and thistles for you . . . by the sweat on your face, because you are dust* (Genesis 3:17–19). And also for the woman: *you will bear children in pain* (Genesis 3:16). And they are all in place also today, and all [the afflictions] that can be seen and felt were not pardoned in the time of your Messiah. However, you say that Gehenna, which is not written about there, has been forgiven, because there is no one who can contradict you. *Send one from among you* (Genesis 42:16), he will come and he will tell. Moreover, far be it for God [to be wicked], for there is no punishment in Gehenna for the righteous because the sin of the first man, their ancestor, because my soul is exactly as close to my father's soul as it is to the soul of Pharaoh, and my soul will not enter Gehenna because of the Pharaoh's sin. The punishments were to the body just as my body is from my father and my mother. Because the two of them (Adam and Eve) became mortal beings, their descendants were thereafter mortal by nature."

46) The same man stood and said: "I will bring another proof that the Messiah already came long ago."

47) I said: "My lord king, listen to me for a moment. There is nothing essential in our law, our truth, or our justice that relies upon the Messiah. For you are of equal or greater [importance] to me than the Messiah. You are a king, and he is a king. You are a gentile king, and he [will be] a king of Israel. The Messiah is nothing more than a king of flesh and blood like

---

32 The smallest monetary denomination.

33 See James R. Davila, *Hekhalot Literature in Translation: Major Texts of Merkavah Mysticism*, Supplements to the Journal of Jewish Thought and Philosophy, v. 20 (Leiden, Boston: Brill, 2013), 69.

34 Nahmanides means "my religion" here. His use of the term *country* is interesting. Since he lived under the royal authority of King James, presumably spoke the same vernacular language, and throughout the disputation account called attention to the king's authority to exert his power over members of the Jewish communities, he seems to be making a claim about ethnic, cultural, and possibly legal distinctiveness.

you. As I worship my Creator in your domain, in exile, torment, and servitude, with *the insults of the nations* (Ezekiel 36:15) *who continuously slander me* (Psalms 102:9), my reward is great because I make offerings to God from my body, and for this I am more and more deserving of life in the world to come. However, when we shall have a king of Israel, according to my [understanding of the] law, he will govern over all nations, and I will be compelled to abide by the laws of the Jews. The reward will not be as great. The root of the law and the division between Jews and Christians, namely your understanding of the essence of divinity, is a very bitter matter. You, my lord king, are a Christian, the son of a Christian man and a Christian woman, and you heard all of your days priests, monks, and preachers talking about the birth of Jesus and they filled your brain and the marrow of your bones with this matter and it comes to you through the force of habit. But the intellect will not accept this thing that you believe, and it is the root of your faith. Nature does not permit it, the prophets never said it. Also a miracle cannot uncover itself in that way, as I will explain with conclusive proof in its place and time. That the creator of the heavens and earth and everything in them would return to the womb of a Jewish woman and grow there for seven months, be born small, and afterwards grow, then be delivered into the hands of his enemies and condemned to a sentence of death, then killed by them, after which, they would say that he lived and returned to his original place is not acceptable to the mind of a Jew or any other man. You speak your words in vain and without cause, for this is the root of the division between us. But we will speak also about the Messiah, as is your desire."

48) Friar Paul said: "Do you believe that he has come?"

49) I said: "No. I believe and know that he has not come, and that there was no man who said or about whom it was said that he was the Messiah other than Jesus. It is impossible for me to accept his messianic nature. The prophet said that the Messiah would *have dominion from sea to sea and to the ends of the earth* (Psalms 72:8). He never had dominion, though he was persecuted by his enemies during his lifetime and hid himself because of them. In the end he fell into their hands and was unable to save himself; how, then, will he save all of Israel? And even after his death he had no dominion, for the power of Rome was not due to him! Even before they believed in him the city of Rome ruled over much of the earth, and after they came to believe in him they lost much of their power. Now the worshippers of Muhammad have greater power than they do. As the prophet said, *no longer does a man need to teach his companion or his brother and say know God because they know me* (Jeremiah 31:33). And it says that *the world will be filled with understanding of the Lord, like waters covering the seas* (Isaiah 11:9). And it says *they will beat their swords*

[into plowshares] . . . and nation will not raise sword against nation and no longer will they study war (Isaiah 2:4). From the time of Jesus until now the entire *earth has been filled with violence* (Genesis 6:11) and oppression; in fact, the Christians spill more blood than the rest of the nations, they are also promiscuous.[35] How difficult would it be for you, my lord king, for these knights of yours, if they *would no longer study war* (Isaiah 2:4). The prophet also said about the Messiah that *he will strike the land with the rod of his mouth* (Isaiah 11:4). The *Sefer Haggadah* that Friar Paul has in his hand interprets this [as follows]: *they say to the messiah king 'a certain nation chastises you,' he says 'may locusts come and destroy you,' they say 'a certain district chastises you,' he says 'let mixed [beasts] annihilate you';*[36] it was not so with Jesus. You are his servants, yet it is good for you that your horses are armored, but this amounts to nothing for you. What's more, I can bring for you many proofs from the words of the prophets."

50) The same man shouted, saying: "Such is his way to constantly make long declarations. I have a question to ask!"

51) The king said to me: "Silence, for he is the prosecutor." So I was quiet.

52) He said: "Your sages said about the Messiah that he would be revered above the angels. It is impossible that this could be anyone other than Jesus, because he is your Messiah and he is divine by nature, and he brought what they said in the *haggadah*: *he will be exalted, lifted up, and very high.*[37] He is more exalted than Abraham, lifted higher than Moses, and higher than the ministering angels."

53) I said to him: "Our sages always say this about all of the pious men, men who were more pious than the ministering angels.[38] Moses our teacher said to the angel 'you do not have permission to stand in the place where I sit.'[39] Concerning Israel in general, he said 'Israel is more beloved than the ministering angels.'[40] But the intent of the author of that *haggadah* is to say about the Messiah that Abraham (our father, on him may there be peace) converted gentiles and he would preach to the peoples his faith in God, he disagreed with Nimrod and was not afraid. And Moses did more than he (Abraham) did. He appeared in degradation before the Pharaoh, the great and evil king, did not ask favor in the wake of the great plague that befell

35 Literally, "they reveal nakedness."

36 A paraphrase of *Midrash Tehillim*, 2:3.

37 According to Chavel, this comes from Yalkut Isaiah, 52:13.

38 Sanhedrin, 93a.

39 *Sifre*, Nitzavim, 308.

40 Hullin 91, 2.

them, and brought Israel out of there. The ministering angels were very alert to the time of the redemption, as it says: *no people made greater efforts in all these matters than Michael your minister* (Daniel 10:21). And it says, *now I shall return to fight with the prince of Persia* (Daniel 10:20). The Messiah will do more than they did. *And his heart was lifted in the ways of the Lord* (II Chronicles 17:6). He will bring and he will command the pope and all the kings of the nations in the name of the Lord, *send forth my people that they may serve me* (Exodus 8:16). He will make for them many great signs and miracles and will not fear them. He will remain in their city of Rome until he destroys it. I will further explain this passage if you so desire." They did not wish me to.

54) Then he brought another *haggadah* that says that the Messiah prays that God will forgive Israel for their transgressions and he received from them afflictions. But he said: *for the dead, yes, I receive afflictions that will revivify the dead, and that will happen in my lifetime. But it will not be solely for the dead of my generation; rather, for all who have died since the first man until now. And just those who died, but even those who were lost at sea and were drowned and those whom wolves and beasts consumed.*[41] Thus, [Friar Paul argued that] the agony of the Messiah that he himself endured is the assassination of Jesus, which he knowingly took upon himself.

55) I said: "Woe to he who has no shame! Jesus did not do all of these things. And he did not raise those who have died since Adam until today. He did not do even one of these things. Moreover, this prayer teaches that he is human, not divine, and thus does not possess the ability to give life. These afflictions are nothing more than his sorrow that he is so delayed and he observes his people in exile *and there is no power in his hand* (Deuteronomy 28:32), and he sees them worship *those who are not gods* (II Chronicles 13:9) and those who deny him and make another [person] Messiah are honored more than his own people."

56) He replied and said: "Now, Daniel said *seventy weeks have been decreed for your people and for your holy city to complete the transgression and to put an end to sin and to forgive iniquity and to bring eternal righteousness and to seal a vision and prophecy and to redeem the most holy of holy ones* (Daniel 9:24). Seventy weeks are [weeks] of years, and those are the 420 years that the Second Temple stood plus the 70 years of the Babylonian exile, and the most holy of holy ones is Jesus."[42]

41 According to Chavel, this is a reference to Midrash Rabbi Moshe ha-Darshan.

42 The Babylonian exile began in 587 B.C.E. when the Chaldeans conquered Jerusalem and a significant portion of the Judean kingdom's elite population was exiled to Babylon. It ended in 538 B.C.E., when the Persians under the leadership of Cyrus prevailed over the Chaldeans.

57) I said to him: "Did Jesus not live more than 30 weeks [210 years] before that time, according to our calculations.[43] Even according to your calculations it was more than 10 weeks [or 70 years before the destruction of the Temple in 70 C.E.]."

58) He said: "Yes, it was. But in one verse it was said *know and understand from the sending forth of the word to return to build Jerusalem with the anointed prince* (Daniel 9:25). He is the Messiah, he is a prince, he is Jesus."

59) I said: "This too is a mistaken interpretation. For the scripture divides the 70 weeks that were mentioned, counting 7 weeks to the Messiah prince, and afterwards counting 62 weeks to *the building with wide spaces and streets*, and after that, counting one and a half weeks when *he will make a strong covenant with many* (Daniel 9:27) then the 70 weeks will be completed. Jesus, whom you call the Messiah prince, did not come for the seventh week, but rather after 60 weeks, and according to your calculations, more [than that]. You could explain the entire portion to me according to your theory and I will respond with an answer, because you will never be able to offer [an adequate] explanation of the matter. However, you have no shame speaking about matters you have not understood. Yet I could instruct you about the Messiah prince, Zerubavel, who came at the time of 7 weeks, as the scripture explains."

60) He said: "How can you call him the Messiah?!"

61) I said: "Cyrus was also called Messiah. And about Abraham, and Isaac, and Jacob, he said *do not touch my anointed ones* (Psalms 105:15). He [Zerubavel] was called prince, so that it [his leadership] would not lift up his kingdom, but he was honored and revered among the people, just as *the most noble of the people were gathered into the people of the God of Abraham* (Psalms 47:10). And now I will make known to you the entire chapter with a clear explanation if you and your friends should desire to learn or you have the heart to understand. And I say before our lord the king and all of his people that there is nothing in this chapter or in the rest of the book where Daniel's words address the end times and the coming of the Messiah except at the end of the book. For there it is explained in the scripture that he said that what he was told in this portion and in other chapters was that he was always praying to know the end, and finally, they told him [the time of] the end in the verse that says: *and from the time the regular offering ends and an appalling abomination set up will be 1290 days* (Daniel 12:11). Now it is possible in the view of these people to explain this verse,

43 As he argued in section 22, he dates the Jesus mentioned in the *aggadah* to the second century B.C.E.

even though it will be difficult for the Jews who are here. He says that from the time that the regular burnt offering ends until the detestable thing that ended it will be devastated—that is, the Romans who destroyed the Temple—there will be 1290 years, because the days mentioned here are years, just as *the redemption period will be a year* (Leviticus 25:29),[44] and also *from year (me-yamim) to year (yamimah)* (Exodus 13:10), and *days or ten* (Genesis 24:55). Later Daniel says *happy is he who waits 1335 days* (Daniel 12:12). He added 45 years. And the meaning is that the Messiah will come within the first span of time and will destroy *the abomination* that worship one who is not God and annihilate it from the world. Afterwards, he will gather the exiled of Israel *to the wilderness of the nations* (Ezekiel 20:35), as it is said *and I will bring her to the wilderness and speak to her tenderly* (Hosea 2:16), and he will bring Israel to their land, as was the case when Moses our teacher, may he be blessed, brought about the first redemption, which took 45 years. Thereafter, Israel will rest on the land *and will rejoice with God, their Lord, and with David, their king* (Jeremiah 30:9), and blessed will be those who wait and tell of those good days. Now, since the time of the destruction, there have been 1195 years. Thus, there remain 95 years until the number Daniel stated. And we hope that he will bring the redemption in that time, because the interpretation is correct and proper. And it is drawing near for those who believe in it."

62) Friar Paul answered: "But your teachers in the *haggadah* said *what are these extra days? They are the 45 days during which the redeemer was concealed from them, when Moses the first redeemer was revealed and hidden from them. Even the final redeemer will reveal himself and be hidden from them.*[45] This indicates that they are referring to a day, (in other words), they are real days, not years."

63) I said: "The Midrash employs the language of the verse, and it references 45 days that were really years, as our rabbis say: *the sage seized on the language of the Scripture.*"[46]

64) Friar Paul said that there is no Jew in the world who would not agree that the meaning of '*yom*' is a real day unless he changes [the meaning of words] according to his desire.

65) He shouted to the king, so they brought a Jew, the first they found and asked him: "What does '*yom*' (day) mean in your language?" He said: "Day."

44 In this example and the two that follow, the Bible uses the words *days* and *year* interchangeably to show that the requisite waiting period for the sale of a house to be legitimated is a full year.

45 *Yalkut ha-mekhiri Hosea*, 518.

46 Baba Metzia 2a. Chavel notes that our contemporary editions use a slightly different formulation: "the language of the world."

66) I said: "My lord king, this Jew is suitable to be a judge for Friar Paul but not for me because '*yom*' speaks in the language of the scriptures about time [generally], such as *on the day that I smote all the firstborn* (Numbers 3:13). And overall days refer to years. And here in particular the scripture speaks about years. It was necessarily thus because he wished to seal the matter, as the angel said to him several times *Shut the words and seal the book until the time of the end, many shall scurry about and knowledge will be increased* (Daniel 12:4). But I am discussing matters of great weight with one who cannot understand and does not believe, so it was appropriate that he would be judged by fools."

67) Friar Arnald de Segora replied: "You see that Jerome interprets *days* here as *days of the people*."[47]

68) I rejoiced at his words and said: "You can recognize from his words that the days in this case are not understood literally, as in other places. Thus he needed to interpret them. I believe that what he called *days of the people* are years, because people say that many days have passed since a certain event, and that refers to many years."

69) The same man [Friar Paul] returned and said: "Their sages say that the Messiah entered the Garden of Eden. The *aggadah* says: *Why did Messiah [enter the Garden of Eden]? Because he saw his ancestors there worshipping idols, and he parted from their path and served God, the Holy One, and God reserved him for the Garden of Eden*."[48]

70) I sneered at him and replied: "Here is my proof that he is the son of idol worshippers and that he is completely human. And God, the holy one, blessed is He, well fortified him when he parted from the way of his ancestors and did not worship idols, as they had. This he would say about God himself." So I took his book from him and read the *aggadah* to them from the beginning. "And it states: *fourteen living people entered the Garden of Eden to search for Serah, daughter of Asher and Bathyah, daughter of Pharaoh*. If Jesus were the Messiah, he would not be with the women in the Garden of Eden, but rather *the heavens would be his throne and the earth would be his footstool* (Isaiah 66:1). It is as I said: The Messiah resides in the Garden of Eden, in the home of the first man before he sinned. So says the *aggadah*, and that is the interpretation."

71) Then our lord the king stood and they departed.

72) On the fifth day of the week, our lord the king set his royal palace as the location for the disputation, saying it should be held without too

47 Meaning epochs.

48 *Derekh Olam Zutah*, Chapter 1. Chavel has pointed out that Nahmanides is clearly using a more expansive version of this text than the one commonly used today.

much pomp. We sat near the entrance to the palace. Friar Paul opened with meaningless words of no interest. Afterwards he said: "I will bring proof from their great sage, who has been without equal for 400 years. His name is Maestri Moses of Egypt,[49] and he says that the Messiah will die and that his son and grandson will rule after him. He does not [say], as you did that he would die in the manner of [ordinary] men." And he asked that someone bring him the Book of Judges.[50]

73) I said to them: "There is no such statement in that book, though I agree that there are those among our sages who say as much, as I mentioned at the beginning. The books of *haggadah* say that the Messiah was born on the day of the Destruction and that he will live forever. It is the opinion of the masters of the simple meaning (of the scripture) that he would be born at the cusp of the time of redemption, and would live for many years and then die in honor and his son would inherit his crown. I already said that this is what I believe. The only difference between this world and the days of the Messiah is our political servitude."

74) They brought Friar Paul the book he requested. He searched in it but didn't find the desired passage. I took the book from his hand and said: "Listen to the words in the book that he brings." And read to them from the beginning of the section: "*the future messiah king will arise within Israel, build the temple, and gather the banished of Israel.*"[51]

75) Friar Arnald de Segora: "He utters lies!"

76) I said to the king: "Until now he was a great sage, and there was none other like him; now he's a liar?"

77) The king rebuked him, and said: "It is not seemly to insult scholars."

78) I said to the king: "He is not lying. I will argue from the Torah and from the prophets that all that he said is true, for the Messiah will gather to him the banished of Israel and the dispersed of Judah and the twelve tribes. Jesus, your Messiah, did not gather a single man from among them, and he did not live during the time of the exile. The Messiah is expected to rebuild the Temple in Jerusalem, but Jesus neither built nor destroyed it, and the Messiah will rule over all the nations. He did not even rule over himself." I read to them a portion [from the Torah] *When all these things come upon you, the blessing and the curse that I set before you* and the end of the passage until *And the Lord, your God, will inflict these curses on your enemies and on your adversaries who pursue you* (Deuteronomy

49 Rather than using the biblical term for Egypt—*Mitzraim*—Nahmanides transliterates the vernacular term *Gipti* or *Egypti*.

50 The final book of Maimonides' *Mishneh Torah*.

51 *Mishneh Torah*, Book of Judges, paragraph 39.

30:1–7). I explained to them that *your enemies* refers to the Christians, and *your adversaries* refers to the Muslims, the two nations that persecute us. But they did not answer. They rose and departed.

79) On the next day,[52] the sixth day (of the week) they made arrangements to meet in the palace, and *the king sat on his seat, from time to time on his seat near the wall* (I Samuel 20:25). The bishop and many of his ministers, and Giles De'Sergon, and Peter Barga, and many knights, and all those who are shunned from the city and the poor of the nation were there.

80) Speaking to the king: "I do not wish to dispute any longer."

81) The king said: "Why not?"

82) I said: "Now many from the [Jewish] community are here, and they all have detained me and begged me, for they are very afraid of these people, of the preachers, who impose themselves and strike terror on the whole world. Also, the great priests and honorable men among them sent [word] to me not to continue. And many knights from your household, my lord king, told me that I am doing great harm to speak before them against their faith. Friar Peter of Girona, a Franciscan scholar, told me that the matter (outcome) is not good. And the people of the city said to the Jews that I should not continue." And indeed, that was the case, but when they saw that it was the king's wish [to continue], they hesitated and all stated that I would continue. The discussion among us was extended on this matter.[53] In the end, I said I would continue the debate. However, the judge permitted that for one day, I would ask the questions and Friar Paul would answer me, since he had asked me and I answered for three days.

83) The king said "Regardless, you will answer." So I agreed.

84) [Friar Paul] stood and asked: "Do you believe that the Messiah described by the prophets will be fundamentally human and divine in his essence?"

85) I said: "At the start, we agreed that we would speak first about whether the Messiah had come as you say, and later we would discuss whether he is God himself. And now you have not demonstrated that he has come, as I have destroyed all of the vain proofs you brought. And I am justified in my assessment, because it is on you to bring proof, for you accepted [this condition] upon yourselves. If you will not concede that I am correct in this judgment, then I take upon myself to bring conclusive proof about this matter, if you will listen to me. After it has been clarified that your Jesus is not the Messiah, there will be no [reason] to debate about the Messiah who will come for us, or if he will be completely human, or what he will be."

52 Friday, July 27, 1263; 19 Av, 5023.

53 That is, the discussion among members of the Jewish community.

86) The wise judges who were there said that the judgment was with me in this matter.

87) The king said to me: "Answer on every matter."

88) I said: "It is true that if the Messiah comes and will be fully man, the son of a man and a woman from their coupling, like me, and will be from the line of David and of his seed as is written, *and there shall come forth from the stem of Jesse* (Isaiah 11:1). It also says *until Shiloh comes* (Genesis 49:10), which means 'his son,' from the word afterbirth (*sheliah)*, for he will have been born like all other people with a placenta. If he were the spirit of God, as you say, he would not be *of the stem of Jesse*. And even if he took shelter in the womb of a woman who was of the seed of David, he did not inherit his kingdom, as daughters and their offspring did not inherit in the Torah as long as there was a male [heir]. David always had male heirs."

89) He said: "The psalmist says: *A Psalm of David. The Lord says to my lord, Sit at my right hand* (Psalms 110:1). Who is it who would call David 'my lord' (*adonai*)—none other than God. And how can [a mere] man sit at the right hand of God?"

90) The king said: "He asks well, for if the Messiah was wholly man from the true seed of David, David would not call him 'my lord.' And if I had a son or grandson from my seed, even if he were to rule the whole world, I would not call him 'my lord.' But I would desire that he call me 'my lord' and that he kiss my hand."

91) I turned and faced Friar Paul and said: "Are you the wise Jew who discovered this new interpretation and was converted in its wake? And are you the one who tells the king to gather for you Jewish scholars to dispute with them about the new interpretations you've discovered? Because we have never heard this until now? Is there not a priest or a child who would not ask this question of the Jews? This is a very old question indeed!"

92) The king said: "Answer it, though."

93) I said: "Now, hear me. King David was the ruler who wrote the psalms with the holy spirit, and he wrote them in order that they would be sung at the altar of God. He himself did not sing them and was not [even] permitted to, as it was forbidden to him according to the law of the Torah. However, he had given the psalms to the Levites for them to sing. The scripture explains this in Chronicles (I Chronicles 16:7). Thus, by necessity he wrote the psalms in language that was appropriate speech for the Levites. Even if [the psalm] said *God spoke to me*, the Levite would have been lying, but it would be plausible were the Levite to say: *God spoke to my lord*, to David, *sit at my right hand*. The meaning of 'sitting' is to say that the Holy Lord, blessed may He be, will protect throughout his days and and rescue him and strengthen him against his enemies. And so it was, for *he raised his spear against eight hundred and killed them at one time*

(II Samuel 23:8). Are there any among these knights who are here before you who could do so with his own strength? This is *the right hand* of God.[54] Indeed, it is written about David, *your right hand has supported me* (Psalms 18:36). And again, *the right hand of God does valiantly, the right hand of God is exalted* (Psalms 118:15–16). And as it is written about Moses, our teacher (peace be upon him), *his magnificent arm marched at the right hand of Moses* (Isaiah 63:12). And he said of the downfall of Pharaoh, *your right hand, Lord, crushes the enemy* (Exodus 15:6). And the scripture says the same thing in other places: *[God sent] Jephtah and Samuel* (I Samuel 12:11), and *you wives of Lemeh* (Genesis 4:23). These are all words of Moses (our teacher) in the Torah. But here he had to express it as [I] indicated. Know that the songs were written with aid of the holy spirit and that they spoke about David and about his son who sat on his throne, he who is the Messiah, for as long as the situation was even slightly in David's favor, so they would be by and large for his son, the Messiah. The right hand of God will support him, as it did David, until he will prevail over his enemies around him and will support him until he will make *all the nations his footstool* (Psalms 110:1). All of them are his enemies, for they subjected his nation and denied his coming and his kingship and some of them made another Messiah. Now it is proper to this poem in the Temple in the days of David and the days of the Messiah, his son, because it refers to *the throne of David and his kingdom* (Isaiah 9:6)."

. . .

97) Again he returned [to his previous line of argument] and brought evidence from the Midrash where they said: [55] "It is written: '*And I will walk among you* (Leviticus 26:12). They likened [this example] to one it resembles, [about] a king who went out for a walk with his laborer in his orchard, but the laborer hid himself. The king asked: 'why do you hide, for, behold, I am like you.' In the same manner, in the future, the Holy one, blessed is He, will walk in the Garden of Eden among the righteous, who will be afraid of Him, in the future to come. The Holy One, blessed is He, will say: 'why do you tremble before me? I am like you. *I will be your God and you shall be My people* (Leviticus 26:12).' Since God said *I am like you* it shows that he turned into a man, like them."

98) I said: "The Midrash he cited is proof against him! This episode refers to the future and will occur in the Garden of Eden. Jesus never

54 What follows is a string of examples demonstrating that the biblical references to God's right hand generally refer to an abstract impersonal force that plays a role in human history. He also indicates that biblical authors frequently refer to themselves in the third person.

55 According to Chavel, this is based on *Yalkut Shimoni'im Katanim*, Behukotai, 672.

walked with the righteous in the Garden of Eden since he was a man. Instead, he was a fugitive from his enemies and his pursuers throughout his lifetime! This Midrash is a parable. It begins: *they constructed a parable with one it resembles*. The meaning is that the righteous of this world cannot understand the truth of prophecy and they cannot perceive the resplendence called *gloria*,[56] as it says: *in a vision I will make myself known to him* (Numbers 12:6). Even Moses, our teacher, trembled [in fear] at the beginning of his prophecy. As it says: *Moses hid his face because he feared . . .* (Exodus 3:6), etc. But in the future, He will clean the souls of the righteous of all sin and of all ugliness, and they will be granted permission to gaze upon the brilliant speculum, like Moses our teacher (may peace be upon him), about whom [scripture] said: *and God said to Moses face to face, as a man says to his friend* (Exodus 33:11). [In the Midrash] they said *behold, I am like you* by way of an example, to show that they should not be trembling and fearful, as they are not afraid of one another. . . ."

99) The same man returned and argued that they said in *Bereshit Rabbah* that "*the spirit of God hovered on the face of the waters* (Genesis 1:2), this spirit is the Messiah."[57] Thus, the Messiah is not a man, but God.

100) I said: "Woe to he who knows nothing and imagines that he is wise and expert. They (the rabbis) also said '*the spirit hovered* this is the spirit of the first man.'[58] Does it state that they said he would be divine? And he who does not know *what is above and what is below*[59] in these books perverts the words of the living God. But the exegete who interpreted this as the spirit of the Messiah explained the verse as referring to the kingdoms, and that the language of the Scripture hints at the future. And it says *and the earth was waste* (Genesis 1:2). This is Babylon, as it says *I looked at the earth and it was waste* (Jeremiah 4:23). *And void (boho)* (Genesis 1:2). This is Media, as it says *and they hurried (yivhilu) to bring Haman* (Esther 6:14).[60] *And darkness*, that is Greece, because they darkened the eyes of Israel with decrees.[61] *On the face of the deep*, this is the wicked kingdom.[62] *And the spirit of God*, this is the spirit of the Messiah. By what justification? [On the basis of the verse] *hovering on the*

56 Meaning Divine Glory. Nahmanides presents this as a Hebrew transliteration from the vernacular.

57 *Bereshit Rabbah*, 2, 4.

58 *Bereshit Rabbah*, 2, 3.

59 *Hagiga* 11b.

60 The noun *bohu* and the verb *yivhilu* are related.

61 Decrees against the Israelite faith and rituals.

62 Rome.

face of the waters, since repentance is compared with water (Lamentations 2:19). Now, the Midrash presents the four kingdoms and the fourth is Rome, after which comes the spirit of God, who is the Messiah, fully human filled with the wisdom and spirit of God, like Bezalel, about whom it was said *and I filled him with the spirit of God* (Exodus 31:3), and Joshua, about whom it is said *and Joshua ben Nun was full of the spirit of wisdom* (Deuteronomy 34:9). It is explained that they were talking about the future Messiah who will come after the fourth kingdom." I could not tell him the meaning of the Midrash, because it is obscure, and they will interpret them with the support of language,[63] though this is not the essential [sense] of the scripture. Such is the case in most places in *Bereshit Rabbah*, as they say in *Vayeitzei Jacob* (Genesis 28:10).[64] I said this to show all of them that he did not know how to read the book that he brought, because his reading of the language was inaccurate.

101) The king then stood, and they all stood.

102) This is an account of all of the disputations. To my knowledge, I did not change a word. Afterwards, on the same day [that the debate ended] I stood before our lord the king, who said: "Let the disputation stand,[65] for I have never seen a man who does not have justice on his side who argued his case so well." That is, as I did. And I heard in the court that the king wanted the preachers (friars) to come to the synagogue on Shabbat, so I remained in the city for eight more days. And they arrived there on the following Shabbat; I answered the king in proper order, for he preached with zeal, saying that Jesus was the Messiah.

103) I rose to my feet and said: "The words of our lord the king, presented before princes and men of honor, are unique since they come from the mouth of an honored and revered prince. Yet, I cannot praise them by agreeing that they are true. I have clear proof and words as bright as the sun showing that what he says is not true. I am unworthy to dispute with him. However, he said one thing that I found amazing. The words he spoke to convince us that Jesus was the Messiah, Jesus himself brought to our forefathers and tried to explain it to them. They discredited his claim to his face, refuting completely and strongly that man who knew and could argue that he was divine, according to your beliefs, even better than the king. If our forefathers, who saw and knew him, did not heed him, how can we believe and hear the king, who knows of the matter only from widespread hearsay from men who didn't know Jesus and were not from his land?"

---

63 Meaning analysis of the language and its usage.

64 In the Hebrew bible, the Pentateuch is divided into portions for daily readings. The title *Vayeitzei Jacob* refers to the portion beginning at Genesis 28:10.

65 In other words, let it stop here.

104) Afterwards, Friar Ramon de Peñaforte rose and preached about the trinity, saying that it is wisdom, will, and power. He stated in the synagogue: "The Master[66] agreed to this in Girona; he accepted the words of Friar Paul."

105) I rose to my feet and said: "Please listen and hear my words, Jews and gentiles. In Girona, Friar Paul asked me if I believe in the trinity. I asked 'what is the trinity? Does it mean that God has three physical[67] bodies like the bodies of men?' He answered, 'No.' 'Or that it was would be one mixed from three, like the bodies mixed from the four elements?' He said, 'No.' 'If so, what is the trinity?' He replied, 'wisdom, power, and will.'" I said, "I agree that God is wise and not stupid, that He has will without emotion, and that He is powerful, not weak. But the term trinity is completely mistaken because wisdom is not an accidental quality of the Creator. Rather, He is one with His wisdom, He is one with His will, and He is one with His power. If so, wisdom, will, and power are all one. And even if there were accidental qualities about Him, it is not the case that the divinity would be three, but rather that He would be one entity enduring three accidental qualities. Our lord, the king, brought one example that his mistaken friends taught him. He said that there are three distinct qualities in wine—color, flavor, and smell—but that it is a singular thing. But this is fully erroneous, for the redness, the flavor, and the smell of wine are separate qualities that can be found on their own elsewhere. There are red and white and other colors of wine. So too with flavor and smell. Moreover, the redness is not the wine [itself], nor is the flavor, nor the smell. Rather, the substance of the wine is the thing that fills the vessels. Thus, it is a body that carries three separate accidental qualities in which there is no unity. If we were erroneously to count, it would be incumbent upon us to refer to four [qualities], because if one were to count the entity that is God, His wisdom, His power, and His will, they are four. Additionally, you should speak of five, because He is living, and life in Him is [a quality] like wisdom. He would then be defined as living, wisdom, power, will, and the divine essence—five. All this is a clear error."

106) Then Friar Paul stood and stated that he believes in the complete unity, along with this, that there are three within Him. And this is a very deep thing that even the angels and ministers on high do not understand.

107) I stood and said: "It is clear that a man cannot believe what he does not know. Thus, the angels cannot believe in the trinity!" His friends quieted him.

108) Our lord the king stood and descended from the Ark of the Law and they left. The next day, I stood before our lord the king and he said to me: "Return to your city and live there in peace." Then he gave me three

66 Nahmanides.

67 The term used here connotes the most base and vulgar elements of physicality.

hundred *dinarim* and I departed from him with great love. May the Lord make me worthy of life in the World to Come. Amen.

DOCUMENT II

The Latin Account of the Barcelona Disputation

In the year of the Lord 1263, on the 20th of July, in the presence of the lord king of Aragon, and many others, barons, prelates, and religious and military persons in the palace of the lord king at Barcelona, when Moses, called Master, a Jew, had been summoned from Gerona by the lord king himself at the instance of the preaching friars, and was present in that same place together with many other Jews who seemed and were believed by the other Jews to be experts, Brother Paulus, after discussion with the lord king and certain friars of the preaching and Minorite orders who were present (not in order that the faith in the Lord Jesus Christ, which because of its certitude should not be put into dispute, should be drawn into the arena with the Jews as if it were a matter of doubt, but that the truth of that faith should become mainifest in order to destroy the errors of the Jews and remove the confident faith of many Jews who, though they could not themselves defend their errors, said that the said Jewish master could sufficiently reply to each and every point which was put to them) proposed to the said Jewish Master that he would prove, with the help of God, through writings accepted and authoritative among the Jews, the following things in order, namely: that the Messiah (of which the interpretation is 'Christ') whom the Jews expect, has undoubtedly come; further, that the Messiah himself, as had been prophesied, must be both God and man; further that he truly suffered and died for the salvation of the human race; further, that legal or ceremonial matter ceased and had to cease after the coming of the said Messiah. When, therefore, the said Moses had been questioned whether he wished to reply to the aforesaid matters, he said and firmly asserted, 'Yes,' and that he would remain, if necessary, for this reason, in Barcelona for a day or a week or a month or even a year. And when it was proved to him that he ought not to be called 'Master,' because no Jew ought to be called by this name since the time of the passion of Christ, he conceded this at least, that it was true for the last 800 years. Eventually it was put to him that when Brother Paul had come to Gerona to discuss with him matters which are relevant to salvation, and expounded diligently, among other things, the belief in the Holy Trinity, both as to the Unity of the Divine essence, and as to the Trinity of the Persons, as held by Christians, he (Moses) conceded that if Christians believed what had been expounded to him, they believed what in truth ought to be so held. And when this was repeated in the presence of the lord king, he did not deny it, but was silent, and so, by his silence, assented. Then in the palace of the lord king the said Jew was asked whether the Messiah who is called Christ had come; and when he answered with the assertion, 'No,' and added that Messiah and Christ are the same, and if it could be proved to him that the Messiah had come, then this ought to be believed about no other than him, to wit Jesus Christ, in whom Christians believe, since no other had come who dared to usurp his name, or had been believed to be the Christ, it was proved to him clearly both by the authority of the Law and the Prophets and by the Talmud, that Christ had in truth come, as Christians believe and preach. To this he was not able to reply. And defeated by irrefutable proofs and authorities, he conceded that Christ, or Messiah, was born 1000 years ago in Bethlehem and later appeared to some people in Rome. And when he was asked where that Messiah is, whom the Jews declared to have been born and to have appeared at Rome, he said that he did not know. Afterwards, however, he said that he lived in earthly Paradise with Elijah. But he said that though had been born, nevertheless he had not yet come, because the Messiah is said to have come only when he assumes dominion over the Jews and frees them and the Jews follow him. Against this reply the authority of the Talmud was adduced, which says plainly that the Messiah will come to them even today, if they listen to his voice and do not harden their hearts, as it says in the Psalm: 'Today if you listen to his voice' (Psalms 95:7). It was added, too, that for the Messiah to have been born among men is the same thing as for him to have come amongst men, and it cannot be otherwise understood. And to these things he was able to make no reply. Further, among the proofs put forward for the advent of the Messiah was adduced that one from Genesis: 'The sceptre shall not pass away from Judah' (Genesis 49:10). Since, therefore, it is certain that in Judah there is neither sceptre nor leader, it is certain the Messiah who was to be sent has come. To this he replied that the sceptre has not been taken away but is merely discontinued, as it also was in the time of the Babylonian Captivity. And it was proved to him that in Babylon they had the heads of the captivity with jurisdiction, but after the death of Christ they had neither leader nor prince or the heads of captivity such as those attested by the prophet Daniel, nor prophet nor any kind of rule as is manifestly plain today. By this, it is certain, that the Messiah has come to them. He, however, said that he would prove that they had the aforesaid heads after Christ, but he could show nothing about the aforesaid, and indeed admitted that they had not had the aforesaid heads for the last 850 years. Therefore it is plain that the Messiah has come, since authority cannot lie. Further, when the said Moses said that Jesus Christ ought not to be called Messiah, because the Messiah, as he said should not die, as it is said in the psalm, 'he asked for life from you and you granted it to him' (Psalms 21:4),[68] but he ought to live for ever, both he and those whom he will liberate he was asked

68 Psalms 21:5 in the Hebrew bible.

whether the chapter of Isaiah, 53, 'Lord, who would have believed . . .' (which according to the Hebrews, begins at the end of chapter 52, where it says, 'Behold my servant will understand . . .') speaks about the Messiah. He firmly asserted that it does not speak of the Messiah at all, but it was proved to him by many authorities from the Talmud, which speak of the passion of Christ and his death, which they prove from the said chapter, that the said chapter of Isaiah is understood of the Christ, and in it the death of Christ and his passion and burial and resurrection are plainly contained. He however, compelled at length by the authorities, admitted that it is understood and explained in reference to Christ. From this it is plain that the Messiah had to suffer and die. Further, since he was unwilling to admit the truth unless compelled by the authorities, when he could not explain the authorities, he said publicly that he did not believe in the authorities which were cited against him, though they were in ancient, authoritative books of the Jews, because, as he said, they were sermons, in which their teachers, for the sake of exhorting the people, often lied. For this reason, he dismissed both the teachers and the scriptures of the Jews. Further, he first denied all, or nearly all, the things which he had previously admitted and which had been proved to him, and then, having been refuted again through authorities and defeated, he was compelled to admit them again. Further, since he could not reply and had been defeated many times in public, and both Jews and Christians were treating him with scorn, he said obstinately in front of everyone that he would not reply at all, because the Jews had told him not to, and some Christians, namely Brother P. de Janua and some respectable citizens had sent to him to advise him not to reply at all. This lie was publicly refuted by the said Brother P. and the respectable citizens. From this it is plain that he was trying to escape from the Disputation by lies. Further, though he had promised in the presence of the lord king and many others that he would answer questions on his faith and law to a small gathering, when the lord king was away from the state he secretly fled away and departed. From this it is plain that he does not dare and is not able to defend his erroneous creed. We, James, by the grace of God king of Aragon, Majorca, and Valencia, count of Barcelona and Urgello, and Don Montispessulanum, truly confess and recognise that each and every one of the words and deeds in our presence and of many others were as is contained above in this present writing. In testimony of this we have caused the seal to be appended in perpetual commemoration.

Translated by Hyam Maccoby, *Judaism on Trial: Jewish-Christian Disputations in the Middle Ages* (London: Littman Library of Jewish Civilization, 1993), 146–50.

DOCUMENT III

A letter from King James I permitting the Dominicans to compel Jews to attend public sermons and protecting the property and freedoms of those who convert

26 August, 1263

To his vassals, bailiffs, justices, committal officers,[69] curates, peace-men, oath-takers,[70] governors, king's ministers, Savalmedinas,[71] Alamins,[72] and our other officials, whether Christian or Saracen, and all of their subordinates, to whom the present letter will have come, salvation and grace. We say and charge you that when the friars of the Order of Preaching Brothers come to you and wish to preach to the Jews or to the Saracens, you should accept those same brothers kindly, and bring Jews and Saracens, young and old, men and women, and, if it should be necessary, compel them to meet face-to-face with the same friars, where and when and however they (the friars) wish, and diligently listen to their words in silence, [and that you should be] punishing those who have disregarded assembling as it was declared, by a fine or other punishment. But you should love those who want to convert and defend them from all injustice and see to it that nobody shall prevail to impede their conversion and baptism, rather that they should hold freely and fully in perpetuity all of their mobile and immobile possessions, both those already possessed and those to be possessed in future, and freedom of every sort, just as other Christians. However if anyone should dare to make conversion an object of reproach to someone by calling the convert an apostate[73] or horn-like or similar name, in such a manner let him (the taunter) experience punishment, whether pecuniary or otherwise, so that the others may hold back from doing it a second time; and may you not change this to any extent.

Translated from D. P. H. Denifle, "Quellen zur Disputation Pablos Christiani mit Mose Nachmani su Barcelona 1263," *Historisches Jahrbuch* 8 (1887): 234–35.

---

69 For a discussion of the development of the office of *vicaria*, see Adam J. Kosto, *Making Agreements in Medieval Catalonia: Power, Order, and the Written Word, 1000–1200* (Cambridge, UK: Cambridge University Press, 2001), 59–64.

70 Those who oversaw the swearing of oaths.

71 Justice ministers in Valencia. This title is derived from the Arabic title *sahib al-madina*, whose responsibilities included overseeing prisons and executing justice in noncapital cases involving Christians. Robert Ignatius Burns, *Islam under the Crusaders: Colonial Survival in the Thirteenth-Century Kingdom of Valencia* (Princeton: Princeton University Press, 1973), 236.

72 Custodians of weights and measures in Valencia. Adapted from the Arabic *amin*, or finance minister. Robert Ignatius Burns, *Medieval Colonialism: Postcrusade Exploitation of Islamic Valencia* (Princeton: Princeton University Press, 1975), 252.

73 That is, a false or insincere convert.

DOCUMENT IV

A letter from James I calling for the burning of copies of one of Maimonides' books on charges that it contained statements blaspheming Jesus

28 August 1263

To vassals, committal officers, bailiffs and the entire group of our other officials and subordinates, to whom the present letter will have come, salvation and grace. Whereas we cannot nor should we ignore blasphemies against our Lord Jesus Christ, whenever and by whomever we have understood that they have been said or made in any manner, we strongly and firmly order you by way of instruction, that on our behalf you must firmly instruct the Jews living under our authority in your counties to show and surrender to you all books that are called *Soffrim*,[74] composed by a certain Jew, Moses son of Maimon, the Egyptian from Cairo, containing blasphemies against Jesus Christ, without delay and difficulty, and without any excuse, so that you make cause the books to be burned in view of the people, once the crime of blasphemy has been put forward, announcing to the aforementioned Jews, that if anyone should retain the aforesaid books and does not immediately surrender them to you, he will be punished just as a blasphemer of our Lord Jesus Christ both on his body and in his property, with due censure.

Translated from D. P. H. Denifle, "Quellen zur Disputation Pablos Christiani mit Mose Nachmani su Barcelona 1263," *Historisches Jahrbuch* 8 (1887): 235.

DOCUMENT V

Letter from James I to the Jewish communities of the Crown of Aragon instructing them to attend Friar Paul's sermons

29 August, 1263

To each and every loyal Jew throughout our realm, wherever they are residing, to whom the present letter will have come, salvation and grace. We command and strictly charge you that when our beloved brother Paul Christiani from the order of preaching friars, whom we send to you for the sake of showing the way of salvation, will have come to you, whether to the synagogues or to your homes or any other locations suitable for the purpose of preaching the word of God or disputing or discussing sacred scripture with you, in public or private or in an intimate conversation, together or separately you must come to him and meekly and favorably listen to him

74 Probably Maimonides' *Sefer Shofetim*, which is part of his exhaustive commentary and distillation of Jewish law.

and respond to his interrogations regarding faith and sacred scriptures to the degree that you know, with humility and reverence and without opprobrium or subterfuge, and provide him with your books, which he needs to show you the truth, and you must pay the expenses which the aforesaid friar incurs from transporting his books from location to location, [books] which he will have caused to be brought in order to demonstrate the truth to you, and the brothers of his order on account of its constitution have a rule that they do not carry expenses, while you charge that to us and deduct it from the tax that you are obliged to pay to us. In addition, we order and strictly command all bailiffs, committal officers, and all of our officials in their entirety, that if the aforementioned Jews should not desire to do the aforementioned things willingly, they [the officials] should compel the Jews by our authority, if they have confidence in our grace or love.

Translated from D. P. H. Denifle, "Quellen zur Disputation Pablos Christiani mit Mose Nachmani su Barcelona 1263," *Historisches Jahrbuch* 8 (1887): 235–36.

DOCUMENT VI

Letter from James I limiting the friars' freedom to compel Jews to attend their sermons

30 August, 1263

To all his vassals, bailiffs, curates, peace-men, justices, and our other officials and subordinates, to whom the present letter will have come, salvation and grace. We command you, that you shall not compel nor shall you permit the Jews of your communities, villages, and places of our jurisdiction to be compelled, including their wives and children, to go to any location outside their *calla iudayca*[75] for the purpose of listening to sermons of any of the preaching friars. But if any brother among the preachers wants to enter any of their communities or synagogues and preach to them in that place, they may listen to him if they so desire. For this we concede to those Jews, that they would not be obliged to go outside their Jewish quarters for the purpose of hearing the preaching of anyone or even to hear the preaching itself in any location through force. And to them we concede this unobstructed by any charter to the contrary granted by me to the preaching friars.

Translated from D. P. H. Denifle, "Quellen zur Disputation Pablos Christiani mit Mose Nachmani su Barcelona 1263," *Historisches Jahrbuch* 8 (1887): 237.

75 The Catalan term referring to physical boundaries of the Jewish community. *Call* (or *calla*) is a Catalan adaptation of the Hebrew word *kehillah*, or community.

DOCUMENT VII

James I's report on a tribunal investigating charges that Nahmanides had blasphemed

12 April, 1265

Let it be known by all that when we, James I etc., caused the Jewish master Bonastruc de Porta of Girona[76] to appear in Barcelona to address the accusation made concerning him to us by the prior of preaching friars of Barcelona, Friar Ramon de Peñaforte, Friar Arnald de Segora, and Friar Paul of the same order, who alleged that he made disparaging comments about our Lord and about the whole Catholic faith and also created a book about the same, from which he then made a transcription and gave it to the Bishop of Girona, in our presence and in the presence of the venerable bishop of Barcelona, Berengario A. de Anglaria, master Berengario de Turri, archdeacon of Barcelona, master Bernardo de Olorda, sexton of Barcelona, Bernardo Vital, Ferrer de Minorisa, and the jurist, Barengario de Vico, and many others, the same Bonastruc responded that he had spoken the aforementioned words during the disputation that took place between himself and the aforementioned Friar Paul in our royal palace in Barcelona, at the beginning of which disputation we granted him permission to say anything he might wish in this disputation. Therefore, [he claimed that] by reason of the freedom granted to him by us and by the aforementioned Friar Ramon de Peñaforte in the aforesaid disputation about the aforementioned things he was not bound in any respect, especially since he had written the aforementioned book, which he gave to the aforesaid bishop of Girona, at his request. In addition, we, James, called king by the grace of God, held counsel with the bishop of Barcelona and those whom we previously mentioned to determine how we should proceed in the matter of the aforementioned Jew. Nevertheless, having taken counsel with them, since we have ascertained that freedom [of speech] would have been given by us and Friar Ramon de Peñaforte to him only for that time, we wanted, by way of sentencing, to banish that Jew from our land for a period of two years and make him burn the books that had been written concerning the aforementioned words. In fact, the aforesaid preaching friars were not at all willing to accept this sentence. Consequently, we, James, called king by the grace of God, concede to you, Master Bonastruc de Porto the Jew, that you need not respond to the preceding charges or

76 This is Nahmanides' name in Catalan. Denifle argued that the Bonastruc de Porta in the document referred to another man, however Heinrich Graetz's challenge to his claim was successful insofar as it has been universally accepted in the subsequent scholarship. See H. Graetz, "Die Disputation des Bonastruc mit Frai Pablo in Barcelona," *Monatsschrift für Geschichte und Wissenschaft des Judenthums* 14 (1865): 428–33.

any of the preceding charges under the power of any person at any time unless it is under our power and in our presence.

Translated from D. P. H. Denifle, "Quellen zur Disputation Pablos Christiani mit Mose Nachmani su Barcelona 1263," *Historisches Jahrbuch* 8 (1887): 239–40.

DOCUMENT VIII

Letter of reprimand from Pope Clement IV to James I

To the illustrious king of Aragon:

Mother Church celebrates feast days, not undeservingly, as she joyously commemorates your magnificent deeds, and redoubles her songs of delight and happiness, in reviewing, nearly every day of late, with delight the fervor of your zeal and the rewards of your diligence, that of so dear and devoted a son. She exults and rejoices in the commemoration of your happy successes, throughout which she virtuously directed the salvation of the Christian people into your hands, with the right hand of the Lord and the courage given to you by Him, against the Saracens, blasphemers of her name and outrageous persecutors of the Catholic faith.

But as for the church of Valencia, a gift so graciously conceded to you by God, so that you might be seen to have the gracious favor of the Concessor and the concession, as is fitting, and that you might abundantly measure its measure from the greatness of the Donor, let your favor come forth in abundance, and let the generosity of your royal piety abound in it so that you will not allow it to wilt in poverty, since it is a new planting, recently uprooted from the hands of treacherous peoples, through you, by divine might, rather, let your royal generosity so honor and endow it, and so protect it in its rights, that whatever worse circumstance which the other neighboring churches have, won't exist, on the contrary that your magnificence, which freed it from the subjugation and impurity of those same peoples, might also free it from the scourges of poverty and dejection. And to that end, let the commendable devotion particularly to your person of my venerable brother, the Bishop of Valencia (a constant zealot for the honor and benefit of you and yours, who we testify, on being appraised of the experience of you and your kingdom, was moved, and whom I confidently and wholeheartedly commend to you for that reason) most effectively motivate you.

But, your highness, in order that your zeal towards the defense of that same orthodox faith, which you tirelessly pursue as a most Christian man, might openly shine out against its enemies on all sides, let your favor be most strong and public in helping it against the Jews, who before all others persecute the Faith and blaspheme the name of Christianity, both blaspheme it more bitterly and persecute it more villainously: as for the rest do not admit Jews to any official positions, and do not promote them to one, but inasmuch as the privileges granted to them by the Apostolic See permit, humble and tame their malice by reining it in. And do not overlook their incorrect blasphemies, but particularly punish the audacity of the one who is said to have written a book about the debate he had in your presence with our beloved son, the pious man Friar Paul, from the Order of Preachers, with many fabricated lies added. And to extend his error, he has reproduced many different copies with plans to send them to various regions. Let the judgment of justice rightly punish his reckless effrontery to such an extent (but without the danger of death or maiming) that the severity of his castigation will make plain how much more he has earned, and the audacity of others will be curbed by his example.

Translated from Shlomo Simonsohn, ed., *The Apostolic See and the Jews*, 8 vols., Studies and texts 94–95, 99, 104–6, 109 (Toronto: Pontifical Institute of Mediaeval Studies, 1988), 1:230–31.[77]

DOCUMENT IX

Letter from Nahmanides to his son, Nahman from Jerusalem.

This document includes important demographic and political information as well as details about daily life in late thirteenth-century Palestine

Letter to Nahman

May God bless you, my son Nahman, and let you see the good of Jerusalem, and see your son's sons, and may your table be like our father Abraham's table. From Jerusalem, the holy city, I write this letter to you. With praise and thanks to the Rock of my salvation, I was granted the right and came peacefully on the ninth day of the month of Elul[78] and remained there in peace until the following day, Yom Kippur. I am facing in the direction to go to Hevron, the city of our fathers' graves and prostrate myself over them and to hew a stone for myself there, with the help of God.

And what can I tell you about the Holy Land? Many are its ruins and great is the horror, and in summary, the holier the place the more devastated it is. Jerusalem is more decimated than the rest, and the land of Judah is worse than the Galilee. With all of this destruction it is still very good. There is a settlement of nearly two thousand; among them are about three hundred Christians, those who escaped the Sultan's sword. But there are none from Israel among them, for they fled from there when the Tartars came, [though] some of them were killed by their swords; just two brothers [remain], dyers who buy their dyes from the government. With them in

77 I am deeply grateful to Anna Lankina, Kat Klos, and Justin Mansfield for helping with the translation of this letter.

78 The twelfth month of the Hebrew calendar, which falls in late summer or early fall.

their home they (Jews) gather until there is a *minyan*[79] and they pray in their house on Shabbat. Now we have urged them and we found a desolated house built with marble columns and a beautiful dome. We took the house for a synagogue, because the city is lawless and anyone who wants to claim ruins, claims them. We made donations for repairs on the house, and they are already under way—they sent to the city of Shechem to bring from there the Torah scrolls that were taken from Jerusalem when the Tartars came. Thus they will establish a synagogue there and they will pray. For many people frequently come to Jerusalem, men and women, from Damascus and Aleppo and all the other districts of the land to see the Temple and to weep over it. He who is worthy to see Jerusalem in ruins, may He deem us worthy to see it also in a complete and restored state, when the glory and spirit (of God) will return. You, my son, and your brothers, and the entire house (i.e., family) of your father, may you be deemed worthy of Jerusalem in good and in consolation of Zion.

Your worrying and forgetful father, who is seeing and rejoicing.

Moses ben Rav Nahman

Translated from Hayim Dov Chavel, *Kitve Rabenu Mosheh ben Nah.man*, 2 vols. (Jerusalem: Mosad ha-Rav K.uk., 1963), 1:367–68.

DOCUMENT X

Selected canons from the Fourth Lateran Council.

Concerning the statement of the Catholic creed, definition of heresy, a call for regulations governing Jewish business and public conduct, and a statement of privileges and rewards for those who participate in renewed military campaigns to the Holy Land. The disputation in Barcelona took place nearly 50 years later, but it built on the multifaceted effort to establish and enforce an ideal of homogeneous Christian orthodoxy throughout Christendom.

FOURTH LATERAN COUNCIL, 1215: CONSTITUTIONS

1. On the catholic faith

We firmly believe and simply confess that there is only one true God, eternal and immeasurable, almighty, unchangeable, incomprehensible and ineffable, Father, Son and holy Spirit, three persons but one absolutely simple essence, substance or nature. The Father is from none, the Son from the Father alone and the holy Spirit from both, equally, eternally without beginning or end; the Father generating, the Son being born, and the holy Spirit proceeding; consubstantial and coequal, co-omnipotent coeternal;

79 A quorum of ten.

one principle of all things, creator of all things invisible and visible, spiritual and corporeal; who by his almighty power at the beginning of time created from nothing both spiritual and corporeal creatures, that is to say angelic and earthly, and then created human beings composed as it were of both spirit and body in common. The devil and other demons were created by God naturally good, but they became evil by their own doing. Man, however, sinned at the prompting of the devil.

This holy Trinity, which is undivided according to its common essence but distinct according to the properties of its persons, gave the teaching of salvation to the human race through Moses and the holy prophets and his other servants, according to the most appropriate disposition of the times. Finally the only begotten Son of God, Jesus Christ, who became incarnate by the action of the whole Trinity in common and was conceived from the ever virgin Mary through the cooperation of the holy Spirit, having become true man, composed of a rational soul and human flesh, one person in two natures, showed more clearly the way of life. Although he is immortal and unable to suffer according to his divinity, he was made capable of suffering and dying according to his humanity. Indeed, having suffered and died on the wood of the cross for the salvation of the human race, he descended to the underworld, rose from the dead and ascended into heaven. He descended in the soul, rose in the flesh, and ascended in both. He will come at the end of time to judge the living and the dead, to render to every person according to his works, both to the reprobate and to the elect. All of them will rise with their own bodies, which they now wear, so as to receive according to their deserts, whether these be good or bad; for the latter perpetual punishment with the devil, for the former eternal glory with Christ.

There is indeed one universal church of the faithful, outside of which nobody at all is saved, in which Jesus Christ is both priest and sacrifice. His body and blood are truly contained in the sacrament of the altar under the forms of bread and wine, the bread and wine having been changed, in substance, by God's power, into his body and blood, so that in order to achieve this mystery of unity we receive from God what he received from us. Nobody can effect this sacrament except a priest who has been properly ordained according to the church's keys, which Jesus Christ himself gave to the apostles and their successors. But the sacrament of baptism is consecrated in water, at the invocation of the undivided Trinity—namely Father, Son and holy Spirit—and brings salvation to both children and adults when it is correctly carried out by anyone in the form laid down by the church. If someone falls into sin after having received baptism, he or she can always be restored through true penitence. For not only virgins and the continent but also married persons find favor with God by right faith and good actions and deserve to attain to eternal blessedness.

3. On Heretics

We excommunicate and anathematize every heresy raising itself up against this holy, orthodox and catholic faith which we have expounded above. We condemn all heretics, whatever names they may go under. They have different faces indeed but their tails are tied together inasmuch as they are alike in their pride. Let those condemned be handed over to the secular authorities present, or to their bailiffs, for due punishment. Clerics are first to be degraded from their orders. The goods of the condemned are to be confiscated, if they are lay persons, and if clerics they are to be applied to the churches from which they received their stipends. Those who are only found suspect of heresy are to be struck with the sword of anathema unless they prove their innocence by an appropriate purgation, having regard to the reasons for suspicion and the character of the person. Let such persons be avoided by all until they have made adequate satisfaction. If they persist in the excommunication for a year, they are to be condemned as heretics. Let secular authorities, whatever offices they may be discharging, be advised and urged and if necessary be compelled by ecclesiastical censure, if they wish to be reputed and held to be faithful, to take publicly an oath for the defence of the faith to the effect that they will seek, in so far as they can, to expel from the lands subject to their jurisdiction all heretics designated by the church in good faith. Thus whenever anyone is promoted to spiritual or temporal authority, he shall be obliged to confirm this article with an oath. If however a temporal lord, required and instructed by the church, neglects to cleanse his territory of this heretical filth, he shall be bound with the bond of excommunication by the metropolitan and other bishops of the province. If he refuses to give satisfaction within a year, this shall be reported to the supreme pontiff so that he may then declare his vassals absolved from their fealty to him and make the land available for occupation by Catholics so that these may, after they have expelled the heretics, possess it unopposed and preserve it in the purity of the faith—saving the right of the suzerain provided that he makes no difficulty in the matter and puts no impediment in the way. The same law is to be observed no less as regards those who do not have a suzerain.

Catholics who take the cross and gird themselves up for the expulsion of heretics shall enjoy the same indulgence, and be strengthened by the same holy privilege, as is granted to those who go to the aid of the holy Land. Moreover, we determine to subject to excommunication believers who receive, defend or support heretics. We strictly ordain that if any such person, after he has been designated as excommunicated, refuses to render satisfaction within a year, then by the law itself he shall be branded as infamous and not be admitted to public offices or councils or to elect others to the same or to give testimony. He shall be intestable, that is he shall not have the freedom to make a will nor shall succeed to an inheritance. Moreover nobody shall be compelled to answer to him on any business whatever, but he may be compelled to answer to them. If he is a judge, sentences pronounced by him shall have no force and cases may not be brought before him; if an advocate, he may not be allowed to defend anyone; if a notary, documents drawn up by him shall be worthless and condemned along with their condemned author; and in similar matters we order the same to be observed. If however he is a cleric, let him be deposed from every office and benefice, so that the greater the fault the greater be the punishment. If any refuse to avoid such persons after they have been pointed out by the church, let them be punished with the sentence of excommunication until they make suitable satisfaction. Clerics should not, of course, give the sacraments of the church to such pestilent people nor give them a Christian burial nor accept alms or offerings from them; if they do, let them be deprived of their office and not restored to it without a special indult of the apostolic see. Similarly with regulars, let them be punished with losing their privileges in the diocese in which they presume to commit such excesses.

"There are some who *holding to the form of religion but denying its power* (as the Apostle says),[80] claim for themselves the authority to preach, whereas the same Apostle says, *How shall they preach unless they are sent?*[81] Let therefore all those who have been forbidden or not sent to preach, and yet dare publicly or privately to usurp the office of preaching without having received the authority of the apostolic see or the catholic bishop of the place,"[82] be bound with the bond of excommunication and, unless they repent very quickly, be punished by another suitable penalty. We add further that each archbishop or bishop, either in person or through his archdeacon or through suitable honest persons, should visit twice or at least once in the year any parish of his in which heretics are said to live. There he should compel three or more men of good repute, or even if it seems expedient the whole neighbourhood, to swear that if anyone knows of heretics there or of any persons who hold secret conventicles or who differ in their life and habits from the normal way of living of the faithful, then he will take care to point them out to the bishop. The bishop himself should summon the accused to his presence, and they should be punished canonically if they are unable to clear themselves of the charge or if after compurgation they relapse into their former errors of faith. If however any

80 2 Timothy 3:5.

81 Romans 10:15.

82 From Pope Lucius III's decree against heretics at the Synod of Verona in 1184.

of them with damnable obstinacy refuse to honour an oath and so will not take it, let them by this very fact be regarded as heretics. We therefore will and command and, in virtue of obedience, strictly command that bishops see carefully to the effective execution of these things throughout their dioceses, if they wish to avoid canonical penalties. If any bishop is negligent or remiss in cleansing his diocese of the ferment of heresy, then when this shows itself by unmistakeable signs he shall be deposed from his office as bishop and there shall be put in his place a suitable person who both wishes and is able to overthrow the evil of heresy.

67. On the Usury of Jews

The more the Christian religion is restrained from usurious practices, so much the more does the perfidy of the Jews grow in these matters, so that within a short time they are exhausting the resources of Christians. Wishing therefore to see that Christians are not savagely oppressed by Jews in this manner, we ordain by this synodal decree that if Jews in future, on any pretext, extort oppressive and excessive interest from Christians, then they are to be removed from contact with Christians until they have made adequate satisfaction for the immoderate burden. Christians too, if need be, shall be compelled by ecclesiastical censure, without the possibility of an appeal, to abstain from commerce with them. We enjoin upon princes not to be hostile to Christians on this account, but rather to be zealous in restraining Jews from so great oppression. We decree, under the same penalty, that Jews shall be compelled to make satisfaction to churches for tithes and offerings due to the churches, which the churches were accustomed to receive from Christians for houses and other possessions, before they passed by whatever title to the Jews, so that the churches may thus be preserved from loss.

68. That Jews should be distinguished from Christians in their dress

A difference of dress distinguishes Jews or Saracens from Christians in some provinces, but in others a certain confusion has developed so that they are indistinguishable. Whence it sometimes happens that by mistake Christians join with Jewish or Saracen women, and Jews or Saracens with Christian women. In order that the offence of such a damnable mixing may not spread further, under the excuse of a mistake of this kind, we decree that such persons of either sex, in every Christian province and at all times, are to be distinguished in public from other people by the character of their dress—seeing moreover that this was enjoined upon them by Moses himself, as we read.[83] They shall not appear in public at all on the

83 See Leviticus 19:19; Deuteronomy 22:5 and 22:11.

days of lamentation and on passion Sunday, because some of them on such days, as we have heard, do not blush to parade in very ornate dress and are not afraid to mock Christians who are presenting a memorial of the most sacred passion and are displaying signs of grief. What we most strictly forbid, however, is that they dare in any way to break out in derision of the Redeemer. We order secular princes to restrain with condign punishment those who do so presume, lest they dare to blaspheme in any way him who was crucified for us since we ought not to ignore insults against him who blotted out our wrongdoings.

69. That Jews not hold public office

It would be too absurd for a blasphemer of Christ to exercise power over Christians. We therefore renew in this canon, on account of the boldness of the offenders, what the council of Toledo[84] providently decreed in this matter: we forbid Jews to be appointed to public offices, since under cover of them they are very hostile to Christians. If, however, anyone does commit such an office to them let him, after an admonition, be curbed by the provincial council, which we order to be held annually, by means of an appropriate sanction. Any official so appointed shall be denied commerce with Christians in business and in other matters until he has converted to the use of poor Christians, in accordance with the directions of the diocesan bishop, whatever he has obtained from Christians by reason of his office so acquired, and he shall surrender with shame the office which he irreverently assumed. We extend the same thing to pagans.[85]

70. That converts to the faith among the Jews may not retain their old rite

Certain people who have come voluntarily to the waters of sacred baptism, as we learnt, do not wholly cast off the old person in order to put on the new more perfectly.[86] For, in keeping remnants of their former rite, they upset the decorum of the Christian religion by such a mixing. Since it is written, cursed is he who enters the land by two paths,[87] and a garment that is woven from linen and wool together should not be put on,[88] we therefore decree that such people shall be wholly prevented by the prelates of churches from observing their old rite, so that those who freely offered

84 The Third Council of Toledo, which met in 589.

85 In this context, "pagans" means Muslims.

86 Colossians 3:9.

87 Ecclesiastes 2:14 and 3:28.

88 Deuteronomy 22:11.

themselves to the Christian religion may be kept to its observance by a salutary and necessary coercion. For it is a lesser evil not to know the Lord's way than to go back on it after having known it.[89]

71. Expedition for the recovery of the holy Land

It is our ardent desire to liberate the holy Land from infidel hands. We therefore declare, with the approval of this sacred council and on the advice of prudent men who are fully aware of the circumstances of time and place, that crusaders are to make themselves ready so that all who have arranged to go by sea shall assemble in the kingdom of Sicily on 1 June after next: some as necessary and fitting at Brindisi and others at Messina and places neighbouring it on either side, where we too have arranged to be in person at that time, God willing, so that with our advice and help the christian army may be in good order to set out with divine and apostolic blessing. Those who have decided to go by land should also take care to be ready by the same date. They shall notify us meanwhile so that we may grant them a suitable legate *a latere* for advice and help. Priests and other clerics who will be in the christian army, both those under authority and prelates, shall diligently devote themselves to prayer and exhortation, teaching the crusaders by word and example to have the fear and love of God always before their eyes, so that they say or do nothing that might offend the divine majesty. If they ever fall into sin, let them quickly rise up again through true penitence. Let them be humble in heart and in body, keeping to moderation both in food and in dress, avoiding altogether dissensions and rivalries, and putting aside entirely any bitterness or envy, so that thus armed with spiritual and material weapons they may the more fearlessly fight against the enemies of the faith, relying not on their own power but rather trusting in the strength of God. We grant to these clerics that they may receive the fruits of their benefices in full for three years, as if they were resident in the churches, and if necessary they may leave them in pledge for the same time.

To prevent this holy proposal being impeded or delayed, we strictly order all prelates of churches, each in his own locality, diligently to warn and induce those who have abandoned the cross to resume it, and them and others who have taken up the cross, and those who may still do so, to carry out their vows to the Lord. And if necessary they shall compel them to do this without any backsliding by sentences of excommunication against their persons and of interdict on their lands, excepting only those persons who find themselves faced with an impediment of such a kind that their vow deservedly ought to be commuted or deferred in accordance with the

89 2 Peter 2:21.

directives of the apostolic see. In order that nothing connected with this business of Jesus Christ be omitted, we will and order patriarchs, archbishops, bishops, abbots and others who have the care of souls to preach the cross zealously to those entrusted to them. Let them beseech kings, dukes, princes, margraves, counts, barons and other magnates, as well as the communities of cities, vills and towns—in the name of the Father, Son and holy Spirit, the one, only, true and eternal God—that those who do not go in person to the aid of the holy Land should contribute, according to their means, an appropriate number of fighting men together with their necessary expenses for three years, for the remission of their sins in accordance with what has already been explained in general letters and will be explained below for still greater assurance. We wish to share in this remission not only those who contribute ships of their own but also those who are zealous enough to build them for this purpose. To those who refuse, if there happen to be any who are so ungrateful to our lord God, we firmly declare in the name of the apostle that they should know that they will have to answer to us for this on the day of the final judgment before the fearful judge. Let them consider beforehand, however, with what conscience and with what security it was that they were able to confess before the only begotten Son of God, Jesus Christ, to whom *the Father all things into his hands*,[90] if in this business, which is as it were peculiarly his, they refuse to serve him who was crucified for sinners, by whose beneficence they are sustained and indeed by whose blood they have been redeemed.[91]

Lest we appear to be laying on men's shoulders heavy and unbearable burdens which we are not willing to lighten, like those who say yes but do nothing,[92] behold we, from what we have been able to save over and above necessities and moderate expenses, grant and give thirty thousand pounds to this work, besides the shipping which we are giving to the crusaders of Rome and neighbouring districts. We will assign for this purpose, moreover, three thousand marks of silver, which we have left over from the alms of certain of the faithful, the rest having been faithfully distributed for the needs and benefit of the aforesaid Land by the hands of the abbot patriarch of Jerusalem,[93] of happy memory, and of the masters of the Temple and of the Hospital. We wish, however, that other prelates of churches and all clerics may participate and share both in the merit and in the reward. We therefore decree, with the general approval of the council, that all clerics,

90 John 13:3 and John 3:35.

91 1 Peter 1:18–19.

92 Matthew 23:3–4.

93 Albert de Castro (died ca. 1213).

both those under authority and prelates, shall give a twentieth of their ecclesiastical revenues for three years to the aid of the holy Land, by means of the persons appointed by the apostolic see for this purpose; the only exceptions being certain religious who are rightly to be exempted from this taxation and likewise those persons who have taken or will take the cross and so will go in person. We and our brothers, cardinals of the holy Roman church, shall pay a full tenth. Let all know, moreover, that they are obliged to observe this faithfully under pain of excommunication so that those who knowingly deceive in this matter shall incur the sentence of excommunication. Because it is right that those who persevere in the service of the heavenly ruler should in all justice enjoy special privilege, and because the day of departure is somewhat more than a year ahead, crusaders shall therefore be exempt from taxes or levies and other burdens. We take their persons and goods under the protection of St Peter and ourself once they have taken up the cross. We ordain that they are to be protected by archbishops, bishops and all prelates of the church, and that protectors of their own are to be specially appointed for this purpose, so that their goods are to remain intact and undisturbed until they are known for certain to be dead or to have returned. If anyone dares to act contrary to this, let him be curbed by ecclesiastical censure.

If any of those setting out are bound by oath to pay interest, we ordain that their creditors shall be compelled by the same punishment to release them from their oath and to desist from exacting the interest; if any of the creditors does force them to pay the interest, we command that he be forced by similar punishment to restore it. We order that Jews be compelled by the secular power to remit interest, and that until they do so all intercourse shall be denied them by all Christ's faithful under pain of excommunication. Secular princes shall provide a suitable deferral for those who cannot now pay their debts to Jews, so that after they have undertaken the journey, and until there is certain knowledge of their death or of their return, they shall not incur the inconvenience of paying interest. The Jews shall be compelled to add to the capital, after they have deducted their necessary expenses, the revenues which they are meanwhile receiving from property held by them on security. For, such a benefit seems to entail not much loss, inasmuch as it postpones the repayment but does not cancel the debt. Prelates of churches who are negligent in showing justice to crusaders and their families should know that they will be severely punished.

Furthermore, since corsairs and pirates greatly impede help for the holy Land, by capturing and plundering those who are traveling to and from it, we bind with the bond of excommunication everyone who helps or supports them. We forbid anyone, under threat of anathema, knowingly to communicate with them by contracting to buy or to sell; and we order rulers of cities and their territories to restrain and curb such persons from this iniquity. Otherwise, since to be unwilling to disquiet evildoers is none other than to encourage them, and since he who fails to oppose a manifest crime is not without a touch of secret complicity, it is our wish and command that prelates of churches exercise ecclesiastical severity against their persons and lands. We excommunicate and anathematize, moreover, those false and impious Christians who, in opposition to Christ and the Christian people, convey arms to the Saracens and iron and timber for their galleys. We decree that those who sell them galleys or ships, and those who act as pilots in pirate Saracen ships, or give them any advice or help by way of machines or anything else, to the detriment of the holy Land, are to be punished with deprivation of their possessions and are to become the slaves of those who capture them. We order this sentence to be renewed on Sundays and feast-days in all maritime towns; and the bosom of the church is not to be opened to such persons unless they send in aid of the holy Land the whole of the damnable wealth which they received and the same amount of their own, so that they are punished in proportion to their offence. If perchance they do not pay, they are to be punished in other ways in order that through their punishment others may be deterred from venturing upon similar rash actions. In addition, we prohibit and on pain of anathema forbid all Christians for four years, to send or take their ships across to the lands of the Saracens who dwell in the east, so that by this a greater supply of shipping may be made ready for those wanting to cross over to help the holy Land, and so that the aforesaid Saracens may be deprived of the most inconsiderable help which they have been accustomed to receiving from this.

Although tournaments have been forbidden in a general way on pain of a fixed penalty at various councils, we strictly forbid them to be held for three years, under pain of excommunication because the business of the crusade is much hindered by them at this present time. Because it is of the utmost necessity for the carrying out of this business that rulers of the Christian people keep peace with each other, we therefore ordain on the advice of this holy general synod, that peace be generally kept in the whole Christian world for at least four years, so that those in conflict shall be brought by the prelates of churches to conclude a definitive peace or to observe inviolably a firm truce. Those who refuse to comply shall be most strictly compelled to do so by an excommunication against their persons and in interdict on their lands, unless their wrongdoing is so great that they ought not to enjoy peace. If it happens that they make light of the church's censure, they may deservedly fear that the secular power will be invoked by ecclesiastical authority against them as disturbers of the business of him who was crucified.

We therefore, trusting in the mercy of almighty God and in the authority of the blessed apostles Peter and Paul, do grant, by the power of binding and loosing that God has conferred upon us, albeit unworthy, unto all those who undertake this work in person and at their own expense, full pardon for their sins about which they are heartily contrite and have spoken in confession, and we promise them an increase of eternal life at the recompensing of the just; also to those who do not go there in person but send suitable men at their own expense, according to their means and status, and likewise to those who go in person but at others' expense, we grant full pardon for their sins. We wish and grant to share in this remission, according to the quality of their help and the intensity of their devotion, all who shall contribute suitably from their goods to the aid of the said Land or who give useful advice and help. Finally, this general synod imparts the benefit of its blessings to all who piously set out on this common enterprise in order that it may contribute worthily to their salvation.

Reprinted from Norman P Tanner, ed., *Decrees of the Ecumenical Councils*, 2 vols. (London; Washington, DC: Sheed & Ward; Georgetown University Press, 1990), 1:230–235 and 265–271.

PART III

CONTEXT

1. *RECONQUISTA* AND THE BOUNDARIES OF CHRISTENDOM

THE DIFFERENCES OF SPAIN

For many, mention of the middle ages calls to mind castles, knights and maidens, religious fervor, and feudalism in France, England, and Germany. This view, often confirmed in college textbooks and History Channel documentaries, explicitly marginalizes—even omits—current-day Spain. What we define and describe as *medieval* plays an important role in this exclusion. Traditionally, historians identified the middle ages as the period that started with the dissolution of Roman political, military, and cultural authority and ended with the rise of humanism and "classical values" in the fifteenth century. Even as historians have finessed and refined the bases for their dating of the beginning or end of the middle ages, the definition of *medieval* builds on a pastiche of political, religious, economic, and architectural markers, most of which are more applicable in the aggregate to Northern Europe (especially France) than to Iberia.

Typically, then, the image many form of medieval Europe is almost uniformly Christian. It is a primitive society, composed of an illiterate and superstitious peasantry, a ruthless militarized aristocracy who adhered to simple but clear values of loyalty and honor, and a cloistered, self-serving clergy. Structured and effective governance, economic vitality, and intellectual pursuit retreated to a small number of monasteries and walled cities. The minuscule Jewish communities that existed were brutally persecuted. Islam remained a distant adversary based overseas.

Like all stereotypes, this one builds upon a kernel of truth. Throughout the middle ages, most of Christian Europe did not experience the benefits of structured, centralized government. Most people—including the elite—were uneducated and illiterate. There was a good deal of local violence, against which few could effectively defend themselves. The church regulated both behavior and morality, relying on the threat of capital punishment by the temporal authorities as a compelling form of persuasion. And

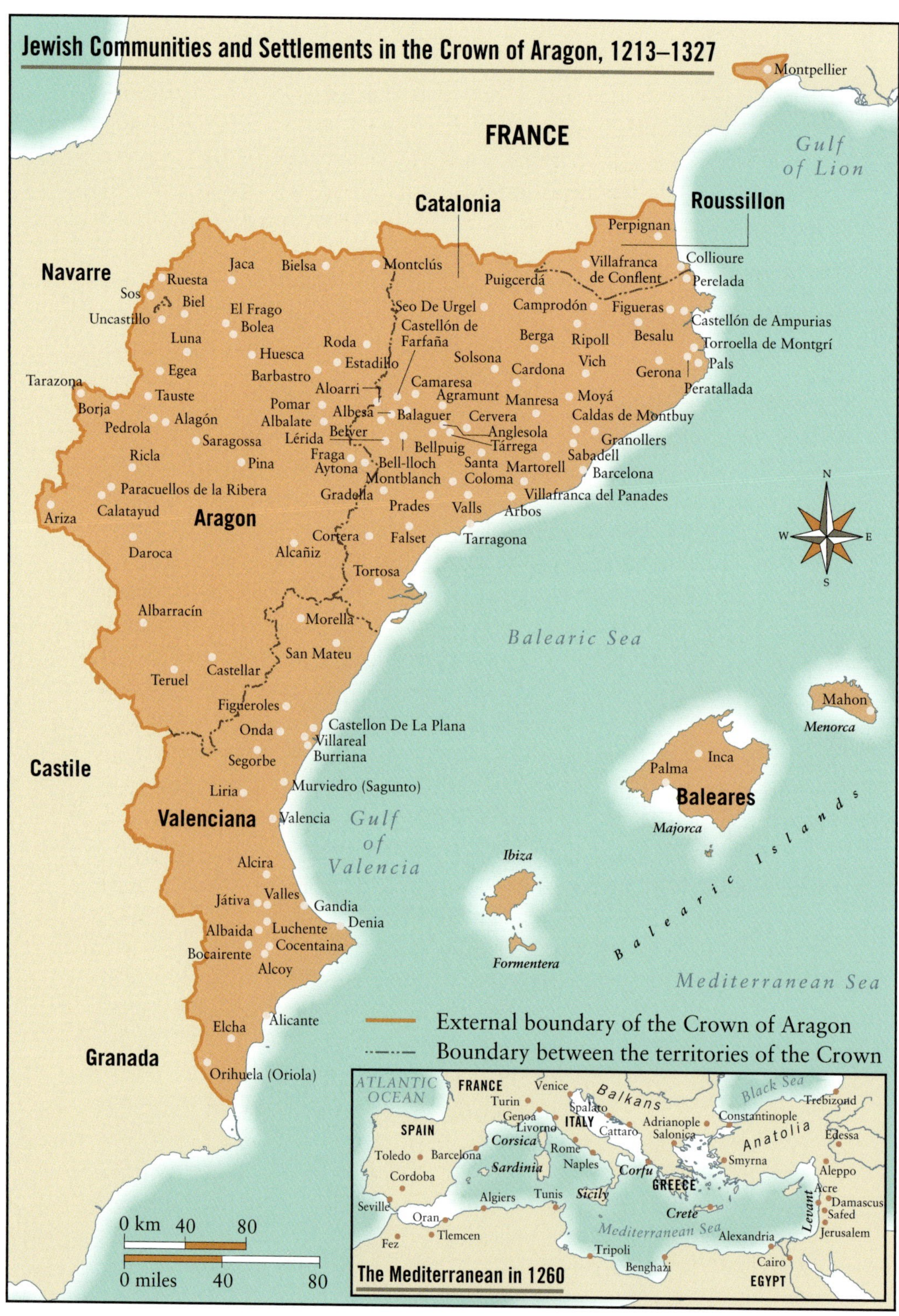

Source: Yom Tov Assis, *The Golden Age of Aragonese Jewry: Community and Society in the Crown of Aragon, 1213–1327* (London: Littman Library of Jewish Civilization, 1997)

most Christians had never encountered a Muslim or a Jew, let alone communities of either.

In many of those respects, Spain was, indeed, different. In contrast to the relatively homogenous Christian populations in what is now France, Germany, and England, the Kingdom of Aragon in northeastern Iberia, where the Barcelona disputation took place, was home to sizable Jewish and Muslim communities. Successful governance demanded that Christian rulers preserve a space in which those communities—called *aljamas* as of the twelfth century—could live in accordance with the laws of their faith. Though they maintained some financial and legal oversight over the shape and contours of Jewish and Muslim community organization, it was in the best interest of the Christian rulers that these communities remain essentially self-governed. Consequently, efforts to unify and purify Christendom in accordance with the dominant ideology of late eleventh- to thirteenth-century western Christendom unfolded at a different pace and more erratically in Iberia than in northern Europe.

Scholars have referred to the relative toleration that shaped social relations among the Christians, Jews, and Muslims in Iberia as *convivencia* (coexistence): three religious communities living in close proximity, sharing economic, cultural, and at times political practices and institutions. Recently, though, many historians of medieval Iberia, and especially of medieval Iberian Jewry, have retreated from using this descriptive term. The tendency to focus too narrowly on interfaith harmony during the caliphate in Cordoba and the twelfth through fourteenth centuries in Christian Spain has rendered *convivencia* a relatively empty, even misleading term. Although Christians, Jews, and Muslims in medieval Iberia did share common languages, aesthetics, and intellectual concerns, while maintaining daily life in an ordered society, they did not live in a society that supported tolerance or equality. Thus, *convivencia* provides a productive model for thinking about interfaith relations in Iberia only when the complexity of social norms finds clear expression as well. Conditions for this multi-faith society were set in motion when the southern tip of Visigothic Spain fell to Muslim invaders in 711. Invading armies, composed of rank-and-file Berbers led by Arab commanders, quickly emerged as the local elite, displacing the Christian aristocracy in part by partnering with the daughters of native Christian elites. Muslim forces swiftly expanded their area of control northward, until Christian armies successfully halted their advancement just north of the Pyrenees in a storied defensive battle led by Charles Martel in 732. Continued assaults by Frankish forces during the second half of the eighth century restored much of the territory that was later called Catalonia to Christian rule by the beginning of the ninth century (Girona in 785 and then Barcelona in 801, under Charlemagne's leadership). Widespread conversion or linguistic and cultural assimilation transformed much of Iberia into an Islamic center within the same timespan.

Since the period of Muslim rule was relatively short-lived in northern Catalonia, Muslim domination had a more subtle impact on the local religion, culture, and language than it did throughout the rest of the Iberian peninsula. The fact of a strong Muslim political, economic, and military presence immediately to the south shaped Catalonia as a frontier settlement. Following the successful conquest of northern Catalonia under Charlemagne, the Carolingians established a series of tributary or client territories governed by counts who were obligated to the Frankish kingdom. Such a close political and military alliance developed and was sustained by necessity. The Franks relied upon their client counts in Catalonia to hold the frontier and prevent further northward Muslim expansion; the leaders of these dependent territories relied upon the Franks for supplies and military support. Close alliances between Catalonia and Provence continued to shape politics and culture on both sides of the Pyrenees through the late thirteenth century. Likewise, beginning in the eleventh century Christian and Muslim leaders on the borderlands forged political and economic alliances with each other to assure local security and lucrative trade.

Demonstrated military and political leadership enabled counts from Catalonia, who had initially derived their authority from the recognition and support of the Franks, to emerge as the legitimate ruling aristocracy. By the early eleventh century, the descendants of tributary counts in Barcelona and Girona began extending their reach to include neighboring counties and then claimed independence from their Frankish patrons. Building upon natural tactical and economic advantages that come with inhabiting a fortified port city, the counts of Barcelona centralized political and military authority around their ancestral territories. Through a series of politically savvy marriages, treaties of alliance, and successful military conquests, they situated themselves as "count-kings" who presided over territories reaching well into previously independent territories in Aragon. Set on incorporating Muslim-controlled territories, they also formalized a policy of expansion.

The Kingdom or Crown of Aragon, a confederation of the counties of Catalonia and the realm of Aragon under the (occasionally contested) leadership of the count-kings of Barcelona, emerged from this movement to consolidate power in 1137. The *Reconquista*, as the systematic effort to commandeer Muslim-ruled territories has come to be known,[1] played a critical role in fortifying the count-kings' power. It also contributed to the formation of a regional Catalonian and later Aragonese political and cultural identity that both preserved local traditions and nurtured a more broadly regional identification with the Crown. When Christian efforts to claim Muslim-held land in Iberia became religiously or ideologically motived is a matter of scholarly dispute. Some argue that Christian leaders immediately envisioned a political and religious necessity to displace Muslim invaders and rebuild a strong Christian kingdom on the ruins of the Visigothic empire.[2] Others claim that an organized effort to evict Muslims emerged gradually from political, economic, and military necessity. Adherents of this approach argue that the Gregorian Reform and the call for and early success of the First Crusade in the late eleventh and early twelfth centuries provided the ideological, theological, and military framework for conceptualizing an organized "reconquest" of formerly Visigothic territories.[3]

Changes in Christian society and culture had a direct impact on the political and religious leadership of al-Andalus. In the late eleventh century relatively weak and fractionalized *taifa* (party or factionalist) kingdoms that had taken hold after the fall of the caliphate called upon the better organized and more militarized Almoravid troops from Morocco to help them defend their positions against Christian advances. The Almoravids brought with them and imposed a more conservative interpretation of Islam than the relatively permissive approach that had emerged in the caliphate and *taifa* kingdoms. This manifested itself in the imposition of increased restrictions on communities of monotheistic religions,

---

1 Joseph F. O'Callaghan provides a complete genealogy of the debate among historians as to whether *Reconquista* or "reconquest" accurately describes the impetus and motivation behind Christian military engagement with Muslims from the earliest period of Muslim conquest through the middle ages. See Joseph F. O'Callaghan, *Reconquest and Crusade in Medieval Spain* The Middle Ages Series (Philadelphia: University of Pennsylvania, 2003), 3–4. I use the term here because it played a significant role in the historiography since the nineteenth century. It also signals that the Christian leaders who organized and pushed to capture Muslim territories from the mid-eleventh century through the mid-thirteenth century were driven by interlaced religious, political, and military motivations.

2 Derek Lomax's authoritative survey of medieval Spain captures this viewpoint clearly: "The Reconquest is a conceptual framework useful to historians but not an artificial one like the Middle Ages. It was an ideal invented by Spanish Christians after 711, and its successful realization has preserved it since then as a historiographic tradition." Derek Lomax, *The Reconquest of Spain* (London: Longman, 1978), 1–2.

3 Thomas Bisson applies this term to the centuries-long process of Christian military conquest of Muslim-held territories; he does not draw attention to *Reconquista* as an ideology that drove political and military actions. See Thomas N. Bisson, *The Medieval Crown of Aragon, A Short History* (Oxford: Clarendon Press, 1986).

or *dhimmi* populations, and military campaigns to extend Muslim rule into Christian-held territories. Similarly, the objective of Christianizing the Iberian peninsula as a clear ideology evolved out of sustained territorial skirmishes both between competing Christian authorities and between Christians and Muslims throughout the eleventh and twelfth centuries. During this period, Christian leaders of Aragon, Catalonia, Castile, Leon, and Navarre competed with one another to secure alliances with the rulers of neighboring *taifa* kingdoms. The larger, confederated Christian kingdoms of Iberia thus emerged directly as a product of the *Reconquista.*

The church in Rome enthusiastically encouraged Christian kings to advance campaigns in former Visigothic strongholds, such as Tarragona and Saragossa, for the purpose of reestablishing bishoprics there. For the papacy, these armed campaigns served a single purpose: to recapture and rededicate the land as Christian. Starting in 1089, just six years before he called for an armed pilgrimage to recapture Jerusalem, Pope Urban II offered indulgences (remission of sins and guaranteed entry to heaven) to recruit knights from France as reinforcements to the Spanish forces. In addition, he explicitly excluded Spanish kings and knights from his call to march on Jerusalem in 1095.

The intensifying push to recapture Muslim lands in Iberia was an outgrowth of the same religious and political impulses that bolstered the crusading movement: an ideal of a unified Christendom, purified of any hint of heterodoxy and the effort to sanctify or reconsecrate buildings and territories that were at one time under Christian rule. Aragon's successful conquest of important strategic and economic settlements, including Huesca (1096), Saragossa (1118), and Tudela (1119), served precisely this goal.

Yet the drive for a purified Christendom occasionally ran at counter purposes with the practical dimension of containing and governing lands recently captured from Muslims. For the long term, Christian conquerors intended to populate formerly Muslim territories with Christian subjects. However, thoroughly depopulating these lands of Muslims would have rendered them functionally insolvent. Few Christians opted to relocate. Those who did lacked the necessary skill and resources to profitably cultivate the land, which meant it would generate neither revenue nor goods. Sustained occupation would then become a political and military liability rather than an asset. In these complicated circumstances it was necessary that Christian rulers permit and even nurture Jewish and Muslim communities in conquered territories.

Initially vanquished and subjected to Christian rule, Muslim communities gradually negotiated more favorable terms of surrender. This transformed them from Muslims living in the *dar al-Islam* (the House of Islam, ruled by a Muslim government according to Muslim law) into *Mudéjares*, Muslim subjects of a foreign occupier. Christian rulers had little interest in proselytizing among Muslims. They were permitted to continue living according to Muslim laws and practices, provided they did nothing to degrade or blaspheme Christian beliefs, doctrines, or saints. *Mudéjares* were also responsible for forming and financing their community institutions and leadership. Moreover, they were encouraged to remain in their towns and homes, continuing in their accustomed occupations. In exchange, they paid the Christian rulers substantial taxes and tributes, which solidified their submission.[4] Tensions between Muslim subjects and Christian authorities certainly arose, sometimes as violent rebellions, but the circumstances of these treaties provided for mostly peaceful conditions.

Jewish communities in conquered territories expanded in both size and significance during the twelfth century in direct relation to military expansion. Christian rulers recruited Jews, especially those who knew Arabic, to serve as colonizing agents. Jews employed as negotiators, scribes, or surveyors either accompanied the troops or followed closely behind to establish the terms of surrender and help secure a peace. They received significant land grants and financial interests in the territories under their command and recruited others to settle in Jewish communities in the new territories.

Maintaining formerly Muslim-held territories as relatively peaceful and productive enclaves of religious minorities laid the ground for further expansion by the individual Christian kingdoms. However, intense competition between Aragon and Castile hindered a unified, coordinated advance against Muslim strongholds in Iberia until the late twelfth century. The Treaty of Cazola (1179) between the two Christian powers solidified an agreement designed to mitigate these debilitating mutual hostilities. Clearly asserting that efforts to expand Christian dominance would continue until Muslim authority had been eliminated from the peninsula, the treaty divided the remaining (or yet-to-be-recaptured) Muslim territories between Castile and Aragon: "Valencia and the entire kingdom of Valencia with all of its territories, inhabited and uninhabited, which belong to it or ought to belong to it" designated for Aragon; the rest of southern Spain reserved for Castile.[5] The Christian realms in Iberia achieved their greatest gains during

4 On Muslim society under Christian rule during the *Reconquista*, see Brian A. Catlos, *The Victors and the Vanquished: Christians and Muslims of Catalonia and Aragon, 1050–1300*, Cambridge Studies in Medieval Life and Thought, 4th ser., 59 (Cambridge, UK and New York: Cambridge University Press, 2004).

5 *Medieval Iberia: Readings from Christian, Muslim, and Jewish Sources*, ed. Olivia Remie Constable, The Middle Ages Series (Philadelphia: University of Pennsylvania Press, 2nd ed., 2012), 207.

the thirteenth century as the struggle to Christianize Iberia was formally shaped as an international enterprise.

Responding to increased Christian attacks, the Almohad caliph from Morocco began aggressive campaigns in the late twelfth century, which escalated during the first decade of the thirteenth century. The Battle of Las Navas de Tolosa (1212) has been hailed by many as the beginning "of the end of Muslim ascendency in Spain."[6] An army composed of knights from Castile, Aragon, Navarre, and Leon, as well as crusaders from France, drove the Almohad forces south of the Guadiana River. The Almohad caliph retreated back to Morocco in the wake of this decisive Christian victory, leaving the remaining Muslim forces rudderless and in disarray. Christian Iberia secured significant strategic and symbolic gains over the course of the thirteenth century, with Castile-Leon laying claim to Cordoba (1236) and Seville (1248) and the Crown of Aragon seizing Majorca (1229) and Valencia (1238). By the middle of the thirteenth century, only Granada remained under Muslim control.

A desire for homogeneous religious and political authority fueled both the initial expansion of Islam into Iberia and the Christian response, the prolonged campaign to establish Iberia as a uniformly Christian stronghold. For the Christian kingdoms, this meant balancing the intensive effort to realize a pure Christendom and the practical necessities of government, which often pulled in the direction of religiously integrated cities and economies. Jewish and Muslim communities enjoyed a period of stability, and, it would seem, cultural and economic prosperity during the height of the *Reconquista*, at a time when Jewish communities throughout much of Europe were beginning to face increasing constriction of their liberties. The circumstances in Spain were, indeed, largely different than in the rest of Europe. In the Crown of Aragon, these conditions also established the possibility and necessity of the formulation of new and original law codes, widespread bureaucratization of royal authority, and the expansion of royal recordkeeping, all of which served a centralized royal government. The fruits of these labors produced political mechanisms that could be used with equal success to protect a public domain in which relatively peaceful interfaith relations reigned, or to destroy it.

---

6 O'Callaghan, *Reconquest and Crusade*, 76. More recently, other scholars have questioned how significant this really was. See Martin Alvira Cabrer, "Las Navas de Tolosa: The Beginning of the End of the Reconquista? The Battle and Its Consequences According to the Christian Sources of the Thirteenth Century," *Journal of Medieval Iberian History* 4, no. 1 (2012): 45–51.

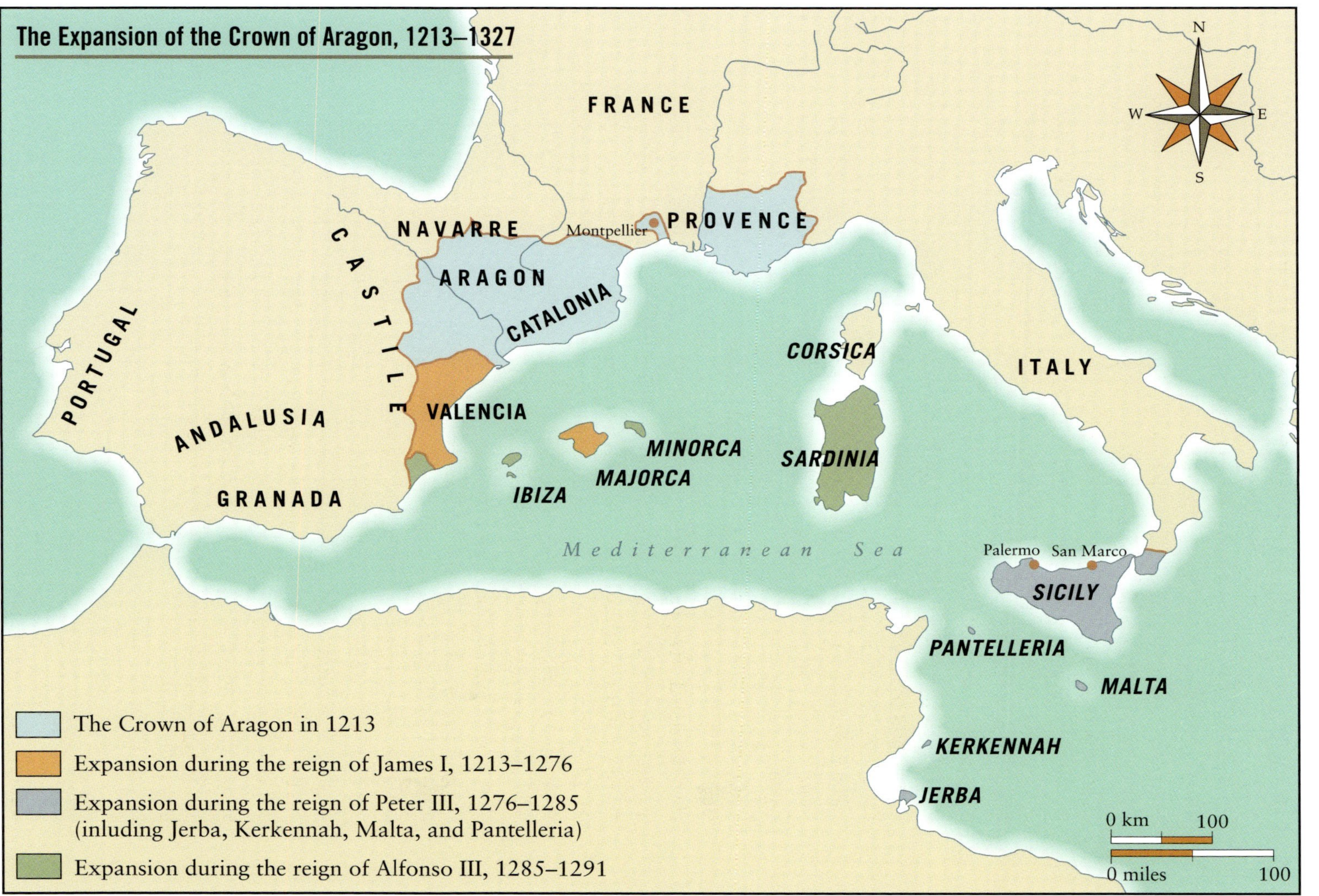

Source: Yom Tov Assis, *The Golden Age of Aragonese Jewry: Community and Society in the Crown of Aragon, 1213–1327* (London: Littman Library of Jewish Civilization, 1997)

2. KING JAMES I THE CONQUEROR (1213–1276)

King James I the Conqueror has been lauded by many scholars as one of the few medieval kings who consistently maintained a policy of beneficence toward Jewish and Muslim communities. Considerable documentary evidence from his royal archives demonstrates a persistent commitment to protecting their religious and political autonomy. And yet the fact that he staged and participated in a public religious disputation, compelled Nahmanides to appear, sanctioned compulsory sermons among Jews and Muslims, and later banished Nahmanides from the kingdom on charges of blasphemy seem to belie this characterization. Does the Barcelona disputation represent a radical departure from his approach to governance, and particularly his policies regarding religious minorities?

James I assumed the throne in the Crown of Aragon in 1213 at the age of five following the untimely death of his father, Peter II. Having inherited the throne at such an early age, James emerged from his minority amid considerable tribulations both within his realm and on its borders. Orphaned at the age of six, James was first made ward of Simon de Montfort, the man responsible for his father's death; later, Pope Innocent III intervened, entrusting him to the stewardship of the Templars, who raised him until he came of age. James I set out early on to fashion himself as a strong, independent, and assertive king in order to win independence from his regents and the Templars, who aspired to continue asserting control over the young king. Many of his projects and accomplishments as king developed directly from this early trajectory toward expanding the parameters of his sovereignty. During his reign, James I nearly doubled the territory of the Crown of Aragon, initiated a process of centralizing and standardizing the structures and mechanisms of government, began to claim the upper hand in his power struggle with the nobility, and expanded the realm's naval power. His military exploits, most especially his successful conquest of Majorca (1229) and Valencia (1238), presented him with tremendous military and economic opportunities and challenges. They also set the foundation for his effort to centralize government throughout the realm by establishing the framework for a mobile and reactive bureaucratic machinery that catalogued and measured demographics, territories, industries, assets, and local authorities. He later implemented all of these information-gathering processes within the kingdom's pre-conquest boundaries with varying levels of success.

From his boyhood, James I actively pushed to shift the balance of power between the king and the nobility in favor of the king.[7] Recognizing that

7 A parliamentary assembly of nobility and clergy that met with the king to advise on issues of governance and taxation. For a discussion of hierarchy and titles of landed elites in the Crown of Aragon, see Bisson, *The Medieval Crown of Aragon*, 73–74.

the ascension of a boy king might pose a great temptation for pretenders to the throne, James's regents wisely obliged all of the municipal and noble leaders in Catalonia and Aragon to swear an oath of loyalty to the young king at a massive assembly of the *Corts*.[8] Such assemblies of the leaders of the estates of the realm, including barons, prelates, and municipal councils, emerged as an invaluable vehicle of royal governance.[9] James I increasingly relied upon the *Corts* as the forum in which he produced and disseminated legislation on fiscal matters—often linked with efforts to raise an army to expand or secure the frontier—as well as issues of local and royal policy. Among the great challenges James I faced was establishing and maintaining peace among the various constituencies within his territories. The ability to travel and move goods safely without impediment within the kingdom provided the foundation for administering justice and commerce in a highly diverse realm composed of people from multiple religious faiths, speaking a variety of languages and dialects, and participating in localized political customs. Because the *Corts* were called at the king's pleasure, subjects were under some obligation to attend. They offered a forum in which the king could nurture a commitment to the peace and security of the kingdom on the part of his subjects by promoting royal plans and policies while granting favors and forging legislation that addressed local concerns.

As a Christian king, James I believed that he ruled faithfully and passionately in the name of God and in defense of God's interests on earth. Nevertheless, like many kings of the age, his relationship with the church was at times quite troubled. In particular, his personal life drew direct papal criticism. He married twice, kept several lovers, sired nine legitimate children, and at least two outside wedlock. In 1246, after the king's relationship with a concubine became public knowledge, the bishop of Girona declined to hear his confession and offer penance. When the bishop refused to budge, James had his tongue lopped off as punishment for insubordination. In addition, he butted heads with the pope over royal privileges granted to Jews and his inconsistent support of preaching missions by Dominicans and Franciscans among Jews in

8 Bisson, *The Medieval Crown of Aragon*, 59.

9 There is some scholarly debate about whether this early assembly was technically a meeting of the *Corts*. See Thomas N. Bisson, "Prelude to Power: Kingship and Constitution in the Realms of Aragon, 1175–1250" in *The Worlds of Alfonso the Learned and James the Conqueror: Intellect and Force in the Middle Ages*, ed. R. I. Burns (Princeton, NJ: Princeton University Press, 1985), 37–39; and Donald J. Kagay, "The Emergence of 'Parliament' in the Thirteenth-Century Crown of Aragon: A View from the Gallery," in *On the Social Origins of Medieval Institutions: Essays in Honor of Joseph F. O'Callaghan*, ed. Donald J. Kagay and Theresa M. Vann The Medieval Mediterranean Peoples, Economies, and Culture, 400–1453, no. 19 (Leiden: Brill, 1998), 228–29.

his realm. Though he pledged several times to go on crusade to the Holy Land, he repeatedly delayed this obligation. James and his assembled army finally set sail for Jerusalem in 1269, only to abort the journey when faced with inclement weather. Regardless, amid these tribulations, over the course of his very long reign, James made strides toward consolidating and systematizing royal power, expanding the kingdom's territory, standardizing royal records and laws, and maintaining a relative peace among the nobility and between Christians, Jews, and Muslims in his realm. He viewed all of these achievements as having been made with God's aid.

James I pursued a somewhat unconventional course in his relations with the church. As Robert I. Burns has demonstrated, the king was both pious and intensely spiritual.[10] James's memoir *Llibre dels fets* reveals that he understood his military and political accomplishments as God's reward for his tireless, dedicated service. His predilection for conducting official royal business in church buildings also attests to his sense that royal authority was both a gift and a service that was thoroughly intertwined with the church. And at the more institutional level, James established himself as an active patron of the recently founded mendicant orders of Dominicans and Franciscans. He also sponsored the establishment of several Dominican *studia* for instruction of Arabic and Hebrew to be used for missionizing purposes. As his participation in the Barcelona disputation and the royal orders he issued shortly thereafter demonstrate, he supported the friars' use of the skills developed there to proselytize among Muslims and Jews.

But James's alliance with the Dominicans and Franciscans was not without controversy. Both orders founded friaries in cities throughout the realm, frequently endorsed by the king. By design, the mendicant orders were directly responsible only to the pope and thus operated outside the typical episcopal hierarchy. The friars' frequent placement of their friaries near parish churches or cathedrals produced tension with local clergy, who feared that these friaries threatened to draw parishioners and thus revenues from the church.[11] Like his use of the *Corts* to quell noble opposition as a means of asserting royal authority, James I's patronage of the mendicants shifted the balance in relations between the crown and the church by effectively bypassing the episcopate.

---

10 This discussion of James's religiosity is indebted to R. I. Burns, "The Spiritual Life of James the Conqueror, King of Arago-Catalonia, 1208–1276: Portrait and Self-Portrait," *The Catholic Historical Review* 62, no. 1 (1976): 1–35.

11 J. R. Webster, "Unlocking Lost Archives: Medieval Catalan Franciscan Communities," *The Catholic Historical Review* 66, no. 4 (1980): 537–50.

Significantly, James I's long reign also ushered in innovations to Aragonese governance and royal recordkeeping. Thanks to the rise of universities in the early thirteenth century, a burgeoning class of literate men trained in mathematics provided an ample pool of skilled bureaucrats who could be deployed throughout the kingdom to keep the books. The availability of relatively inexpensive and abundant supplies of paper, a product of paper production workshops acquired by the Crown in Valencia, facilitated the preservation of transactions that previously might have been deemed private or inconsequential. The archive of written records from this period, therefore, offers historians a rich body of evidence representing social, legal, and economic conditions from a cross-section of Aragonese society during much of the thirteenth century.

Economic challenges drove a wide-ranging effort to keep a running register of royal assets and expenses. Likewise, efforts to maintain recordkeeping and governmental processes also shaped the structure and outcome of royally administered justice. The fiscal archives from James's reign (especially in its later years), therefore, provide a remarkably rich source of information about the delegation of royal authority and practices of government. During the king's minority, at a point when the royal *fisc* was very nearly empty due to the poor management of James's father, Peter II, James and his regents appointed Templars to serve as bookkeepers and accountants for the king. They divided the kingdom into administrative units, with each assigned its own royal agent. This facilitated the production of records, including a running tabulation of debts owed by and to the king, payments made, collection of revenue for specific projects or campaigns, and standardization of local coinage. James maintained these practices within the pre-conquest boundaries, then streamlined them in Valencia and Majorca.

These records point to a hybrid method of governance, combining standardized and well-documented procedures (such as the annual collection of taxes and fees), combined with the more ad hoc, but also well documented, means of raising funds through specific lines of credit extended to the king.[12] Royal authority emerged from the ability to dispense favors and privileges in exchange for pledges of loyalty, annual rents, and military

12 For a detailed discussion of finances during King James's reign, see Thomas N. Bisson, "The Finances of the Young King James I (1213–1276)," in *Medieval France and Her Pyrenean Neighbours: Studies in Early Institutional History*, Studies Presented to the International Commission for the History of Representative and Parliamentary Institutions, LXX (London: The Hambledon Press, 1989), 351–91; and Thomas N. Bisson, "The Fiscal Power of James the Conqueror (ca. 1230–1276): A Provisional Study," in *Jaume I: Commemoració del VIII centenari del naixement de Jaume I*, ed. Maria Teresa Ferrer i Mallol (Barcelona: Institut d'Estudis Catalans, 2011), 249–57.

support. The archives thus reveal solid foundations for as well as possible fissures in the structure on which royal power rested. Because they detail royal favors as well as royal debt, the fiscal archives shed light on the delicate balance of negotiations that enabled the king to grant mutually beneficial privileges to the barons, Jewish and Muslim communities, and the towns in the Crown of Aragon. Naturally, though, the benefits of such privileges were seldom timeless; moreover, arrangements that benefitted one constituency could prove detrimental to another and potentially sow discord.

Among the most important contributions made during King James I's reign was the proliferation of written legislation. This legal turn was, according to Thomas N. Bisson, a "remarkable efflorescence of legal codifications," that included municipal charters, a general code of law for Valencia based on a Roman model, and privileges and regulations for Jewish and Muslim communities, among others.[13] Individually and in the aggregate, this turn toward codification solidified and systematized local traditions related to baronial privilege, execution of justice, and the collection of revenue. In addition, because they were subject to royal approval, the legal codes in some cases succeeded in balancing baronial and royal interests, which provided the framework for economic expansion benefitting the nobility, municipalities, and the crown.

Maintaining stability in Valencia and Majorca posed a very different set of challenges. The long-term goal was to colonize these territories with Christian settlers; for the shorter term, it was in the king's interest to preserve native Muslim populations, or *Mudéjares*, as subjects on recently conquered land. The economic benefit of preserving and collecting taxes from existing urban markets, production of goods in artisanal workshops and agricultural settlements, and trade routes also brought political and military challenges. James implemented policies in Majorca and Valencia that had served him well in Catalonia and Aragon. He issued charters and localized privileges to discrete communities of *Mudéjares* and Jews that offered relative self-governance, including religious and judicial autonomy in exchange for paying taxes and fees. As was the case in Catalonia and Aragon, many of the people charged with collecting and recording these taxes were Jews, who served as tax collectors and bailiffs.

The early effort to colonize these conquered territories also spurred the immigration of Jews both from the north—especially from southern France and northern Catalonia—and from southern Iberia and Morocco. The knowledge of Arabic and relative familiarity with Muslim customs and

13 Bisson, *The Medieval Crown of Aragon*, 75.

culture among Andalusian and north African Jews made them a highly valued asset. And the king had good reason to prefer Jewish agents to local Muslims, who resented having been conquered and subjugated to Christian rule. Given James's uneasy relationship with the nobility, landed Christian elites from the north posed a different set of difficulties. Often suspected of forging alliances to restore a greater degree of parity between the *Corts* and the king, many among the nobility were perceived as a threat to royal stability. Unlike their Muslim and Christian counterparts, Jewish administrators did not have access to powerful allies who could work to undermine royal authority. Any privilege offered to a Jewish individual (or community) therefore remained a private and time-bound contract between the king and that person.

A firsthand account of James I's military and political successes has been preserved in *Llibre dels fets*, the earliest vernacular royal memoir of the middle ages. Composed over the course of many years, it narrates the entire duration of James's reign, allowing a rare view of a king processing the challenges of leadership and authority.[14] It gives voice to the king he was, as well as to the king he hoped he would be remembered by his subjects and in history. Spanning his entire lifetime, it also provides a glimpse at how some of his leadership traits may have developed. For example, his ambivalent relationship with the aristocracy began early on. Stories about his childhood hint that the pleasure the nobility enjoyed while exploiting his vulnerability as a youth stung James throughout his life. The *Corts* provided a setting in which he could neutralize aristocrats' individual schemes, while acknowledging their crucial role in governance and maintaining his authority. This literary endeavor, paired with his concerted effort to collect and maintain archives of royal authority, marks James I's reign as one of the most completely documented in the middle ages.

James I's reign ended in 1276 no less dramatically than it began. He died at the age of 68 after sustaining a battle wound as he fought to protect his interests in Valencia. From his early youth until his final battle, James continuously renewed his role as an independent and powerful sovereign. As a practical outcome of this approach to governance, his policies and decisions at times may appear incongruous and inconsistent. His approach to regulations of Muslim and Jewish communities provide a vivid example. Maintaining security and peace in the conquered territories of Valencia and Majorca proved a constant struggle. In Valencia especially the

14 D. Smith and H. Buffery, *The Book of Deeds of James I of Aragon: A Translation of the Medieval Catalan Llibre Dels Fets*, Crusades Texts in Translation; 10 (Aldershot: Ashgate, 2003).

population bristled against Christian rule, resulting in persistent *Mudéjar* rebellions nearly from the time of their defeat. James I struggled throughout his reign to quell Muslim unrest through treaties and charters. But, when necessary, he engaged in persistent military engagement. Similarly, his committed patronage of the mendicant friars led him to sponsor the Barcelona disputation and endorse preaching campaigns in synagogues. Due to his commitment to and reliance on Jews as agents of his government, however, he placed limitations on when and where the friars could conduct these preaching campaigns. These policies, which might seem contradictory to the modern eye, enabled him to maintain his autonomy and independence as a ruler.

3. THE JEWS OF MEDIEVAL SPAIN

JEWS IN EARLY CHRISTENDOM

Even during periods of intense crusading, "reconquest," and concerted efforts to purify Christendom, Jewish communities in the Crown of Aragon experienced growth, religious and cultural development, and political advancement. These apparently incongruous circumstances are indicative of the distinctive status of Jews in medieval Christendom as well as the exceptional demographic and religious history of Spain.

Christianity emerged from the Jewish messianic tradition. Sharing a common scriptural and historical origin laid the foundation for a contested, if sturdy bond between the two faiths. Both claimed the sole legitimate interpretation of the Hebrew Bible and, whether actively or implicitly, built interpretive traditions intended to negate the other's claim. However, the structure of biblical revelation permits that chosenness be bestowed to just one people at any time. Christianity accepted the authority of the historical and prophetic traditions but adapted them to support the unique historical circumstance of Jesus's life and teachings. Early Christian theologians dedicated considerable energy to the project of delegitimizing Jewish chosenness while asserting that the true covenant had legitimately passed to the Christian people who represented *verus Israel*, the true Israel.

Augustine of Hippo offered what became the most enduring and practicable approach to this problem. Struggling to demonstrate that contemporary Jews were bathed in error, while also preserving the timeliness and sanctity of the revelation in the Hebrew Bible, Augustine joined many of his contemporaries in reading the destruction of the Second Temple and the persistent diaspora of the Jews as evidence that the Jews' place in history had passed to Christians. Contemplating why Jews continued to exist and interpret the Hebrew Bible literally in the wake of the new revelation, Augustine couched his reflections in the historical circumstances that signaled their fall from divine favor. As such, their continued existence as Jews in dispersion served as a testament to the nations that God played an active role in human history. To support this argument he turned to Psalm 59:12[15] as his prooftext: "slay them not lest my people forget; scatter them by your power and bring them down." Augustine understood the Jews to be the guardians of the Hebrew Bible and its law; a people who, by their very nature, preserved a bygone era.

From the perspective of Christian theology, the Jews in the diaspora, as the people who received the first revelation, remained stubbornly resolved to apply biblical law literally in the physical world. But their assumption that Judaism was frozen in a pre-Christian time, of course, represents a view from outside. Even prior to the destruction of the Temple in 70 C.E., Jewish communities scattered around the Roman empire had developed localized interpretive traditions. By the fourth century, distinct centers of authority had emerged in Palestine and Babylonia around schools of teachers and redactors. The school of rabbis assembled in Palestine under the leadership of Rabbi Judah ha-Nasi in the early third century compiled and redacted the Mishnah. This body of literature contains legal traditions relating to nearly every aspect of Jewish life and ritual in the diaspora, as well as lore about and exegesis by the leading rabbis of the early generations.

The Mishnah elaborates and comments on precepts and practices delineated in the Hebrew Bible without echoing or conforming to its structure, chronology, or organizational principals. The Jerusalem Talmud and the Babylonian Talmud, which together include commentaries on the Mishnah as well as the product of many generations of teaching and tradition, are built around the six "orders" (*sederim*) or thematic groupings that comprise the organizational structure of the Mishnah.[16] The style of both Mishnah and Talmud is distinctive. Since portions of the Talmud are presented as a transcription of active discussion and debate, they provide a

15 This verse appears in 59:12 according to the Hebrew bible; 58:12 according to the Vulgate.

16 Since the Talmud contains an incredibly varied body of opinions, debate, and forms of storytelling, there is considerable scholarly debate about whose authorial hand composed it and what it represents. Some argue that the Talmud is a compilation of generations of rabbinic debate preserved, compiled, and reproduced as a guide for subsequent generations, while others hold that the document that has come to us today is the product of later redactors who used this multigenerational debate to privilege a particular school of rabbinic teachings. The literature on this is enormous. For a brief and accessible introduction see Richard Kalmin, "The Formation and Character of the Babylonian Talmud," in *The Cambridge History of Judaism, Volume IV: The Late Roman-Rabbinic Period.* (Cambridge: Cambridge University Press, 2006), 840–76.

widely diverse array of information: multiple—sometimes contradictory—findings on questions of law, interpretive methods and biblical exegesis, as well as lore about rabbis' lives, including homilies, tales about their behavior within and outside the academy, and genealogies of traditions. In short, rabbinic teachings and interpretations provided the common foundation on which most of diasporic Jewry built practices and traditions that preserved biblical precepts but adapted them to local contingencies.

THE VISIGOTHIC PERIOD

The earliest evidence of a Jewish presence in Iberia comes from inscriptions from the late Roman empire, the earliest of which date from the third century.[17] Church councils and legal codes provide further evidence of Jewish life in late Roman and early medieval Spain. At the time of their arrival, Jews held the status of citizens of the Roman Empire, which meant they were free to settle the colonized territories, hold slaves, own property, and serve as senators. With the increasing Christianization of the Roman empire, social relations between Jews and Christians came under more scrutiny. Early canon law, for example, such as the Council of Elvira (ca. 305), contains several canons restricting Jewish–Christian social interaction—in particular, activities that nurtured a sense of intimacy, such as dining together and marriage.

The long history of medieval Spanish Jewry is one of extremes: periods of significant persecution and religious repression juxtaposed with periods of high cultural, political, and social integration; long periods during which the historical record is virtually silent about Jewish life or culture, in contrast with long periods replete with extensive documentation of all sorts. To piece together information about the size, structure, and activities of Spanish Jewish communities prior to the tenth century, historians have at their disposal very limited sources. Nearly all of these are legal codes produced by rulers of the dominant society, rather than internal records of Jewish communities themselves. Legal sources as a rule depict society as the lawmakers felt it should be, not necessarily as it was. Since it is impossible to ascertain how widely early laws were disseminated or implemented, it is also very difficult to know how they affected the lives of Jews.

The consistent attention Jews garner in legal codes has led many scholars to believe that the Jews of Spain attained a position of relative wealth and authority from the third to the sixth century. As Roman citizens, their religious difference was protected by the law as long as they refrained from

17 David Noy, *Jewish Inscriptions of Western Europe: Italy (excluding the City of Rome), Spain and Gaul*, 2 vols. (Cambridge: Cambridge University Press, 2005), 1:238–62.

proselytizing and buying, selling, or holding Christian slaves. When the Visigothic King Reccared undertook to update the Roman law codes in 589 by bringing ecclesiastical and civil law under the jurisdiction of the king, he supplemented these injunctions with the stipulation that the children of a union between a Jew and a Christian must be baptized. For many scholars, the repetition of these regulations at church councils and in legal codes demonstrates that Christians and Jews alike chose not to abide by restrictions on social intercourse and that interfaith relations were relatively natural until the early seventh century.

Jews of Visigothic Spain suffered serious restrictions on their religious practices and freedoms for first time during the reign of Sisebut (611–621). Unlike his predecessors, Sisebut abandoned Roman practice regarding Jews and called for compulsory conversion of Jews married to Christians, removal of all Christian slaves and workers from Jewish households, compulsory re-Christianization of those who had converted to Judaism, and removal of Jews from positions of authority over Christians. Later, he legislated the universal forced baptism of all Jews living in his realm.

Whether the policy of mass conversion was successful demographically or theologically is a matter of debate. Many of Sisebut's contemporaries, including Isidore of Seville, one of the leading intellectual and religious figures of the day, opposed it; subsequent rulers and church leaders struggled in the aftermath with baptized Jews who returned to Judaism, raised their baptized children in Jewish homes, or used subterfuge to shield their children from baptism.[18] There is no scholarly consensus about either the motives or the success of these restrictive policies. Some argue that Visigothic leaders were, by definition, so weak that implementing these laws must have been impossible. Others suggest that Visigothic legislation created an early form of crypto-Judaism akin to the secret practice of Judaism that emerged in late medieval Spain in the wake of mass forced conversions. The true impact is probably somewhere in between. Likely, a handful of the Jews either relocated to less restrictive environments or concealed their Judaism, while others found means of accommodation that facilitated their continued residence in Iberia.[19]

---

18 For a highly innovative interpretation of this evidence see Wolfram Drews, "Jews as Pagans? Polemical Definitions of Identity in Visigothic Spain," *Early Medieval Europe* 11, no. 3 (2002): 141–82.

19 Hagith Sivan, "The Invisible Jews of Visigothic Spain," *Revue des études Juives* 159, no. 3 (2000): 369–85. Sivan suggests that the fact that historical records from Jewish communities omit mention of these persecutions may be indication that Jews suffered less under Visigothic rule than the legal documents might imply.

AL-ANDALUS

Documentary silence obscures the contours and details of Jewish life in Iberia during the early period of Muslim rule as well. Arabic accounts of the Muslim conquest report that some Jews had worked with the invading soldiers who arrived on the shores of Granada in 711 to secure victory against Visigothic defenders. The earliest of these sources, however, date from the ninth and tenth centuries, around the same period when records of Jewish cultural activity and leadership in Muslim society come to light. Consequentially, it is difficult to determine whether such reports were accurate or were mostly the product of latter-day lore reflecting contemporary realities. Still, since there is extensive evidence that well-established, socially and culturally integrated Jewish communities resided in Iberia as of the early tenth century, there is reason to assume a continuity of settlement.

The Muslim conquest of Iberia attests to the theological appeal of Islam and to the power of Muslim armies. Islam encouraged local populations to convert; Muslims also reserved a protected status for peoples of the book (*ahl al-kitab*) who lived in accordance with revealed scripture and accepted a monotheistic God. Such communities were allowed to continue practicing their traditions in accordance with their laws as administered by their religious authorities. In exchange, they paid a poll tax (*jizya*) that signaled their acceptance of the subjugated status of religious minorities, or *dhimmi* populations.[20] The Jewish communities in al-Andalus relied on the Geonim, the rabbinic authorities in Babylonia, as their religious authorities. Their status as *dhimmi* communities facilitated the establishment of local traditions and teaching, but directed and overseen by the stable rabbinic courts in the east.

By the late ninth century, Muslim society and culture in al-Andalus actively nurtured productive relations among Muslims, Jews, and Christians. Spurred by a marked gender imbalance among the ethnic Arab elite, conquerors married indigenous Christian women, some of whom converted to Islam. Mutual familiarity with customs and behaviors across religious

---

20 The Pact of Umar, attributed to an early caliph in Syria, presents a clear and succinct idealized expression of the conditions of *dhimma* status. See http://legacy.fordham.edu/halsall/source/pact-umar.asp, accessed May 2, 2016. A different version is printed in *Muslim and Christian Contact in the Middle Ages: A Reader*, ed. Jarbel Rodriguez, Readings in Medieval Civilization and Cultures XVII (Toronto: University of Toronto Press, 2014), 2–4. In a recent book on *dhimma* status in al-Andalus, Janina Safran entirely disaggregates the history of religious minorities in Muslim Iberia from the Pact of Umar because this text testifies to conditions in a very different time and place. Her book provides a fascinating reconstruction of the legal, social, and cultural fabric of medieval al-Andalus. See Janina M. Safran, *Defining Boundaries in al-Andalus: Muslims, Christians, and Jews in Islamic Iberia* (Ithaca, NY: Cornell University Press, 2013).

and ethnic lines fostered in the offspring of these unions an ability to navigate the aesthetic and theological realms of Islam and Christianity. Though these relations were at times colored with animosity and unease, they set the foundation for a public culture that included, even welcomed, active participation of *dhimmi* peoples. Even outside elite circles, the native population—converts as well as *dhimmi* communities—also adopted Arabic as their *lingua franca* and were thus poised to contribute to the dominant society at all levels.

In 929, amid an extended period of political, economic, literary, architectural, and social growth, Abd al-Rahman III, emir of Cordoba, established al-Andalus as a caliphate, an independent Muslim state. Having broken free from and, indeed, challenging the political and theological authority of the Abbasid Empire in Baghdad, al-Rahman solidified complex social and economic conditions that supported a multi-ethnic, multi-faith elite that lasted beyond the disintegration of the caliphate in 1009.[21] Jewish communities in particular enjoyed a period of great cultural vitality, thanks to a concerted effort among some to master and contribute to Muslim society and culture. Most notable—and most visible—among these figures were two men who made their mark as military and diplomatic leaders: Hasdai ibn Shaprut and Ismail ibn Naghrela (better known as Samuel ha-Nagid). Both of these men situated themselves within the Muslim court, prospered as a result of significant contention among the various factions represented in the court, and served as important leaders within the Jewish communities as well.

Hasdai ibn Shaprut (915–ca. 975) emerged as a politically savvy leader who was an equally astute pilot of his own career. A noted physician who also may have served as customs officer under Abd al-Rahman III, Hasdai rose to favor in the court by demonstrating himself valuable in establishing diplomatic relations between the caliphate and various Christian rulers. He helped forge relations between Abd al-Rahman and the German emperor, Otto I. He also brokered an alliance between the caliph and the Christian leader, Sancho I of Leon who, in the throes of a struggle for power, turned to Abd al-Rahman for aid.

Hasdai ibn Shaprut played an equally significant role in advancing Jewish society and culture. In Cordoba he supported an independent center of Jewish learning, and he sponsored a rising school of Hebrew poetry that echoed the forms and aesthetics of Arabic poetry during this period. Farther afield, he maintained communication with Jewish communities

21 Jonathan P. Decter, "Before Caliphs and Kings: Jewish Courtiers in Medieval Iberia," in *The Jew in Medieval Iberia*, ed. Jonathan Ray (Boston: Academic Studies Press, 2013), 5–6.

around the world, earned the designation as head of the Jewish community of al-Andalus from the Gaon in Baghdad, and, perhaps most famously, initiated a correspondence with the king of Khazaria about the nature of Jewish power.[22]

Samuel ha-Nagid followed ibn Shaprut's example as a visible and successful figure in the Muslim court. Born at the end of the tenth century, during a period of momentous change and political turmoil for Muslim al-Andalus, ha-Nagid attained a position of authority and influence within Jewish and Muslim society as a result of his talents as a scribe and writer of letters in the court in Granada. Whereas Hasdai ibn Shaprut benefited from the centralization of power under a single caliph, Samuel ha-Nagid ascended to power in part due to the factionalization of power and loyalty under the *taifa* rulers. He was a gifted strategist who commanded respect and capitalized on the need for loyal and trustworthy leaders in the kingdom of Granada. Eventually, he ascended to the position of vizier. In this capacity, he led a Muslim army in battle against Muslim soldiers serving other Muslim rulers. Samuel ha-Nagid also exerted considerable influence in the Jewish community. He was an accomplished Hebrew poet who served as patron for other poets, while also supporting and reinforcing localized schools of Jewish law and interpretation.

Muslim society in al-Andalus offered great opportunity for those with the requisite talent and wherewithal to make themselves indispensible, in spite of the fact that achievements like Samuel ha-Nagid's were in direct conflict with a strict interpretation of *dhimma* law. And there is evidence that a good number of Jewish men attained positions of respect and authority. Jewish communities at large also enjoyed relative prosperity and peace during this period. But since it was not a fully open or tolerant society, individuals and communities faced serious dangers in the event of a misstep, whether proven or merely perceived. The case of Samuel ha-Nagid's son Joseph ibn Naghrela provides a vivid example. After his death, Samuel ha-Nagid's title and position passed to Joseph. While Samuel ha-Nagid consistently demonstrated himself to be a generous, fair, well-valued leader who cultivated allies, Joseph ibn Naghrela ran afoul of the Muslim elite. Following the untimely and perhaps suspicious death of his patron, Joseph's enemies accused him of murder and then exacted retribution by executing him and massacring much of the Jewish community of Granada; survivors scattered and resettled in other communities.

---

22 English translations of Hasdai ibn Shaprut's letter and the king's reply can be found in Curt Leviant, *Masterpieces of Hebrew Literature: Selections from 2000 Years of Jewish Creativity* (Jewish Publication Society, 2010), 159–69.

With the rise of Almoravid rulers in al-Andalus in 1086, who adopted a more conservative interpretation of Islam than did the caliphs or the *taifa* kings, a more strictly enforced subjugation of religious minorities slowly emerged as the norm. *Dhimmi* populations in previously cosmopolitan cities, like Granada and Seville, suddenly found themselves shut out of the corridors of politics and culture. Under Almohad rule, a more extreme Muslim faction that began to exert authority in al-Andalus during the second half of the twelfth century, the protections of *dhimma* status eroded completely.

Because these extremist policies were at least partially initiated as a reaction to military incursions led by Christian kings from northern Iberia in their effort to "reconquer" Muslim-held territories, the native Christian population especially endured a more heavily regulated existence. Though Jews did not face the same specifically retributive legislation, many found the new conditions intolerable. Some sought refuge either in northern Christian territories or in the Middle East and North Africa, where their skills as linguists, philosophers, poets, or physicians might prove valuable. The itinerant life these men adopted suggests that the transition was both unwelcome and difficult, a supposition supported by the fact that several composed poetic or theological works that attest to their sense of displacement. Judah ha-Levi (ca. 1075–1141), Petrus Alfonsi (late-eleventh to mid-twelfth century, exact dates unknown), and Moses ben Maimon, or Maimonides (1138–1204) all produced works expressing awareness and anxiety that they were living in a time of great political and religious transformation.

Judah ha-Levi, a gifted Hebrew poet who was also trained in Arabic and philosophy, arrived in the recently Christianized Toledo in the early twelfth century. He remained for just a short time before embarking for Egypt. From there, he intended to continue on to Palestine, where he hoped to spend his final years, but it is not clear that he ever arrived. Ha-Levi wrote some 800 poems, many of which provide details about his life and travels. However, he is perhaps best known for *The Kuzari*, his imaginings of a series of theological and philosophical disputations between the Khazar king and, respectively, an Aristotelian philosopher, a Christian, a Muslim, and a Jew. Originally composed in Judeo-Arabic, this text was translated into Hebrew and circulated among northern European Jewish communities in the thirteenth century.[23] As formulated by ha-Levi, the Khazar king, in the midst of his discussion with the Jew, recognized

23 Adam Shear, *The Kuzari and the Shaping of Jewish Identity, 1167–1900* (Cambridge and New York: Cambridge University Press, 2008), 38–39.

Judaism to be true and decided to convert to Judaism, bringing his entire kingdom with him—in spite of the generally degraded social and political status of the Jewish people.[24] In *The Kuzari*, ha-Levi used his knowledge of Christianity, Islam, and philosophy to make his case that of all the philosophies, Judaism alone is rooted in true revelation that had been preserved in an uninterrupted and authentic chain of tradition. The fictionalized story based on historical circumstances solidified his argument. This text may also testify to a deeper concern on his part that during periods of strife Jews would seek refuge in the dominant faith, whether it be Christianity or Islam.

The life and writings of Petrus Alfonsi provide some indication that ha-Levi's fear of Jewish apostasy was not entirely unwarranted. Petrus Alfonsi converted from Judaism to Christianity in 1106 in the recently conquered town of Huesca, under the patronage of King Alfonso I of Aragon. Petrus later composed an anti-Jewish disputation in which he informs his readers of the time and place of his conversion and puts Christianity in direct dialogue with Judaism and Islam. His text is all the more poignant since he figures the Jewish disputant as himself prior to his baptism, and the Christian disputant as himself after his conversion. Though he provides little information about theological or emotional struggles that drove him to convert, Petrus's *Disputatio contra judaeos* offers a glimpse at the cultural and intellectual agility of Jews raised in this milieu and the difficulties they faced as the political and religious authorities in their world were displaced.[25] Following his conversion, Petrus migrated north. He spent some time in England in the court of Henry I, and possibly in France as well, where his *Disputatio* was well received for its introduction to Judaism, Islam, natural philosophy, and rational theological debate.

If Judah ha-Levi expressed ambivalence about the cultural legacy of Iberia, and Petrus Alfonsi displayed alienation from Judaism and Spain, Moses Maimonides' relationship with Iberia was less troubled. Maimonides and his family fled Cordoba after the rise of the Almohads, who adopted a radical policy requiring all Jews and Christians to accept Islam. Those who refused could emigrate or face execution. Possibly traveling as Muslims, perhaps having nominally converted to forestall attack, Maimonides and his family settled first in Fez, then Palestine, and finally in Fustat (Cairo),

---

24 The opening section of *The Kuzari*, which also bears the title *The Book of Refutation and Proof: On the Abased Faith* in the Judeo-Arabic original, is available at http://legacy.fordham.edu/halsall/source/kuzari.asp, accessed on May 2, 2016.

25 For an excellent English translation, see Petrus Alfonsi, *Dialogue against the Jews*, trans. Irven Michael Resnick, Fathers of the Church, v. 8 (Washington, DC: Catholic University of America Press, 2006).

where they remained. Maimonides entered the service of an emir as a physician. It was in Fustat that he wrote his great works, *The Mishneh Torah*, his philosophical work *The Guide for the Perplexed*, as well as a large number of medical tracts. Nevertheless, he lamented his exile from al-Andalus, which he identified as his intellectual home, and he unambivalently brought this identification with him into exile.[26]

JEWISH LIFE IN CHRISTIAN SPAIN DURING THE RECONQUISTA

These three exiles, of course, represent a very limited sample of the Jews of al-Andalus who settled throughout the Middle East, North Africa, and Europe in the wake of reinterpretation of *dhimma* law under the Almoravids and Almohads. Many found their way to Catalonia, where Jewish communities had been established at least since the late eleventh century. The *Reconquista* also brought immigrants from recently conquered territories who sought opportunity and stability in the north, while continuing efforts on the part of Christian kings to secure or purify Christendom brought exiles from northern Europe. The *lingua franca* among the native Jews was Catalan, but the steady influx of Arabic-speakers also meant that they bore the religious and cultural inflection of al-Andalus.

Catalonia was both prosperous and cosmopolitan. The proximity of such cities as Barcelona (the capital of Catalonia) and Girona to the Pyrenees in the north and the Mediterranean to the east made this region a geographic, political, and cultural crossroads: between Christianity and Islam, between France and Spain, and between the unified Crown of Aragon and the independent principalities and counties that were joined under the Crown. Successful conquest of Majorca in the early thirteenth century by King James I brought increased trade in such items as silks, spices, grain, cotton, weapons, and dyes, which set the foundation for a complex credit-based economy. Jewish populations of Catalonia and Aragon were integral to this economic boom. Jews emerged as interested merchants and financiers of the military conquest of Majorca, bureaucrats—record keepers and translators—working for the Crown, and creditors and moneychangers vital to the "repopulation" of formerly Muslim territories.

Efforts to expand into Muslim-held territories intensified with the dissolution of the caliphate in the eleventh century. During the first phase of this expansion, Christian noble families who were most loyal to count-kings assumed authority over newly acquired territories. However, as kings

26 Joel L. Kraemer, *Maimonides: The Life and World of One of Civilization's Greatest Minds* (New York: Doubleday, 2008).

fortified their own royal authority, nobility and powerful elites posed an increasing threat in these conquered lands. Bitter political struggles among Christians, then, shaped Jews as an asset during the early *Reconquista.* Viewed as loyal and dependable subjects who brought valuable skills, including a knowledge of Arabic, this class of "Jewish Courtiers" played a vital role in the conquest of Muslim territories.[27] Many were native subjects in the Crown of Aragon, but their ranks also included visitors or immigrants from southern Iberia or North Africa. They served as bailiffs, tax collectors, traders, and record keepers. They also provided a crucial source of tax revenue. In contrast with Christian communities, which were obliged to tithe to the Church, Jewish communities paid the Crown directly.

Jewish communities in northern Iberia developed as formal political units in tandem with the same political movement that propelled the solidification of royal powers and as part of the same cultural impetus. The mid-twelfth century saw a proliferation of legal charters and statutes delineating the legal status of individuals and corporate entities like cities. Such charters formalized relationships based on vassalage or mutual dependence and benefit in documents that ideally provided a clear determination of the rights and responsibilities that preserved social order. Production of legal records did not assure a society governed by law, but it established the institutions and practices necessary for a society of law to function. Jews participated in this process not just as agents of the crown; formal Jewish communities as political units also began to take form under the guidance of Jewish leaders in the late twelfth century.

Documentary evidence of internal Jewish governance and its relation to the dominant society remains scant until the early thirteenth century. Indeed, prior to 1150, there is no documentary evidence showing that formal Jewish communities existed at all. Conditions and legal protections of Jewish autonomy grew more precise over time, shifting, in the words of Elka Klein, from "autonomy by default" in the late eleventh and early twelfth centuries, to an "autonomy by design" by the thirteenth century.[28] Historians map this evolution in legal charters. For example, the *Fuero* of Teruel (1176), a charter delineating the legal status of a frontier city, defined the Jews as *servi* (slaves or servants) of the king, a status

27 I borrow the term "Jewish Courtiers" from Jonathan Ray, in *The Sephardic Frontier: The Reconquista and the Jewish Community in Medieval Iberia, Conjunctions of Religion and Power in the Medieval Past* (Ithaca, NY: Cornell University Press, 2006), 17–22. His definition is based on the fact that these Jewish officials possessed horses and carried arms, as did the nobility.

28 Elka Klein, *Jews, Christian Society, and Royal Power in Medieval Barcelona* (Ann Arbor: University of Michigan Press, 2006), 72.

that distinguished Jews from others governed or protected by this document.[29] Since each community negotiated for (or received) conditions and privileges independently, these were locally determined by the lord, count, or king who claimed jurisdiction over the place of Jews in each settlement.

As religious minorities, Jews in Iberia, as elsewhere in western Christendom, functioned as autonomous and self-governing communities. In Catalonia and Aragon the formal organized communities were known as *aljamas*, or *kehillot* (*kehillah* = singular) in Hebrew.[30] Each *aljama* was governed by a local body of elected officials, referred to in the Hebrew documents as *berurim*. The political and demographic character of each community was locally determined; thus election processes, the number of officials elected, the roles allotted to them, and the titles of elected officials varied from one *aljama* to the next. All who participated in an election generally paid a minimum tax. Practical administrative power, though, rested in the hands of the wealthiest local families: members of the intellectual and social elites, including financiers, traders in luxury items, physicians, and merchants involved in overseas trade. They oversaw the institutions fundamental to Jewish ritual, including the Jewish slaughterhouses and burial grounds, as well as the collection of revenue. They also made decisions permitting individuals to travel, engage in certain businesses, or enter as new members of the community.

It is impossible to identify general mechanisms of *aljama* governance, since each *aljama* ran according to unique guidelines and few Hebrew documents dealing with the structure of *aljamas* remain from the period before the second half of the thirteenth century. However, royal documents that discuss Jews and Judaism give some indication of how *aljamas* functioned in relation to the Crown. During the time of King James I *aljamas* enjoyed significant freedom. The only practical matters of Jewish community administration with which King James was officially concerned were the collection of taxes for the royal *fisc* and overseeing elections of judges

29 David Abulafia, "'Nam iudei servi regis sunt, et semper fisco region deputati': The Jews in the Municipal 'Fuero' of Teruel (1176–7)," in *Jews, Muslims and Christians in and around the Crown of Aragon*, ed. Harvey Hames and Elena Lourie (Leiden: Brill, 2004), 97–123. For a similar case in Castile see Maya Soifer Irish, "Tamquam domino proprio: Contesting Ecclesiastical Lordship over Jews in Thirteenth-Century Castile," *Medieval Encounters* 19, no. 5 (January 1, 2013): 534–66.

30 On the origins of Jewish community institutions see Klein, *Jews, Christian Society, and Royal Power*, 26–50. On the structure of Jewish communities in Spain see Yitzhak Baer, *A History of the Jews in Christian Spain: From the Reconquest to the Fourteenth Century*, 2 vols. (Philadelphia, PA: Jewish Publication Society of America, 1961), 1:212–36.

(*dayyanim*) and *berurim*.[31] Until the turn of the fourteenth century, leadership positions in local *aljamas* remained under the control of only a small number of elite families who maintained close ties with Christian rulers.[32] The position of rabbi was, through the thirteenth century, an honorary one held by those well known for their mastery of rabbinic interpretation. In many cases, rabbis played no formal role in community governance.

For the community to function it was necessary that individuals have at least a basic understanding of the fundamentals of Jewish law and custom. Responsibility for educating youth in basic Torah study resided with individual families. As most Jewish communities until the late fourteenth century did not have established schools for the education of all students, individual families contracted teachers for the instruction of their children. In some communities, philanthropists provided for the education of the poor. For more advanced education in biblical interpretation and Talmud, students turned to *yeshivot* (*yeshivah*=singular), Talmud academies formed around eminent scholars. *Yeshivot* bore the flavor of the master's distinctive interpretations and teachings. Nahmanides, for example, led an important academy in Girona, which attracted students from around the Jewish world. An early proponent of the mystical movement Kabbalah, Nahmanides attracted many students who sought his innovative yet systematic approach to Torah study. Nahmanides' cousin, Jonah Gerundi, presided over his own *yeshivah* in Barcelona during the early thirteenth century, offering an approach deeply rooted in moralist and pietist approaches to Jewish learning. Among their many disciples were several very influential rabbis; for instance, Solomon ibn Adret, who studied under both men, became the leading rabbi in the Crown of Aragon during the late thirteenth century. Hundreds of his *responsa* (correspondence on matters of *halakhah*, or Jewish law) and original writings are extant today, providing a tremendous storehouse of information about Jewish life throughout the region.

The conditions necessary for maintaining active Jewish life in the diaspora varied widely from one settlement to the next. Jewish leaders were challenged to reconcile Jewish law with diverse cultural and social demands, while also preserving the integrity of rabbinic practice. The rabbinic tradition represented in the Talmud also endorsed political and cultural independence. Leaders of the *aljamas* vigorously protected their local autonomy against challenges or incursions from leaders of distant

31 Yom Tov Assis, *The Golden Age of Aragonese Jewry: Community and Society in the Crown of Aragon, 1213–1327*, (London: The Littman Library of Jewish Civilization, 1997), 88–109.

32 For a broad discussion of Jewish community governance see Assis, *The Golden Age of Aragonese Jewry*, 67–160.

Jewish communities. The freedom of local Jewish leaders to define the parameters of proper social conduct, ritual practice, and protocols for education and interpretation was tremendously important for the preservation of tradition and stable leadership. The Talmud also provided model ordinances regulating public behavior, such as business practices and relations with gentiles.

Authority for interpretation of Jewish law and issues of contention among Jews—marriage, divorce, bequests, business contracts—fell to the Jewish court (*bet din*) and community leaders. Local Jewish cultures developed in conjunction with the economic, political, and cultural climate of the dominant society. Jewish community governments expected that Jews would automatically turn to the *aljama's bet din* for administration of legal claims and disputes. However, municipal and royal archives in the Crown of Aragon hold substantial evidence that Jews also sought protection in royal courts. Business agreements and wills, for example, composed in Latin and copied in Hebrew, point to a fairly intricate set of links between Jewish and Christian political cultures at the ground level. The rising notarial class in the Crown of Aragon under James I provided an alternative to the Jewish community scribe (*sofer*). By the thirteenth century, institutions of the *aljama* required that all business and legal transactions adhere to rabbinic law. In the case of wills, this meant that the conditions under which one might record a last will and testament were clearly delineated by Talmudic tradition: rabbinic law demands that all testators be in good heath and standing when dividing property, and that the bequeathal follow a line of succession in keeping with biblical traditions of inheritance. While all legal documents held sway in royal courts regardless of which authorities composed them or in which language they were written, royal notaries placed none of the limitations of rabbinic law on legal transactions.[33] The fact that a significant number of Jews chose to conduct their business through notaries employed in the royal courts indicates that neither the taboo on appealing to gentile courts, nor the Christian affiliation of the notaries, marked the public sphere as foreign or dangerous for many Catalonian Jews.

Historians look to the willingness of the dominant society to allow Jews a place in the public sphere, combined with Jews' production of original Jewish learning and culture, to measure whether a given community attained success and stability in a diaspora settlement. Certainly by these gauges the medieval Crown of Aragon was a hospitable, even nurturing

33 Elka Klein, "Splitting Heirs: Patterns of Inheritance among Barcelona's Jews," *Jewish History* 16, no. 1 (2002): 49–71.

setting for Jewish life and culture. Until the late fourteenth century, Jewish communities benefitted from royal patronage, thrived culturally and financially, and enjoyed relative continuity and stability of settlement. As a general rule, the Crown showed no interest in Jewish or Muslim ritual, practice, or learning. King James's endorsement and participation in the Barcelona disputation is an exception. In this instance King James's obligations to the church, particularly to the pope and the Dominicans and Franciscans, who served as his representatives, trumped concerns about Jewish autonomy. But the fact that Jewish life in the Crown of Aragon in the wake of the disputation changed so little is significant. The structures of the *aljamas* remained strong, Jews continued to be vital to the governance of territories captured during the *Reconquista*, Jewish learning prospered even as the friars monitored Jewish books, and the communities continued to swell as migrants from less hospitable settings kept flowing into Aragon.

From the modern perspective, the significance of the disputation perhaps resides in what it shows us about the nature of interfaith hostility in the medieval Crown of Aragon. It is beyond question that the disputation, from the Jews' perspective, was an unwelcome disruption that challenged the community's sense of place and security. However, it also reveals a very high level of social and cultural integration of Jews in Christian society. To sustain a sophisticated theological dialogue, both sides would have needed access to a vocabulary and idioms for technical discourse, similar understandings of the shape and contours of history and God's role in it, and a clear understanding of the difference between the two worldviews. As is true in any society, the success of a minority population in mastering the codes of the dominant culture does not preclude the possibility that everyday interactions may be tinged with open hostility or even violence. In the case of medieval Iberia, it does mean that Jews were able to navigate their way through the intricacies of Christian society and contribute to it intellectually and economically, while also preserving a distinct zone of Jewish life and learning.

4. DISPUTATION IN MEDIEVAL SOCIETY AND CULTURE

Disputation traces its roots as a philosophical form back to classical antiquity. The great philosophical works by Plato and Aristotle, which served as the central models of Roman and medieval philosophical method and style, use the dialogue form because it is a pleasing and compelling means of demonstrating the power and agility of a disciplined human intellect. Dialogue appealed, among other reasons, because it presented ideas in a dynamic fashion while personifying each claim, allowing the reader (or observer) to judge the legitimacy of each argument and counterargument based on its merits. Introducing doubt by posing challenging questions resulted in greater clarity and certainty in the face of a sound, true argument. As many early Christians were educated in philosophy, sometimes having sampled multiple philosophical schools, they naturally gravitated toward philosophical modes of demonstrating the truth of their claims, both in debate about correct doctrine with fellow Christians and in confrontations with detractors.

Because dialogue and formal disputation are also productive pedagogical tools, they continued shaping early Christian theological discourse through the sixth century at least. Augustine of Hippo (354–430), influenced by neo-Platonic philosophy, employed various forms of dialectic in his works. In addition to composing a handful of short dialogues early in his career, including one against Manichaeism, he also lauded meditative dialectic as a reliable, even preferred means of arriving at the truth. Likewise, Boethius (ca. 480–524), inspired by the philosophy of Plato and Aristotle, translated many of the great Greek philosophers' works from Greek to Latin and incorporated dialogic form in his *Consolation of Philosophy*. The relatively wide circulation of these texts by the tenth century firmly established the place of some form of rationalism in the toolbox of medieval schools.

Whether disputation continued playing a formative role in western Christendom following the dissolution of the Roman Empire has been an issue of contention. Some argue that because Christianity is rooted in doctrine and indisputable truth, leaving little room for doubt or argument, disputation, which introduced questions as a means of grappling with multiple possibilities, eventually gave way to dogma as defined by the church.[34] Others convincingly maintain that a more organic continuity preserved Christian meditation and reflection in Western monasteries through the middle ages, even though the production of original dialogues and disputations tapered off.[35] Pedagogical techniques in Benedictine monasteries preserved dialectical method as part of the standard curriculum used to train monks about the scriptures and exegesis. In cathedral schools throughout Europe, as well, disputation as a pedagogical device provided a forum for controlled intellectual competition among students.

---

34 Richard Lim, *Public Disputation, Power, and Social Order in Late Antiquity* (Berkeley: University of California Press, 1995).

35 Alex J. Novikoff, *The Medieval Culture of Disputation: Pedagogy, Practice, and Performance* (Philadelphia: University of Pennsylvania Press, 2013); Olga Weijers, *In Search of the Truth: A History of Disputation Techniques from Antiquity to Early Modern Times* (Brepols, 2014).

The eleventh century saw a gradual shift from passive reception of dialectic, to the active expression of disputation in secular learning. Anselm of Bec[36] (1033–1109) is frequently credited with having played a decisive role in reinvigorating disputation in European schools and paving the way for the rise of the university.[37] Under the tutelage of Lanfranc at the abbey of Bec in Normandy, he contributed to a developing school of rationalist theology that was directly influenced by Aristotelian philosophy. Over the course of his career, which brought him later to England, Anselm wrote seven works in dialogue form and presented many key questions of Christian faith concerning God's nature in the form of philosophical precepts. In the wake of his concerted effort to refine dialectical methods in his teaching and writing, disputation reemerged as a valuable tool for demonstrating the fundamental truth—or lack thereof—of crucial theological claims.

This intellectual revival came hand-in-hand with a proliferation of new schools, some geared toward the training of clerics, others devoted to learning for the sake of learning. By the mid-twelfth century, disputation, whether undertaken in the form of controlled interpersonal exchange, systematic presentation of theses and antitheses in a treatise, or in a tract posing purely textual questions and answers, became central to the training in schools throughout western Europe. A renewed interest in the methods and forms of classical learning undergirded this movement, as did a concern with systematization of disciplines such as grammar, law, medicine, theology, and religious—particularly anti-Jewish—polemic.

With the foundation of universities, which evolved out of urban cathedral schools at the beginning of the thirteenth century, disputation served a variety of purposes across disciplines in the standard curriculum. As in the cathedral schools, university masters in law, theology, and grammar organized classroom lessons around disputations related to interpretations of texts. Because it imposed a predetermined structure on textual analysis, this methodology, later (often derisively) called scholasticism, imposed discipline and order on the process of interpreting challenging texts. The master or a student would pose a question about tensions, contradictions, or lack of clarity in a given passage, propose a thesis, then a contrary thesis, and finally offer a judgment. The conversation could involve anywhere from one individual to several people. Disputation

36 Known as Anselm of Canterbury after he became the city's archbishop.

37 For a complete and thoughtful discussion of Anselm's role in reanimating the disputation as a pedagogical and discursive form, see Novikoff, *The Medieval Culture of Disputation*, chapter 2, and Alex J. Novikoff, "Anselm, Dialogue, and the Rise of Scholastic Disputation," *Speculum* 86, no. 2 (April 2011): 387–418.

preserved a certain level of control over the trajectory of interpretation of authoritative sources. At the same time, though, this mode of discussion revealed additional tensions or contradictions and thus brought further questions to the fore.

Disputation also played more ceremonial roles in university culture in the form of examinations. These varied considerably depending upon the school. Masters also participated in performative public disputations, known as *quodlibet* disputations, to highlight their own intellectual prowess. A scholar could build his reputation and attract a circle of students as a result of an exceptional performance. Audiences included masters and students from the faculty and possibly visitors from outside. In the schools of theology, the master performing in a *quodlibet* disputation fielded questions from anyone in attendance on any topic. Responses followed the same structure as classroom disputations, though without warning of what the next question might be or who might ask it. As qualification for degree, universities also required students at all levels to demonstrate their disputation skills in a formal public demonstration. Classroom instruction in the dialogical method prepared students for the formal conclusion of their education and their entry into the ranks of masters.

The dialogical structure of presenting and weighing opposing arguments also shaped the written works those educated in universities produced. Given the place and importance disputation attained in the medieval intellectual world, it is no surprise that it had a significant impact in many areas of medieval life. The emerging university trained members of the professional classes applied systematic thinking to the study and application of law, medicine, tax collection, recordkeeping, and in the business of the ecclesiastical and royal authority. In its most rarified form, among theologians and philosophers, scholasticism produced a class of intellectual elites who claimed possession both of the truth and of the only trustworthy means of demonstrating the truth; an inability to master or mobilize these skills signaled a moral deficiency.

Members of Dominican and Franciscan mendicant orders made extensive use of disputation in their campaign to stamp out heresy. Viewing the rational dialectic employed by university-trained scholars as a model, mendicant friars developed a distinctive preaching style, which they utilized in marketplaces throughout Christendom. In addition, the friars' methods emerged as decisive in the effort to protect orthodoxy when Pope Gregory IX established the papal Inquisition under the authority of Dominicans in the 1230s to rid Christendom of heresy. Their weapon of choice was careful interrogation intended to extract the truth and set offenders on the right path. During the second half of the thirteenth century, Ramon de Peñaforte dedicated considerable energy to honing arguments and methods intended to gut Judaism. Later, Ramon Martí produced a polemical encyclopedia containing arguments against Judaism and Islam, along with prooftexts from their sacred texts to support these arguments.

ANTI-JEWISH POLEMICS

Live and literary disputations played a vital role in Jewish–Christian relations since the birth of Christianity. Because Christianity emerged from Jewish and Greco-Roman culture, early defenders of Christianity adopted methods of proof and argumentation native to both contexts. The use of rational, systematic, and controlled exchange intended to demonstrate the truth (or falsehood) of a given argument or belief played a vital role in shaping the contours of Christian doctrine and distinguishing Christianity from Judaism.

Christian anti-Jewish disputation literature dates back to the second century. Literary disputations about theology staged as dramatic human encounters were successful didactic devices both because they invited the audience to witness firsthand the development and refutation of arguments, and because readers almost inevitably form a connection with the protagonist. The earliest known post-biblical anti-Jewish polemic, Justin Martyr's (ca. 100–ca. 165) *Dialogue with Trypho*, dates from the mid-second century, when Christianity was just beginning to form a coherent theology.[38] Having set the drama in the marketplace, where men of letters exchanged ideas and opinions, the author/protagonist presented himself as a philosopher who had been well-trained in various schools of thought. He calls upon sources whose authority his opponent also recognizes, including the Hebrew Bible, Plato's philosophy, and history. In contrast, his Jewish opponent Trypho, whose arguments mimic the structure and vocabulary of a sound philosophy, reasserts the singular truth of the letter of the law.

While disputation remained an important pedagogical tool among Christians, the urgency of proving through argument that Christianity superseded Judaism waned following the conversion of Rome. Heresy and internal factionalism displaced Judaism as a threat to the continuity and authority of the church. By the sixth century, Christians produced polemical tracts aimed at reiterating the complete fallacy of Jewish biblical interpretation and the Jews' persistent blindness. These tracts largely repeated tried-and-true scriptural arguments dating back to the fourth and early fifth centuries, when real dialogues with Jews served clear social and cultural purposes. The focus of the polemical enterprise shifted with the solidification of Christian theological principles and the increasing marginalization

---

38 For an English translation see http://www.ccel.org/ccel/schaff/anf01.viii.iv.html, accessed May 2, 2016.

of Jews living among Christians during the early middle ages. What was once an outwardly directed genre, aimed at converting Jews or convincing non-Christian gentiles that Judaism had ceased to matter, became an inwardly directed genre, intended to fortify Christian values and beliefs by delineating (or inventing) an outside opponent. As Amos Funkenstein has argued, "polemics *with* Jews became polemics *against* them."[39] And though Christians lauded Jewish conversion, the pressing effort to push them toward conversion also waned.

The return to rational argument as the preferred basis for demonstrating truth during the high middle ages reintroduced disputation as a polemical tool and added a new urgency and immediacy to the debate. Beginning at the end of the eleventh century, examples of rational *contra judaeos* disputation literature proliferated. Most of these are grounded in well-known points of interpretive difference between Judaism and Christianity, presenting Jews as purely literal or carnal in their reading of the Hebrew Bible and thus unable to see that the messianic age had begun. There is good reason to believe that Jews and Christians discussed and debated theological differences on an individual basis. However, public disputations such as the Barcelona disputation, in which kings played an instrumental role and leaders from the Jewish community were obliged to defend Jewish texts and practices, stand out as a departure from the relatively nonconfrontational literary genre.

With this gradual shift first to rational argument and then to disputations interrogating the beliefs, literature, and practices of Judaism, anti-Jewish polemic took on a new tone, structure, and purpose. The same systematic and rational thinking that drove the development of new schools and methods during the eleventh and twelfth centuries also had an impact on the perception of Jews and Judaism. A substantial number of the new polemical tracts were written in dialogue form, frequently with the suggestion that the text grew out of a conversation with Jews in which the author participated. That these texts were intended for an educated Christian audience is clear. All were composed in Latin using a technical scholarly style and vocabulary. Most reinforce the common refrain that Jews are stubborn in their ignorance and therefore unconvertible. And few of them offer new or innovative material.

The most influential polemical dialogues written in this period share some central features: a compelling explanation for the production of the work highlighting the author's expertise and identifying the author as a character in the dialogue; an effort to foreground specific theological issues, like the unity of God or divine incarnation; and an intelligent but stubborn

39 Amos Funkenstein, *Perceptions of Jewish History* (Berkeley: University of California, 1993), 174 (emphasis added).

Jewish opponent. These works showcase the theologian's skill in crafting an argument, not success in missionizing. For example, *A Disputation of a Jew and a Christian*, written around 1092 by Gilbert Crispin (ca. 1045–1117), abbot of Westminster and a student of Anselm of Bec, presents a traditional debate around frequently contested scriptural passages couched in the language and assumptions of philosophy. It professes to record a conversation between the author and a Jewish man who visited the abbey on business. Gilbert committed the exchange to writing, he claims, because witnesses to the discussion asked him to do so. Interestingly, the dialogue is relatively egalitarian and natural—the Jewish character initiates some of the lines of questioning and provides developed answers. He expresses admiration for the Christian arguments but remains steadfastly committed to Judaism.

Likewise, Peter Abelard (1079–1142) frames his *Dialogue between a Philosopher, a Jew, and a Christian* as the report of a dream he had in which scholars representing each of the faiths—Judaism, Christianity, and philosophy—ask him to mediate and judge the outcome of their debate. That testing the rationality of Jewish theology and practice is foremost among Abelard's goals is clear from the structure of the text: the Jew debates directly with the Philosopher, leaving the debate between the Christian and the Philosopher for a later chapter. The Jewish character poses the questions of discussion and gives voice to many of the arguments that are frequently leveled as evidence that Jews had been displaced by Christians as the true people of God.

A small subset of literary disputations drew attention to the fact that the author himself had converted—though not as a consequence of convincing rational argument. Petrus Alfonsi and his contemporary Herman the Jew (ca. 1107–ca. 1181) both juxtapose the impetus for their conversion with the theological debates included in their texts. In the case of Petrus, his prior conversion provides a vehicle for introducing new information about contemporary Judaism to a Christian audience. Though he touches on scripture-based arguments, the truly original contribution of his work can be found in his arguments against precepts included in the Talmud. In contrast, the central story in Herman the Jew's text is his conversion. He describes a disputation between himself as a young man and Rupert of Deutz, a well-known abbot and author of his own anti-Jewish tract. Here the disputation is one of several unsuccessful efforts to persuade him to accept Christianity.[40]

---

40 See Jean Claude Schmitt, *The Conversion of Herman the Jew: Autobiography, History, and Fiction in the Twelfth Century*, trans. Alex J. Novikoff (Philadelphia: University of Pennsylvania Press, 2010), for an excellent treatment of Herman and an English translation of the text.

Two lesser-known disputations at Ceuta in Almohad North Africa (1179) and Majorca (1286) deviate from these literary disputations in some important ways.[41] Both represent theological disputations between Genoese businessmen and Jews they met on their travels. Though there are questions about the authenticity of these conversations, in part because the latter replicates sections of the former, neither has been attributed to a known theologian. More striking, and not unrelated, is the fact that the Jewish character in each text converts to Christianity at the conclusion of the disputation. It is no accident that these men succeeded in converting their interlocutors, the authors assert, because they were more accomplished disputants than any theologian.

Medieval Jewish polemical disputation literature departs from this model. Jewish authors in France and Spain during the twelfth and thirteenth centuries produced an impressive body of polemical tracts composed in the disputation genre.[42] Like many of the fictional Latin disputations, these often open with a rationale for the composition. In his *Book of the Covenant*, for example, Joseph Kimhi (ca. 1105–ca. 1170) explains that he wrote his text as a polemical guide for anyone who might be challenged by apostates to Christianity.[43] In contrast to the defensive posture Kimhi assumes, Judah ha-Levi's *The Kuzari* provides the elaborate frame-story of a king having called representatives of philosophy, Christianity, Islam, and Judaism to present the central tenets of their respective faiths. The representative of Judaism scores an early victory by convincing the king to convert. Though ha-Levi based his text on a historical event, the disputation in this case mostly serves a Jewish fantasy of justice delivered by an objective, impartial, and rational observer. More commonly, though, Jewish disputation literature professed to serve the practical purpose of supplying a guide for anyone who might find himself in an impromptu debate.

Each of these literary disputations likely reflects a kernel of real personal encounters between the members of the two faiths, and all signs seem to indicate that these were relatively friendly, voluntary encounters.

---

41 On Ceuta see Maya Soifer, "'You Say That the Messiah Has Come . . .': The Ceuta Disputation (1179) and Its Place in the Christian Anti-Jewish Polemics of the High Middle Ages," *Journal of Medieval History* 31, no. 3 (2005): 287–307; and on Majora see Ora Limor, "Polemical Varieties: Religious Disputations in 13th Century Spain," *Ibéria Judaica* 2 (2010): 55–79, and Ora Limor, *Vikuah Mayorkah, 1286: Mahadurah bi'kortit u-mavo* (Jerusalem: ha-Universitah ha-Ivrit bi-Yerushalayim ha-Fakultah le-mada'e ha-ruah, 1985).

42 For a thorough analysis of this body of literature see Robert Chazan, *Fashioning Jewish Identity in Medieval Western Christendom* (New York: Cambridge University Press, 2004).

43 Joseph Kimhi, *The Book of the Covenant of Joseph Kimhi*, trans. Frank Talmage (Toronto: Pontifical Institute of Mediaeval Studies, 1972).

In sharp contrast, the coerced disputations arranged during the thirteenth century subjected Jews and Judaism to intensive public scrutiny. Beginning in the late twelfth century, the church committed considerable resources and attention to defining and maintaining orthodoxy within Christendom. Many factors contributed to this turn. Among the most decisive were devastating military losses over the course of the twelfth century in the Holy Land, an increasingly politicized and powerful papacy aided by a cadre of university-trained clerics, and a concerted political and military campaign to undermine a wealthy, powerful heretical sect in southern France, known as the Albigensian Crusade. A direct interest in the nature of rabbinic literature and Judaism emerged at the same time, likely as a consequence of the same political and religious transformations. The Fourth Lateran Council of 1215 crystalized these goals in an ideological and systematic package.[44]

The Dominican and Franciscan friars were instrumental in mobilizing the investigation of Jewish texts. Both movements were founded during the first half of the thirteenth century for the explicit purpose of pursuing and protecting orthodoxy among Christians and missionizing among non-Christians. Among the converts they attracted were a handful who dedicated themselves to introducing the friars to dangerous, theologically interesting, or offensive elements of post-biblical Jewish literature. This exposure of Jewish books as a possible site of blasphemy and evidence of Jewish recognition and rejection of Christian theology drove the obligatory public disputations between Christians and Jews.

In most of these cases, the debate took place in a royal court, often before the king, conflicting Jewish and Christian accounts remain, and vocal converts played a crucial role either in instigating the investigation or in arguing the case. Unscripted public theological disputations with Jews served much the same purpose as university disputations. They provided the friars a means of demonstrating their own credibility, worth, and authority. And the very act of calling Jewish teachers and leaders to defend their foundational literature posed a direct challenge to the authority of those figures within their communities.

The first of these disputations was effectively an investigative trial of the Talmud on thirty-five charges of blasphemy brought by the convert Nicholas Donin. The disputation took place in 1240 in Paris. Two rabbis were obliged to answer to charges against the text. These included specific allegations that the Talmud contained derogatory references to Jesus and Mary as well as accusations that Jews treated the Talmud almost as if it

---

44 See Document X in Part II, pages 123–133.

were revealed scripture. A Latin summary and two Hebrew narratives of the trial remain; they agree about the basic points of contention but provide very different pictures of what transpired during the meeting.[45]

Hebrew and Latin documents do agree, however, about the outcome. The jury of clerics found that the Talmud contained offensive and absurd statements, and thus condemned it to destruction. Thousands of volumes were set aflame in 1242. However, there is considerable debate about whether this event can be described as a disputation at all. Recent scholarship suggests that the clerics allowed the rabbis no opportunity to speak, whereas the Hebrew reports of the event present Rabbi Yehiel of Paris responding to each claim eloquently and at length. Indeed, Rabbi Joseph ben Nathan Official, the author of the earliest Hebrew account, wrote the text in the form and genre of a true disputation.[46]

The Barcelona disputation was the second of these coerced public debates about post-biblical Jewish literature. Whereas the simple fact that the church imposed Christian authority on Jewish books and behavior distinguished the Paris disputation as new and unique, it was the mode of argument the friars pursued that marked the Barcelona disputation as a true revolution in Christian–Jewish polemics. Friar Paul, a convert who claimed expertise in rabbinic learning, argued that the Talmud showed that the rabbis recognized Jesus as the Messiah but chose not to accept him, and that the Talmud itself held evidence of Jesus's messianic nature. Nahmanides, as the preeminent rabbi and teacher of his day, defended the way Jews interpreted and taught rabbinic texts. Embracing the demands of the disputation genre, he challenged the assumptions and foundations on which Friar Paul based his arguments, claiming the friar had fundamentally misunderstood his sources. The Hebrew and the Latin accounts of this event agree that a disputation took place, but disagree as to shape and

45 For a recent translation of the central documents, see John Friedman, Jean Hoff, and Robert Chazan, *The Trial of the Talmud: Paris, 1240*, Mediaeval Sources in Translation 53 (Toronto: Pontifical Institute of Mediaeval Studies, 2012).

46 This fact has been the focus of much scholarly attention. Harvey Hames has suggested that the author of the Hebrew report of the Paris disputation self-consciously mimicked Nahmanides' report of the Barcelona disputation: Harvey J. Hames, "Reconstructing Thirteenth-Century Jewish-Christian Polemic: From Paris 1240 to Barcelona 1263 and Back Again," in *Medieval Exegesis and Religious Difference: Commentary, Conflict, and Community in the Premodern Mediterranean* (New York: Fordham University Press, 2015), 115–27. Yehudah Galinsky, on the other hand, argues that Rabbi Joseph ben Nathan Official wrote his accounts of the Paris trial much later and as a very deliberate effort to portray the event as a disputation akin to Nahmanides' encounter, rather than a trial: Judah Galinsky, "The Different Hebrew Versions of the 'Talmud Trial' of 1240 in Paris," in *New Perspectives on Jewish-Christian Relations; In Honor of David Berger*, ed. Elisheva Carlebach and Jacob J. Schacter, The Brill Reference Library of Judaism, v. 33 (Leiden: Brill, 2012), 109–40.

content of that exchange. Evidence suggests that Friar Paul had the opportunity to refine and redeploy his polemical arguments in a second public disputation in Paris in the early 1270s. Like the confrontations in Paris in 1240 and Barcelona in 1263, this encounter took place in public in the presence of the king and members of the Jewish community were obliged to answer Friar Paul's accusations.[47] In this case, however, only a Hebrew account written by an observer, rather than a participant in the debate, survives. Nevertheless, it is clear that Friar Paul gained the patronage of at least two kings and made extensive use of his polemical strategy over the course of the second half of the thirteenth century.

Anti-Jewish polemical arguments based on rabbinic sources like those advanced by Friar Paul during the Barcelona disputation and the subsequent encounter in Paris had a significant and enduring impact on the way that some mendicant friars conceptualized their missionizing effort. Shortly following the Barcelona disputation, Ramon Martí, also a member of Ramon de Peñaforte's school, produced two works in which he adapted and applied the same kinds of arguments Friar Paul pioneered at the disputation.[48] In *Capistrum Iudeorum* (*The Muzzle of the Jews*, 1267) and *Pugio Fidei* (*Daggers of Faith*, 1278), Martí crafted his arguments in direct response to objections and claims Nahmanides voiced during the disputation.[49] Martí gained access to extensive collections of Jewish works through his participation in the oversight and censorship of Jewish books that James I authorized beginning in 1264. In addition, he trained friars in Hebrew and Arabic at Dominican language schools in Barcelona and Tunis, possibly to help hone and improve polemic based on

---

47 On the second Paris disputation, see Cohen, *Living Letters of the Law: Ideas of the Jew in Medieval Christianity* (Berkeley: University of California Press, 1999), 334–42. Also see Joseph Shatzmiller, *La deuxième = controverse de Paris: un chapitre dans la polémique entre chrétiens et juifs au moyen âge*, Collection de la Revue des Études Juives (Paris and Louvain: E. Peeters, 1994); Hames, "Reconstructing Thirteenth-Century Jewish-Christian Polemic"; and Harvey Hames, "Reason and Faith: Inter-Religious Polemic and Christian Identity in the Thirteenth Century," in *Religious Apologetics—Philosophical Argumentation*, ed. Volkhard Krech and Yossef Schwartz (Tübingen: Mohr Siebeck, 2004), 267–84.

48 R. Chazan, *Daggers of Faith: Thirteenth-Century Christian Missionizing and Jewish Response* (Berkeley: University of California Press, 1989); and more recently, Syds Wiersma, "The Dynamic of Religious Polemics: The Case of Raymond Martin (ca. 1220–ca. 1285)," in *Interaction between Judaism and Christianity in History, Religion, Art and Literature*, ed. Marcel Poorthuis, Joshua Schwartz, and Joseph Turner (Leiden: Brill, 2009), 201–17.

49 Adolfo Roblès Sierra, ed., *Raimundi Martini Capistrum Iudaeorum*, 2 vols. (Würzburg and Altenberge: Echter Verlag; Telos Verlag, 1990–1993). There is no modern edition of *Pugio Fidei*, but a seventeenth-century printing is available online: http://sammlungen.ub.uni-frankfurt.de/freimann/content/pageview/260942, accessed May 2, 2016.

rabbinic texts.[50] In *Pugio Fidei*, Martí assembled an exhaustive catalogue of passages—likely with the help of a team of scholars—that could be used to refute Jewish practices or to support Christian claims that Jesus was the Messiah. He reproduced these texts in the original language and in translation, and supported them with fully developed, nuanced arguments. This text occupies a middle ground between traditional polemical tracts and coerced disputations. Many scholars believe that Martí designed *Pugio Fidei* as a sourcebook or guide for friars preaching among Jews. His intent was to take full control of Jewish sources and thus leave Jews no line of defense.

Polemics involving rabbinic sources continued to play an important role in Christian–Jewish theological debates well into the fourteenth century. During the first half of the fourteenth century, another convert from Judaism produced a body of polemical literature that seems to have grown organically from a deep understanding of rabbinic literature and exegesis. Alfonso of Valladolid (formerly Abner of Burgos, ca. 1270–ca. 1345) directly engaged some of the central texts and teachings of Judaism while also addressing the psychological and social impediments to Jewish conversion. The fact that Alfonso wrote his polemical works for a Jewish audience in either Hebrew or Spanish, rather than Latin, marks his oeuvre as truly distinctive. His major work, *Moreh Tzedeq* (*Teacher of Righteousness*), is a long and elaborate dialogue between a teacher who promotes a Christian interpretation of Jewish teachings and his stubborn student.[51] To present Christianity as the true revelation, Alfonso utilized Jewish sources of authority, traditional biblical and Talmudic exegetical arguments, philosophical arguments, Jewish polemical works (including a Hebrew account of the Talmud trial of

50 Jeremy Cohen, "The Christian Adversary of Solomon Ibn Adret," *Jewish Quarterly Review* 71, no. 1 (1980): 48–55; and Jeremy Cohen, *The Friars and the Jews: The Evolution of Medieval Anti-Judaism* (Ithaca: Cornell University Press, 1982), 129–69. Ryan Szpiech takes a different view, arguing that Martí's primary objective in mastering this literature was to counter possible accusations that his evidence had been fabricated or manipulated. See Ryan Szpiech, *Conversion and Narrative: Reading and Religious Authority in Medieval Polemic*, The Middle Ages (Philadelphia: University of Pennsylvania Press, 2012), especially 121–42.

51 This text remains only in Spanish translation under the title *Mostrador de justicia*. For a modern printing, see Abner of Burgos and Walter Mettmann, *Mostrador de justicia*, Abhandlungen der Nordrhein-Westfälischen Akademie der Wissenschaften, Bd. 92 (Opladen: Westdeutscher Verlag, 1994). Translations of extended passages from this text and various others by the same author can be found in Yitzhak Baer, *A History of the Jews in Christian Spain: From the Reconquest to the Fourteenth Century*, 2 vols. (Philadelphia, PA: Jewish Publication Society of America, 1961), 1:327–54. For a thorough, exhaustive study of this work see Ryan Wesley Szpiech, "From Testimonia to Testimony: Thirteenth-Century Anti-Jewish Polemic and the *Mostrador de Justicia* of Abner of Burgos/Alfonso of Valladolid" (PhD Dissertation, Yale University, 2006).

1240 and Nahmanides' disputation account), and stories of personal experiences. This was a potent combination that stamped his interpretations with authenticity and authority.[52] Alfonso's mode of polemical argument was both more intimate and more threatening than the approaches of Nicholas Donin and Friar Paul, both of which involved a program of highly choreographed coerced public encounters.[53] Alfonso's polemical works did find an audience and circulated within the Jewish community. A substantial record of correspondence between Alfonso and members of the Jewish community remains, as do extensive Jewish responses to his writings.[54]

The impact of polemics using rabbinic sources resounded through the fourteenth century. Evidence of an additional compulsory disputation has been preserved in a late fourteenth-century Hebrew polemical work by Moses ha-Kohen of Tordesillas. In the 1370s Moses, who had already endured torture and violence at the hands of zealous Christians intending to force him to accept baptism, defended Jewish interpretations and rituals in a disputation with two apostates in the Castilian city of Avila—an event endorsed by the king. After the disputation concluded, a Christian-born follower of Alfonso of Valladolid appeared on the scene demanding the opportunity to debate about Talmudic evidence with Moses ha-Kohen and threatening to arouse public animosity against Jews and Judaism should he refuse. In the wake of these public exchanges, Moses composed *Ezer ha-Emunah* (*Support of Faith*), a handbook intended to aid others who might encounter similar challenges.[55] This text shares some similarities with accounts of the Paris and Barcelona disputations. Moses ha-Kohen demonstrated a familiarity with previous Jewish polemical works, including Nahmanides' disputation account. However, while these works grew out of and responded to challenges posed during public disputations in which the author was compelled by Christian authorities to defend his practice and learning in a public spectacle, Moses ha-Kohen did not present his text as an account of the event itself. In addition, and more importantly, no parallel Christian account of this event remains.

The final coerced public disputation for which Christian and Jewish accounts remain took place in Tortosa, 1413–1414. The convert in this

52 Szpiech, *Conversion and Narrative*, 143–73, especially 147–54.

53 According to Ryan Szpiech, Ramon Martí is not among the many Hebrew and Latin sources directly referenced in the *Moreh*. Szpiech, "From Testimonia to Testimony," 314 and 643–63.

54 Szpiech, "From Testimonia to Testimony," 309–29.

55 For a biography and edition of this work, see Yehuda Shamir, *Rabbi Moses Ha-Kohen of Tordesillas and His Book* Ezer ha-Emunah*: A Chapter in the History of the Judeo-Christian Controversy*, Études sur le judaîsme mediéval, t. 7 (Leiden: E. J. Brill, 1975). Also see Hanne Trautner-Kromann, *Shield and Sword: Jewish Polemics against Christianity and the Christians in France and Spain from 1100–1500* (Tübingen: Mohr, 1993), 148–51.

case, Gerónimo de Santa Fe, formerly Joshua ha-Lorki, incorporated arguments from previous public disputations; however, this event took place in such completely different political and religious circumstances that it is almost incommensurable with the previous forced disputations. Convened during a period of institutional turmoil within the church by Pope Benedict, one of three pretenders to papal authority, this disputation served as a sort of show trial to bolster his political credibility. It took place twenty years after the violent riots that brought about the forcible conversion of nearly one-third of the Jews in Iberia, and the violent death of another third. In the wake of this devastation, Gerónimo and his supporters hoped the Tortosa disputation would undermine the foundation of faith within the diminished Jewish communities. Their tactic was generally successful. Perhaps as many as twenty representatives appeared at the disputation in the papal court in Tortosa to defend Judaism; several among those converted before the disputation ended. A Hebrew and a Latin account remain, and here, too, the author of the Hebrew version, Solomon ibn Verga (ca. 1460–1554), trained attention on heroic actors, but did not concern himself with meticulous historical accuracy. The Latin text, however, is a detailed daily chronicle kept by a papal notary.

If the church intended for these compulsory public disputations to serve as missionary tools designed to help Jews recognize the truth of Christianity through argument and peaceful persuasion, then it is worth noting that the Paris and Barcelona disputations failed in this effort. Arguably, even the Tortosa event failed on those terms, since it seems likely that many who converted did so because circumstances of Jewish life had become untenable, not necessarily because rationally formulated arguments persuaded them. Yet the genre of disputation provided a sufficiently powerful narrative form such that several Jewish authors applied it themselves when recounting theological exchanges with Christians—even when those exchanges did not involve any real debate, as would appear to be the case in the 1240 Paris event. Consequently, we must carefully distinguish between the events as they occurred and the texts that document them.

Disputation as a means of establishing the truth played a decisive role in shaping western European culture. In addition to the well-known and often reviled methods of scholastic pedagogy and philosophy that emerged from the medieval cathedral schools and universities, dialogical expression spilled over into the realm of Jewish textual expression. Dialogue and debate played a central role in rabbinic culture. The Talmud is packed with exchanges and disagreements about proper practice and interpretation. However, rarely do they conclude in a decisive resolution with a single view prevailing. More typically, various viewpoints appear, side by side; some attain preferred status through practice and precedent, but the others remain as a reminder of alternative interpretations.

PART IV
HISTORIOGRAPHY

MODERN AND MEDIEVAL TRACES OF THE BARCELONA DISPUTATION

In 1263, Nahmanides, one of the most prominent rabbinic scholars and teachers of his time, was summoned by King James I of Aragon to appear at the royal palace in Barcelona. There he would defend the normative interpretation of the canonical texts of Judaism in a public debate with Friar Paul, a convert from Judaism to Christianity. At issue was the Jewish claim that the Jewish messianic redemption was still imminent. Nahmanides defended the Jews' continued expectation of messianic redemption against evidence culled by Friar Paul from Jewish sources that the rabbis of the Talmud believed the Jewish Messiah had already come in the person of Jesus. After the public disputation came to an end, Nahmanides returned to his home in Girona, where he resumed his regular activities.

We know of the Barcelona disputation from several sources. Nahmanides penned a detailed firsthand account in the form of a dialogue that claims to report the debate just as it happened. But a separate report written in Latin that bears the royal seal of the Crown of Aragon and was likely composed by Friar Paul presents an alternative view. Other sources inform us of a controversy that erupted some years following the disputation around a first-person account that Nahmanides wrote and gave to the bishop of Girona. An investigation took place, Nahmanides was charged with blasphemy, and was then banished from the Crown of Aragon for a period of two years. Letters from Nahmanides and other Hebrew sources indicate that he relocated to Palestine, where he later died, never having returned to Iberia.

In the aggregate, the documents regarding the disputation raise nearly as many questions as they answer, in part because they offer such very different perspectives on the event. The author of the brief Latin account adopts virtually no stylistic flourish. He crafts it as a chronological protocol presenting the basic outline of the debate. Periodically, he intersperses a statement that appears to reproduce Nahmanides' own language, which casts Nahmanides as utterly confused and unable to communicate or defend even the basic precepts of his faith. In this version, the dispute seems to last just one day, after which Nahmanides steals away from town to avoid further debate as the king is detained by other business. Nahmanides' Hebrew account, by contrast, is a highly stylized dialogue that professes to replicate the disputation as it unfolded. The author's use of the authorial "I" adds to the plausibility and power of the account because it makes the reader a first-person observer of the drama. Not surprisingly, in his own account Nahmanides thoroughly outmatches Friar Paul. Moreover, in this version the disputation lasted four days, after which the king praises Nahmanides for his performance and bestows upon him a gift of cash as a token of his gratitude.

Royal and papal sources, too, help clarify events that unfolded in the aftermath while raising additional yet unanswerable questions. In particular, the royal documents that were written in the summer of 1263 attest that the king's loyalties were split between a strong dedication to the friars' preaching campaign and a commitment to preserving and protecting the Jewish communities in his realm. That ambivalence emerges again in a series of missives, written between April 1264 and sometime in 1266, by Pope Clement IV and King James concerning charges brought by the friars that Nahmanides blasphemed in a report of the disputation that he wrote, presumably in Catalan, and presented to the bishop of Girona. The king satisfied the friars' demand that Nahmanides be punished for this offense, but then ran afoul of the pope and his mendicant representatives when he commuted a limited term of punishment. The friars refused to accept the punishment, and James I released Nahmanides from any further demands of the friars unless they were issued in the king's presence. After a letter of stern reprimand from the pope to the king, the archive falls silent. No document remains to clarify whether Nahmanides' departure for Palestine was a personal choice or mandated by royal order. Once again, these documents indicate that James I strove to maintain a manageable balance between serving the interests of his faith by supporting the church and the interests of Jewish community leaders, who were concerned that increased church oversight of Jewish literature would have a deleterious effect on Jewish life and learning in the Crown of Aragon.

The sources related to the Barcelona disputation and the event they report are captivating for readers today because of what they reveal as well as what they obscure. Both accounts provide what seems to be unmediated access to a unique event. But the simple fact that these authors constructed complete narratives, with a beginning, middle, and end, protagonists, adversaries, and human drama, transformed their versions of the disputation into something that bore little resemblance to the event that took place in Barcelona in 1263. Narratives, in contrast to the events of life, organize details in a structured, coherent, meaningful fashion. To do so, the creators of narratives necessarily omit or downplay details that take the story off course, while emphasizing or elaborating others that serve the trajectory of the story and interest of the storyteller. Both disputation accounts conclude with the end of the debate in Barcelona and the dispersal of the participants. They largely agree about the agenda and topics discussed, some of the arguments each disputant advanced, and specific points of contention between the two sides. Both firmly assert that they provided a true and complete report of the disputation. Yet, as we have seen, the style, structure, and focus of the narratives differ dramatically.

Medieval public disputations were necessarily conducted in an atmosphere tinged with adversity and discord. And the authors of documents recounting them intended to reproduce, or at the very least to recall, the deep tension that gave the discussion gravity in the first place. But this is just part of the picture. Disputations could be successful *only* if sufficient common ground existed between the two sides to enable a clear expression of the difference between the disputants' interpretations. In terms of the language in which the debate took place, this is merely a statement of the obvious. But at the level of politics, culture, and religion, the points of intersection and divergence are more fundamental yet more difficult to pin down. In the controlled atmosphere of a public disputation, issues that were not likely the stuff of everyday intercourse either among Jews or between Jews and their Christian neighbors found direct expression. And since victory in a debate with an opponent who was either mute or incompetent was no victory at all, each party needed to present his arguments in a manner that would elicit discussion and response from his adversary. The process of building rhetorical boundaries between Judaism and Christianity, therefore, might also have had the unexpected and perhaps contradictory result of reaffirming the points of contact between the two traditions. The same general considerations apply to the production of textual records or narrative representations of such debates. It can be taken for granted that no medieval religious disputation account is devoid of partisan biases.

As the title of this book implies, what was at stake in the disputation was the ability to claim possession of the truth. But the same stakes have been at play for modern scholars as they have written about and tried to make sense of the documentary evidence remaining from the Barcelona disputation and the events that unfolded in its wake. The details of many—indeed, most—events from the medieval past have been lost for lack of documentary evidence, but the evidence representing Jewish and Christian perspectives of the Barcelona disputation is relatively abundant. The documents provide sufficient evidence to support multiple and very different interpretations of how the disputation may have unfolded. But how can we use conflicting sources to make sense of what happened at the disputation or in its aftermath? Do the methods of critical and rigorous scholarship provide the necessary tools to differentiate between multiple perspectives and to extract useful information from them? Are they equally reliable sources? What kind of information about the Barcelona disputation, Jewish and Christian culture in medieval Aragon, and interfaith relations might these sources reveal?

To begin addressing these issues, we must first investigate the history of the production and transmission of both texts. Each poses a very distinct set of challenges. The Latin version bears excellent provenance. It remains in two very similar copies, one in the royal registry at the Archive of the Crown of Aragon and the other in the episcopal curia of Girona. The fact that it was kept in both repositories suggests that it was commissioned or at least authorized by the king, who attended the event, or by his agents.[1] This author remains anonymous, but the text locates the event on a specific day—July 20, 1263—which implies that the document may have been written shortly thereafter. Were other copies made and circulated to a broader readership? Was it intended primarily to preserve a record of the disputation, or did the author hope to use the account for other purposes? It is virtually impossible to answer these questions definitively, since records of wider distribution or the author's intent are lost to history. But the fact that this text exists in two important institutional repositories may indicate that the author wrote it as an official record of the event.

Several factors make the transmission history of Nahmanides' disputation account considerably more difficult to nail down. None of the remaining manuscript copies of this document were made by Nahmanides' hand.[2] Indeed, the earliest copy, possibly dating from the thirteenth century, is a short fragment that contains just a small portion of the debate presented in later versions of the full text. Manuscript copies that are closest in form and content to the critical edition in common use today do not begin to appear before the fourteenth century, sometime after Nahmanides' death. How closely might these copies resemble the text Nahmanides wrote? Might these copies contain scribal errors, emendations, or additions?

1 For a detailed analysis of this text and its critics, see Robert Chazan, *Barcelona and Beyond: The Disputation of 1263 and Its Aftermath* (Berkeley: University of California Press, 1992), 39–44.

2 Ursula Ragacs at the Institute of Jewish Studies, University of Vienna, is compiling a new critical edition of this work, for which she is conducting a comprehensive and systematic review of all the known extant manuscripts of Nahmanides' text. This discussion relies on her painstaking work, especially: Ursula Ragacs, "Edieren oder nicht edieren. . . ? : Überlegungen zu einer Neuedition des hebräischen Berichtes über die Disputation von Barcelona 1263. Teil 2: Dei Hanschriften," *Judaica* 65, no. 3 (2009): 239–58.

Modern critical editions of the text, including the one from which the version presented in this volume was translated, have been redacted from manuscripts dating from the seventeenth and eighteenth centuries, which are, themselves, copied and compiled from various, possibly deeply flawed, manuscripts [Figure 1]. Moritz Steinschneider, one of the early fathers of

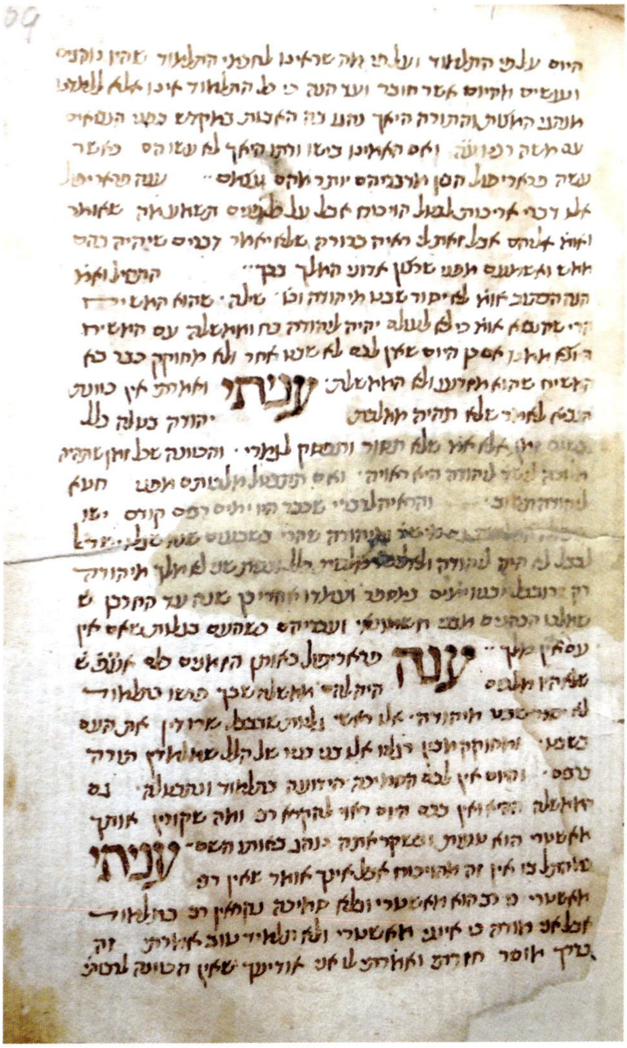

Figure 1. As is the case with many medieval manuscripts, water damage, discoloration, and tears have rendered some words difficult to decipher on this page of a fifteenth-century copy of Nahmanides' disputation account. This portion of the document contains the debate about Genesis 49:10 and the scepter of Judah, one of the central issues addressed in both the Hebrew and Latin disputation accounts. The scribe signals changes of voice by magnifying the opening word of each exchange: "I answered . . . He answered."

MS Oxford, Bodleiana, Opp. Add. 36 = Neubauer 2425/8, 69 r.

the academic study of Judaism,[3] published the first modern critical edition of the Hebrew text based on these late sources in 1860. In keeping with professional scholarly practices, Steinschneider strove to produce as complete and flawless an edition of Nahmanides' account as possible. To this end, he identified versions of the text that he believed to be both comprehensive and similar enough that they may have come from a single original source. Comparing the texts, he applied his considerable expertise in Jewish literature and scholarship to fill in gaps or identify and correct scribal mistakes. While Steinschneider made the text widely available to scholars, his edition either produced or reproduced a number of textual errors. However, because one of his base manuscripts vanished during the Second World War, scholars working since the end of the war have been unable to reconstruct or check his critical process.

Producing a critical edition is painstaking work. It demands from the scholar a keen sense of the language, literary traditions, and social and cultural practices that contribute to an author's understanding of the world, as well as a feel for the audience. Critical editions play a crucial role in developing and sustaining modern historical discussions. Especially before the rise of digital reproduction, it was through critical editions that scholars around the world were able to engage in focused discussion on a common version of a given text. Yet, in practical terms, a critical edition is a new and entirely original work, produced by an editor who carefully evaluated and reconciled multiple recensions of the same text. Because the editor does everything in her power to narrow the differences between various versions of the text, the critical edition is explicitly and by definition not identical to the work penned by the original author.

But, because Nahmanides' account had a troubled life from its very inception, the difficulties scholars face in trying to trace its transmission and transformation run deeper than issues connected with redaction. The royal letter from 1265 that describes charges that Nahmanides had committed blasphemy states that he included those offending statements in an account of the disputation, presumably in Catalan, which he then gave to the bishop of Girona.[4] Does this provide any evidence that the Hebrew and

3 Steinschneider was a pioneer of the *Wissenschaft des Judentums* school (meaning "the scientific study of Judaism"), which developed during the first half of the nineteenth century in Germany. Closely linked with the Reform movement, members of this school sought to subject the rituals and texts of Judaism to critical analysis in order to situate Judaism within the world of history as a subject worthy of examination. The *Wissenschaft* movement produced many critical editions of texts that are central to the study of Judaism and Jewish history, providing the foundation for a professional school of scholarship.

4 See Document VII in Part II, pages 120–21.

Catalan texts were related in form or content? Arriving at a conclusive answer to this question is all but impossible. No known manuscript of the Catalan document remains. The only evidence available for comparison between the Hebrew document that exists today and the document Nahmanides reportedly gave to the bishop is a very brief mention in the same letter describing the rabbi's defense at a tribunal. Here some key details do seem to mesh. The letter states that Nahmanides claimed that he had been granted freedom of speech by King James I and Friar Ramon de Peñaforte during the disputation and that this freedom should naturally be extended to his description of the event. Many manuscript copies of the Hebrew text include a passage in which the friars grant Nahmanides freedom of speech. This connection is intriguing, but, once again, it also raises questions about the reliability and accuracy of Nahmanides' text.

MODERN SCHOLARLY DEBATE

Concerns about the process by which Nahmanides' text was transcribed and transmitted had some impact on this debate in modern scholarship, but scholars have more consistently questioned whether details in either the Hebrew or the Latin disputation account had been fabricated and, if so, for what purpose—in other words, whether either of the two accounts is plausible or reliable. Debates over historical authenticity emerged at the intersection of religion, modern nationalist politics, and professional scholarship. Though the political and national landscape has completely changed, questions about the character of this literature and its authors continue to influence the way the Barcelona disputation fits into narratives of Jewish, medieval, and Spanish history.

The earliest professional historical analyses of the Hebrew and Latin accounts do not subscribe to the same conventions of objectivity that scholars profess today. Rather, they updated the medieval polemical project by framing it in the modern scholarly methods of textual criticism. Heinrich Graetz, one of the leading figures in the movement to build a method for the scientific study of Judaism, *Wissenschaft des Judentums,* presented such an approach first in his comprehensive *History of the Jews* in 1863 and again in a short article published in 1865.[5] He took Nahmanides' account entirely at face value and understood the abundance of detail

5 Heinrich Graetz, *Geschichte der Juden von Maimuni's Tod (1205) bis zur Verbannung der Juden aus Spanien und Portugal*, Geschichte der Juden von den ältesten Zeite bis auf die Gegenwart/H. Graetz, 7–8. Bd (Leipzig: C. B. Lorck, 1863); and H. Graetz, "Die Disputation des Bonastruc mit Frai Pablo in Barcelona," *Monatsschrift für Geschichte und Wissenschaft des Judentums* 14 (1865): 428–33. The central argument in this article concerns the identity of the rabbi investigated and exiled in 1265. Graetz definitively identifies him as Nahmanides.

provided as a clear sign of its accuracy. The Latin report, he concluded, must have deliberately misrepresented the proceedings in hopes of repairing any damage that Nahmanides' successful refutation of Friar Paul's arguments may have caused to the ongoing mission to convert the Jews.

Writing at a time when history was deeply rooted in the work of building and fortifying national institutions and traditions, Graetz believed that prominent Jews throughout history acted primarily *as Jews* in a world that, often as not, placed significant impediments before them. His analysis largely focused on the incommensurability between the Latin and Hebrew accounts in terms of style as well as content. Graetz thus used his examination of the disputation documents as an opportunity to suggest that powerful men in Latin Christendom, and in the Church in particular, routinely falsified the historical record pertaining to Jewish–Christian relations during the middle ages. Nahmanides, in Graetz's view, defended Judaism heroically and, though he had been cornered by a considerably more powerful opponent, he successfully put his adversary to shame.

Graetz's approach to Jewish history in general drew criticism from some of his most prominent colleagues in the field, who felt that his work defaulted too easily to the celebratory and veered away from critical analysis. However, his article on the Barcelona disputation drew its most outspoken criticism from the well-known and influential medievalist Heinrich Denifle.[6] Himself a Dominican and a Vatican archivist who wrote substantial works on Thomas Aquinas, the history of the University of Paris, medieval mysticism, and, later in his life, on Luther, Denifle took issue with the thrust of Graetz's argument as well as with his scholarship. However, his response was also explicitly polemical in tone. A careful reading of the Hebrew account in comparison with all of the relevant Latin texts, in Denifle's view, exposed this text as a deliberate fabrication by Nahmanides, who intended to conceal the fact that he failed miserably in his task. In addition, Denifle asserted that Graetz's interpretation was marred by his failure to take into account all of the sources or to accept the friars' interpretation of the Talmudic passages in question.

Both Graetz and Denifle apparently subscribed to expectations akin to those of their medieval predecessors: that disciplined rational disputation revealed which disputant possessed the single, indisputable truth. Neither

6 D. P. H. Denifle, "Quellen zur Disputation Pablos Christiani mit Mose Nachmani su Barcelona 1263," *Historisches Jahrbuch* 8 (1887): 225–44. Denifle also took issue with Graetz's argument about the identity of the individual referenced in the Latin documents concerning the investigation of the rabbi for blasphemy, but his critique is clearly aimed at the broader interpretation presented in the article.

subjected the sources representing his own views to close scrutiny. Both accepted the authority and reliability of their own sources without question, even as they subjected those authored by the opposing side to intense criticism. In spite of their capacity for astute critical readings of texts, both scholars advanced arguments that confirmed their own theological and political commitments and assumptions. This level of critical partisanship in the service of scholarship seems quite alien to many of us today. Indeed, scholarship intended to support or defend national or theological ideals has long since fallen out of favor. In its place has arisen an interest in work that both highlights the complexities of society, culture, and daily life in the past and confronts head-on unflattering or uncomfortable turns in our collective past. This approach to history requires unflinching critical analysis of revered authoritative sources and a concerted effort to maintain objectivity.

But scholarly conclusions can be very powerful and influential—sometimes enduringly so. The arguments made by Graetz and Denifle built upon and responded to an early printing of the disputation account in *Satan's Darts of Fire, or the Secret and Horrible Books of the Jews against Christ, God, and the Christian Religion*, published in 1681 by the Christian Hebraist Johann Christoph Wagenseil [Figure 2].[7] As the title conveys, Wagenseil collected and edited a large selection of texts, reproduced them both in the original language (he worked in Hebrew, Greek, Arabic, and German) and in Latin translation, and then added commentary. Graetz's effort to recast Nahmanides' performance in the Barcelona disputation in heroic terms was part of his larger project to reclaim the Jewish past for a *Jewish* history, as we would say today, to return agency to Jews of the past. Denifle's response recognized and strove to neutralize Graetz's efforts to valorize medieval Jews and Judaism. The struggle between Graetz and Denifle for sole legitimate claim of the documentary evidence from the Barcelona disputation and its interpretation set the agenda for subsequent treatments of the event and its documentary legacy.

More recently, scholars have focused on questions about what motivated both the investigation of Jewish books by mendicant friars and royal sponsorship of their efforts. The Augustinian principle that Jews and Judaism should be preserved as a remnant of and witness to God's first

7 Wagenseil, Johann Christoph, *Tela ignea Satanae: Hoc est, arcani, et horribiles Judaeorum adversus Christum Deum, et Christianam religionem libri 'Aνεκδοτοι. Sunt vero: R. Lipmanni Carmen memorial; Liber Nizzachon vetus autoris incogniti; Acta dispvtationis R. Jechielis cum quodam Nicolao; Acta disputationis R. Mosis Nachmanidis cum fratre Paulo Christiani, et fratre Raymundo Martini; R. Isaaci Liber Chissuk Emuna; Libellus Toldos Jeschu* (Altdorfi Noricorum, Excudit J. H. Schönnerstaedt,1681), vol. 2, 23–60.

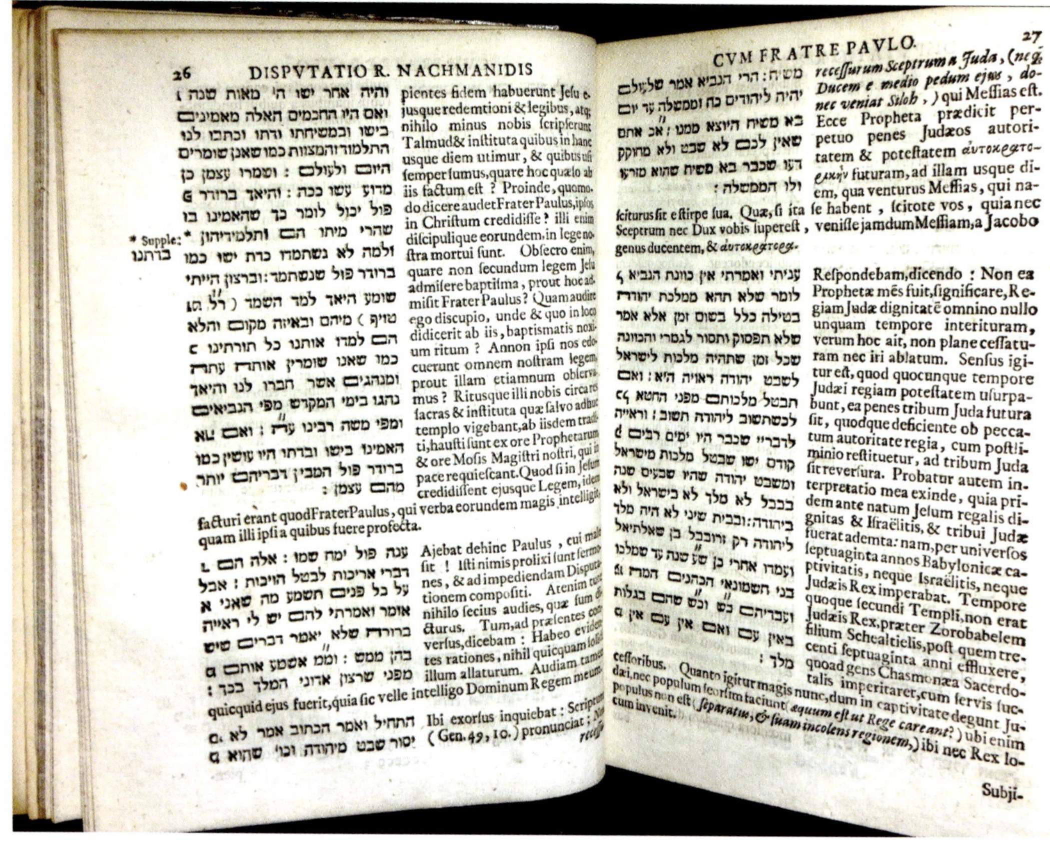

Figure 2. The Protestant scholar, Johann Christoph Wagenseil, who compiled the *Tela ignea Satanae*, was an important German Christian Hebraist (a Christian who mastered Hebrew in order to engage and understand Jewish theology and interpretations). In this collection, he reproduced several Jewish polemical or anti-Christian tracts in the original language along with Latin translations. This page contains the same portion of text presented in Figure 1. Note that Wagenseil added punctuation that was not included in the manuscript.

Wagenseil, Johann Christoph, *Tela ignea Satanae: Hoc est, arcani, et horribiles Judaeorum adversus Christum Deum, et Christianam religionem libri 'Ανεκδοτοι. Sunt vero: R. Lipmanni Carmen memorial; Liber Nizzachon vetus autoris incogniti; Acta dispvtationis R. Jechielis cum quodam Nicolao; Acta disputationis R. Mosis Nachmanidis cum fratre Paulo Christiani, et fratre Raymundo Martini; R. Isaaci Liber Chissuk Emuna; Libellus Toldos Jeschu* (Altdorfi Noricorum, Excudit J. H. Schönnerstaedt,1681), vol. 2, 23–60. British Library, General Reference Collection 223.k.26–27.

revelation provided a rationale for the protection of medieval Jews and Judaism by the church. Clerical toleration of Judaism is striking, since the church otherwise acted to effect theological uniformity within the physical and political boundaries of Christendom. The forced disputations thus signal a shift in the status quo of Jewish religious autonomy based on the

Augustinian principle of toleration. A good deal of scholarship has sought the theological and political impetus for this change in ecclesiastical Jewish policy. One thread in this debate examines the evolution of Christian engagement with the Talmud in the broad context of Christian efforts to eradicate heresy and other forms of heterodoxy from western Christendom, while another draws the contextual frame with a tight focus on transformations in Christian–Jewish relations. Undergirding both are the questions about the intended audience for these polemical works and for what purpose they were being developed.

Several scholars have traced a shift from a relatively passive model of toleration of Judaism on the part of the church to a more confrontational approach to contemporary Judaism that focused attention on Jewish books. Of interest to these scholars is the impact changes in Christian thinking had on Jewish communities. Jeremy Cohen, for example, trained attention on the slow transformation and application throughout the middle ages of Augustine's enduring principle that Jews and Judaism should be preserved as a witness to the truth of Christianity.[8] The understanding of Judaism that supported Augustine's view was necessarily rooted in a deep-seated assumption that Judaism itself remained unchanged since the time of the crucifixion. Cohen argued that the mendicant friars' interest in things Jewish emerged from their charge to purge Christendom of heresy.[9] Because Jewish history and practice had been subsumed in the Christian redemption narrative, Jewish books and learning fell within Christian jurisdiction and were thus subject to scrutiny and regulation. Thus, Friar Paul's innovative reading of rabbinic literature and his argument that these works impeded Jews' acceptance of Christianity are a direct outgrowth of arguments that had been expressed in previous decades: that contemporary Judaism was heretical precisely because it was shaped by rabbinic teachings, rather than strict adherence to strictures of the Hebrew Bible. Insofar as it wrested interpretive authority from Jewish leaders, this strategy fell in line with mass burnings of rabbinic literature for blasphemy and/or heresy following the Paris disputation and thereafter as well as efforts to remove offensive material from the Talmud through ecclesiastical censorship. Thus, Cohen argued, the polemical program the friars undertook functionally abrogated the Augustinian principle by criminalizing Judaism.

8 Jeremy Cohen, *Living Letters of the Law: Ideas of the Jew in Medieval Christianity* (Berkeley: University of California Press, 1999).

9 Jeremy Cohen initially advanced this argument in his first book, *The Friars and the Jews: The Evolution of Medieval Anti-Judaism* (Ithaca: Cornell University Press, 1982), especially chapter 2; he later refined the argument in *Living Letters of the Law*, 325–62.

Robert Chazan focused instead on the relationship between the rhetorical thrust of the friars' arguments to ascertain their objectives. Based on a review of the Barcelona disputation texts as well as Ramon Martí's *Pugio Fidei*, Chazan concluded that the friars' primary objective was to persuade the Jews of Christian Europe to convert to Christianity. Unlike Cohen, whose assessment of Christian polemical strategies and anti-Jewish rhetoric directed attention to a new theological valuation (or devaluation) of Judaism that resulted in restrictions placed on Jewish religious and economic liberties, Chazan mined Jewish responses to polemical tactics in order to assess the friars' motivating goals for employing Jewish books in missionizing efforts. Disputing Cohen's argument that the friars' anti-Jewish polemical program was designed to render Judaism untenable according to the terms defined by Christendom, Chazan argued that these developments should be viewed instead in the context of efforts to bring Jews into the Christian fold.[10]

Because Jewish books and ritual were the subject of these polemical works, most scholars, including Cohen and Chazan, have understood Jews to be their primary audience and the object of this polemical strategy. Robin Vose has proposed a revision of this general approach.[11] Vose challenged the assumption that Friar Paul, Ramon de Peñaforte, and Ramon Martí's intrusive investigation of Jewish learning and practice were indicative of the activities of goals of the order as a whole. Instead, he adopted a contextual frame that was firmly grounded in the local grassroots dimensions of the friars' ministerial duties in the Crown of Aragon. Members of the Dominican order as a whole directed the vast majority of their preaching campaigns toward Christians during the thirteenth and fourteenth centuries. Evidence from the Dominican archives indicates that the friars largely resorted to missionizing among Jews, which occasionally included intimidation, as a means of ministering to the Christian laity. Such practices, according to this view, were a necessary defense against Jewish influence resulting from social contacts, informal religious discussions, and royal and even clerical protection of Jewish communities.

There is also a sizable and varied scholarship on the intent behind the authorial decisions that shaped Nahmanides' account of the debate.

10 For the direct response to Cohen's conclusions, see Robert Chazan, *Daggers of Faith: Thirteenth-Century Christian Missionizing and Jewish Response* (Berkeley: University of California Press, 1989), especially 169–81. Cohen asserted the arguments to which Chazan responded in *Friars and the Jews*.

11 Robin J. E Vose, *Dominicans, Muslims, and Jews in the Medieval Crown of Aragon*, Cambridge Studies in Medieval Life and Thought. Fourth Series (Cambridge, UK; New York: Cambridge University Press, 2009), 133–61 pertains to the activities of Friar Paul, Ramon de Peñaforte, and Ramon Martí and the Barcelona disputation.

Since the direction and tenor of the previous secondary scholarship play an important role in shaping the questions addressed by subsequent authors, the issues of comparative reliability and facticity continue to guide disputation scholarship. Indeed, this may speak to the relative silence among historians of medieval Christianity or medieval society and culture about this event. However, in the wake of Denifle's article, many Jewish historians have subjected Nahmanides' text to close scrutiny. This body of work also reflects more contemporary concerns and theoretical principles. That Nahmanides' Hebrew account was not a perfectly accurate or precise record of the disputation has, by now, been accepted by nearly all scholars in the field. The question of what Nahmanides or modern scholars could or ought to have committed to writing undergirds much of this more recent literature. Two distinct interlaced lines of argument emerged over the course of the twentieth century. The first grapples with Nahmanides' motive for writing the text and his intended audience, while the second examines his intent behind advancing specific arguments in his account.

Efforts to reconstruct Nahmanides' motives for writing the account have led several scholars to home in on one central question: why would he write and circulate an account in Hebrew (and even more so in Catalan!) containing material that was sure to draw the friars' attention, when he knew from hard experience that they were monitoring Jewish literature and learning? This question also emerges as a product of Graetz's effort to recharacterize Nahmanides and his performance in the disputation. The very fact that his work drew a conviction for blasphemy posed a direct challenge to assumptions about his skill as a leader within the Jewish community and a representative of the Jews in the Christian world. Nahmanides' bold assertion that he did not believe the *aggadah* that Friar Paul brought as evidence and that Jews were not obliged to accept the authority of *aggadot* formed one crucial pivot of scholarly debate. Disputes about whether the *aggadot* carried the same authority as other rabbinic works had caused divisions within European Jewish communities at the beginning of the thirteenth century. Jeremy Cohen has suggested that Friar Paul's conversion was precipitated by a dramatic disillusionment with the authority of traditional rabbinic sources, and with the *aggadah* in particular.[12] For some, Nahmanides' noted position as an early teacher of the Kabbalah, a mystical interpretation of Judaism in which the various meanings of

12 Jeremy Cohen, "The Mentality of the Medieval Jewish Apostate: Peter Alfonsi, Hermann of Cologne, and Pablo Christiani," in *Jewish Apostasy in the Modern World*, ed. Todd Endelman (New York: Holmes and Meier, 1987), 20–47.

aggadot acquired tremendous significance, seemed out of keeping with this statement.[13] The disputation account, according to this reading, was intended to mend any rifts that may have occurred within the Jewish community as a result of Nahmanides' controversial statements during the public debate.

Along similar lines, Robert Chazan has suggested that Nahmanides wrote this text as a guidebook for others who might find themselves forced to defend Judaism in another disputation.[14] Questions about the accuracy of Nahmanides' account motivate this line of argument as well. Taking for granted the assumption that Nahmanides fabricated—or at least elaborated—portions of the Hebrew account to provide a clear and accessible polemical guide, this argument firmly situates the Hebrew account in the increasingly rigorous effort among Christians, particularly the mendicants, to missionize among Jews. Chazan's approach is notable for reading Nahmanides' account against a rich contextual framework built on an analysis of royal politics and relations with the church. His argument has thus effectively changed the course of scholarly debate on the disputation and its sources. Many more recent studies take Nahmanides' effort to guide future readers through the labyrinth of confrontational Christian anti-Jewish polemics as a point of departure.[15] Largely tracking the continuing influence of Nahmanides' Hebrew account on the way Jewish leaders recorded and understood Christian theological challenges, these works accept that Nahmanides' account was pivotal and widely circulated.

Much scholarship on the Hebrew disputation account presumes a direct identity between the document that we have today and the text Nahmanides composed. But there is also a smaller body of scholarship that directly challenges this assumption. A different set of concerns sparked Jaume

13 In particular, see Martin A. Cohen, "Reflections on the Text and Context of the Disputation of Barcelona," *Hebrew Union College Annual* 35 (1964): 157–92. In contrast, Marvin Fox sees no conflict between Nahmanides' view of *aggadot* in his exegesis and in his disputation account. See Marvin Fox, "Nahmanides on the Status of Aggadot: Perspectives on the Disputation at Barcelona, 1263," *Journal of Jewish Studies* 40, no. 1 (1989): 95–109.

14 Robert Chazan, *Barcelona and Beyond: The Disputation of 1263 and Its Aftermath* (Berkeley: University of California Press, 1992). Chazan has also developed this argument in numerous articles and book chapters.

15 See, for example, Harvey J. Hames, "Reconstructing Thirteenth-Century Jewish-Christian Polemic: From Paris 1240 to Barcelona 1263 and Back Again," in *Medieval Exegesis and Religious Difference: Commentary, Conflict, and Community in the Premodern Mediterranean* (New York: Fordham University Press, 2015), 115–27; and Ursula Ragacs, "Christian-Jewish or Jewish-Jewish, That's My Question . . . ," *European Journal of Jewish Studies* 5, no. 1 (2011): 93–114.

Riera i Sans's reading of the disputation documents.[16] Because no copy of the text from the thirteenth or even fourteenth century is similar enough in style and detail to present itself as source for the version that exists today, he suggests the late fifteenth or early sixteenth century as a possible date of composition.[17] So late a date of authorship, Riera i Sans argues, would also account for the unique dramatic and fictional flourishes used in this document. The author's sense of showmanship, ironic sense of humor, and self-consciousness about the pomp of courtly rituals are narrative techniques and themes typical of literary production during the Italian Renaissance, and not, in his view, of Jewish authors in the late thirteenth century. Instead, he argues that the Hebrew account was written by an unknown scholar who could not believe widespread reports that the talented exegete and legal authority had faltered so embarrassingly in the public debate with Friar Paul. Acting on the same concerns, Ursula Ragacs is conducting a systematic study of the manuscript tradition in the hope of stripping away additions and changes imposed on the text as it was copied and recopied over the generations.[18]

Source criticism is crucial to historical research. Conventions of modern historiographic practice insist that documentary evidence, to the degree possible, be reliable and authenticated. In a field like medieval Jewish history, in which the chains of evidence are marred by significant gaps, the problem of source authentication is an especially troubling one. Even a faint shadow of doubt about the provenance or validity of a widely accepted source can significantly compromise both the document and the historical story it tells. But to what degree must questions about the authenticity of a text be couched in terms of evidentiary proof? Given the notions of authorship and authority practiced during the medieval and early modern periods, along with premodern methods of storing, transmitting, and preserving texts, modern scholars possess few guarantees that accepted documentary sources are what they started out as, what they appear or claim to be, or, for that matter, what we think they are. That very uncertainty provides the basis for a hearty, continuing debate

16 J. Riera i Sans, "Les fontes històriques de la Disputa de Barcelona," in *Disputa de Barcelona de 1263 entre Mestre Mossé de Girona i Fra Pau Christià*, ed. E. Feliu (Barcelona: Columna Edicions, 1985), ix–xv.

17 The fact that several Jewish authors, including Alfonso of Valladolid (c. 1270–1345), refer to or quote from Nahmanides' disputation account makes this argument difficult to credit.

18 Ragacs, "Edieren oder nicht edieren . . . ? " *Judaica* 62, no. 2 (2006): 157–70; and Ursula Ragacs, "Edieren oder nicht edieren . . . ?: Teil 2: Die Handschriften," *Judaica* 65, no. 3 (2009): 239–58.

about what the past looked like and what impact it might have on the present. Historians piece together their representation of the past from disparate, often fragmentary textual evidence. This project, especially when applied to the analysis of the premodern world, is characteristically a complex one. Since historical narratives are inevitably informed by a wide array of factors, including historical or social memory (a body of common knowledge about the past as it pertains to a group, whether it be a national, cultural, or social past), the process of interpreting documents, the questions asked of evidence, and the kind of information sources yield to any given scholar will necessarily be shaped by the trajectory of analysis followed by those who interrogated the sources in the past as well as individually determined interests, biases, and bodies of knowledge.

It is the task of the historian to give meaning to the subject of her study by projecting its story through a contextual lens. The parameters of what makes historical subjects and how contexts emerge are quite broad. Historical subjects can include anything from an individual, event, cultural or social themes, political movements, place, time period, or object. And context is a highly mutable and porous construct. It assumes that "situational" conditions, whether on a large scale, including a vast society or time period, or a smaller scale, contained within circumscribed cultural or social parameters, determine meaning and significance.[19] As such, historical context is a powerful explanatory device or causal agent that can encompass national, cultural, social, economic, religious, familial, class, or temporal factors, and context is as much defined by the subject of study as it is by the scholar's analytical methods. Until now, most studies of the Barcelona disputation and its documentary sources have been set firmly in the context of Jewish history. The conventions of critical research demand that when entering a new field of study, scholars must master and engage previously published studies in the field. But the same conventions demand that novices in any field carefully reassess and critique the methods, arguments, and conclusions of those who preceded them. The Barcelona disputation has significant implications for Jewish history, but also for the history of medieval Christianity, the Crown of Aragon, medieval royal authority, and medieval intellectual history, to name just a few.

---

19 On the emergence and development of context as a theoretical device, see Peter Burke, "Context in Context," *Common Knowledge* 8, no. 1 (2002): 152–77.

MAKING THIS BOOK: SOURCES, HISTORICAL NARRATIVE, AND VISUAL MEDIA

WHY A GRAPHIC HISTORY?

I first encountered the Barcelona disputation during an undergraduate Jewish history class at UCLA. Everything about it captivated the budding historian in me. The disputation took place in the royal court under royal sponsorship. The two remaining accounts of the event are in perfect agreement about some details but are diametrically opposed about others; also, both sources appear to have been written by the main figures who were involved in the debate, each representing his own perspective. In addition, there was (and still is) an active and heated modern historiographic debate about the veracity, authorship, and reception of these texts, as well as the immediate significance and consequences of the disputation. The wide variety of documentary problems and compelling scholarly arguments provided for me a perfect illustration of just how interesting and exciting medieval history can be. But it also provided a hard lesson in the significant challenges any scholar faces in communicating a single critical narrative while preserving the integrity of multiple textual voices. A chance encounter with the relatively new genre of "graphic history" suggested it as an approach that might provide an opportunity to engage in a different sort of discussion with and about the key sources. It was my intention to use graphic signs to draw readers' attention to the historiographic issues that made—and continue to make—the Barcelona disputation so interesting to me.

Writing this book was, in many ways, unlike any historical project I had undertaken before. Conceptualizing the graphics themselves, in collaboration with the artist, Liz Clarke, demanded that I devote myself to details and issues that I had often thought about but had never incorporated into my own analysis or arguments. Many of these touched on concrete physical characteristics, including questions related to fashion, the dimensions of interior spaces, and the transformation of physical spaces of power and authority over time. Difficulty in locating, verifying, and reconciling sources is something of an occupational hazard for us medievalists. We often take it for granted that our understanding of events—even very well known and extensively documented events—will suffer evidentiary gaps. This difficulty became much more acute for me as I tried to formulate concrete answers to Liz's practical questions about how to depict the central people and places in the graphic history. Graphics, of course, demand that artists and authors make editorial decisions about representation.

What a character looks like, his body language, facial expressions, the color palette, even the weight of the lines contributes to interpretive work the graphic itself does. Pictorial or sequential graphic narrative allows the historian to tell a story while using graphic markers to show which texts informed her interpretation. This book grew out of my fascination with the gaps in an apparently comprehensive and sequential record of the Barcelona disputation, and my belief that it is precisely the ambiguity of the textual record that makes this case both fascinating and an ideal tool for demonstrating the power and significance of documentary sources—even texts that now exist only as traces in other documents and memory, like the account Nahmanides gave to the bishop of Girona. These very issues thus shaped the decisions that Liz and I made as we constructed every frame of this graphic history.

Several factors guided the way we chose to depict the historical figures and places that populate this work. We had to consider very carefully what kinds of evidence to use to inform our decisions about how people or buildings should be depicted, especially in cases where direct evidence has not been preserved either through illustrations or prose descriptions. And along the same lines, we had to consider the implications of using medieval illustrations and illuminations as the basis for selecting characterizations of historical figures. As Marc Epstein has pointed out in his analysis of medieval illuminated Passover *Haggadot*,[20] we cannot assume that any given illumination might offer insight as to how people in the middle ages saw the world: "Barcelona in 1320 was not Barcelona in 1325, and Mainz in 1300 was not Speyer in 1300. The localization of a given work to one town or another, has the potential to alter iconographic readings, closing down some possibilities for interpretation and opening up others, so that all readings must be contingent."[21] In short, medieval images can inform our sense of the aesthetics of an artist (or a patron who commissioned the work), but not necessarily of a generic *medieval* aesthetic, of the medieval world as a whole, or, most importantly for our project, of the reality of attire, interior spaces, or streetscapes in Barcelona in July 1263. The material reality of that time and place is lost to us. As a result, Liz and I were mindful that transferring the fruits of traditional scholarship to a medium that, by offering pictorial representations, makes aesthetic demands and prescriptions, raises some sticky methodological and theoretical questions:

20 The text that lays out the ritual and liturgy for the Passover Seder. Because it played an important role in domestic ritual, many surviving examples of these texts are illuminated, some in very rich, ornate style.

21 Marc Michael Epstein, *The Medieval Haggadah: Art, Narrative, and Religious Imagination* (New Haven: Yale University Press, 2011), 7.

What might the graphic interpretation contribute to the historian's task of contextualizing, presenting, and analyzing documentary evidence? What are the ramifications of mixing graphic narrative and critical historical analysis, two fairly rigid and in some senses diametrically opposed forms of representation? Are the demands of these two forms of exposition compatible? Complementary?

PROBLEMS OF PORTRAYAL

In many ways, *Debating Truth* is a rather conservative work of history. Based on a discrete body of documentary evidence, it presents an interpretation of the chronology and significance of an historical event and embeds that event in a straightforward cultural, religious, and political context. But whereas authors of traditional historical analyses can (and often do) develop multiple lines of argument simultaneously, the text and narrative in a sequential graphic history must remain relatively spare and simple. Much of the complexity, then, must find expression through imagery—in particular, the portrayals of characters and their emotions, as well as visual cues about the time and place of the action, the mood generated, chronology of events, and narrative strategies of sources. In the process of producing characters and a series of images to represent the Barcelona disputation in the distinctive visual vernacular of sequential graphics, Liz and I had to start our collaboration by making a series of decisions about the aesthetic of the graphic history and the physical qualities of the people who populate it. We were immediately confronted with some rather tricky questions: Were there visual cues, whether anatomical or sartorial, that might have distinguished Jews from Christians in thirteenth-century Catalonia? How might Nahmanides have viewed the Christian figures he encountered? What were symbolic markers of masculinity, power, or wisdom? And were they reflected in any way in medieval figural representations?

Medieval illuminations, stained glass windows, reliquaries, frescoes, and sculptures provide countless representations of historical and contemporary people depicting modes of medieval attire and countenance. Yet medieval art historians are quick to note that medieval art was not a literal or realist mode of representation. As Sara Lipton has argued, "[m]edieval images served many purposes: they glorified God, embodied sanctity, told tales, radiated authority, and inspired miracles, but they did not reflect reality."[22] And medieval Christian artistic representations of Jews, in fact, provide an excellent case in point. Jewish, or more accurately, Judaic figures

---

22 Sara Lipton, *Dark Mirror: The Medieval Origins of Anti-Jewish Iconography* (New York: Metropolitan Books, 2014), 21.

appear most frequently—in fact, almost exclusively—as biblical characters in Christian art through the thirteenth century. But precisely because Christian theologians hailed their biblical past as venerable and holy, while at the same time degrading it as outmoded, these depictions were often ambivalent. Lipton argues that until the fourteenth century, "Jewish" figures in art—those adorned in symbolically recognizable biblical clothing—were overwhelmingly stylized in a manner that specifically served Christian theological purposes; only very rarely did these images include representations of contemporary Jews of any sort (let alone "denigrated or distorted ones").[23] Thus, these images provide almost no information about the actual status or appearance of Jews in medieval Christian society. Nor can we assume that checking them against figural representations of Jews in illuminated Hebrew texts would provide a corrective.[24] Hebrew illuminations from this period share many of the prominent aesthetic conventions of Christian art. Indeed, there is substantial evidence that Jewish patrons employed Christian illuminators and that Jewish artists worked in Christian workshops.[25] Thus, there is nothing to suggest that illustrations in medieval Hebrew texts, such as the Passover *haggadot* that were produced in the late thirteenth and early fourteenth centuries, were meant as accurate or realistic depictions of Jewish fashion, characteristics, rituals, or behaviors.

In spite of the problematic nature of thirteenth-century imagery, characterizations in *Debating Truth* were informed in some measure by representations of the historical figures. A relatively good number of medieval depictions of King James I remain today. However, the details of his appearance change depending on where and when the image was produced. Many images of James I that were produced during his lifetime present him as clean-shaven [Figure 3]. Beginning in the first quarter of the fourteenth century, though, artists typically represented James I with an impressive beard [Figure 4]. Many medieval depictions of kings from this period do include beards, perhaps as a symbol of authority, power, and stability. Indeed, this idealized image of a powerful, bearded King James the Conqueror holds

---

23 Ibid., 133. Also see Pamela Anne Patton, *Art of Estrangement: Redefining Jews in Reconquest Spain* (University Park: Pennsylvania State University Press, 2012).

24 On the theoretical and methodological evolution of Jewish art history and interpretations of Jewish images, see Eva Frojmovic, "Buber in Basle, Schlosser in Sarajevo, Wischnizter in Weimar: The Politics of Writing about Medieval Jewish Art," in *Imagining the Self, Imagining the Other: Visual Representation and Jewish-Christian Relations Dynamics in the Middle Ages and Early Modern Period*, ed. Eva Frojmovic, Cultures, Beliefs, and Traditions, v. 15 (Leiden; Boston: Brill, 2002), 1–32.

25 Joseph Shatzmiller, *Cultural Exchange: Jews, Christians, and Art in the Medieval Marketplace* (Princeton: Princeton University Press, 2013), 113–40.

Figure 3. Though some images of King James I that were produced during his lifetime represent him as bearded, this one, like many from the same period, show him clean-shaven. This image, which dates from the 1260s, comes from a series of three panels painted to honor a marriage joining two important noble families in Montpellier.

Paredal ou ai d'entrevous n° 5 - Le roi Jaume Ier partant à la chasse. Peinture à la détrempe sur panneau de bois (vers 1260)—25,8 × 43 cm. Musée Languedocien de Montpellier, collections de la Société archéologique, http://www.mediterranees.net/moyen_age/jaume/iconografia/roi_chasseur.html.

today in Spanish monumental and commemorative art, so that he is nearly always depicted as bearded and larger than life [Figure 5].

In a realm where the royal court traveled regularly throughout the kingdom, it is possible that coins and artistic depictions that altered the king's countenance would have appeared unacceptable and perhaps even off-putting to subjects who had encountered him. The fact that most images produced during James I's lifetime represent him as clean-shaven suggests that the beard may have been added after his death to satisfy later idealized conceptions of royal authority and power.[26] In spite of the beard that sprouted from James's face in the fourteenth century, we opted for a clean-shaven king [Illustration 1].

26 However, Robert I. Burns called attention to a late portrait that pictures a beard and short white hair, which he suspects might be an accurate representation. See R. I. Burns, "The Spiritual Life of James the Conqueror, King of Arago-Catalonia, 1208–1276: Portrait and Self-Portrait," *The Catholic Historical Review* 62, no. 1 (1976): 4.

Figure 4. Later medieval depictions of King James I consistently represented him with a beard. In contrast with the image in Figure 3, which offers a rather lifelike and approachable portrait of the king, this miniature from a fourteenth-century copy of James's memoir presents the king as authoritative and intimidating. His posture, beard, and ceremonial goblet help solidify this commanding image of the king.

Jaume le Conquérant—*Llibre dels Feits*, Manuscrit dit « de Poblet »—ms 1, fol.27 r (1343), Bibliothèque de l'Université de Barcelone, http://www.mediterranees.net/moyen_age/jaume/iconografia/diner.html.

While there is no shortage of images of the king, no images of Nahmanides or Friar Paul remain. The representations that appear in the graphic history are entirely the product of Liz's creative work, along with some minor suggestions from me. In creating these images, we were especially concerned that ascribing specific physical characteristics to historical figures whose appearance has not been preserved could inadvertently endorse or reify stereotypes about ethnicity, social class, or nationality. This was an especially sensitive issue with regard to representing Nahmanides,

Figure 5. Adopting the heroic image of medieval royal authority that marked later medieval representations of King James I, modern depictions of the king, such as this stamp from 1977, present him as larger than life, with a well-groomed beard and an exaggeratedly regal bearing.

http://www.canstockphoto.com/images-photos/king-aragon.html#file_view.php?id=11220336.

Illustration 1.

who remains a towering figure in traditional Jewish learning and culture. I felt it was essential to avoid reinforcing modern (or, for that matter, medieval) stereotypes of Jewish features or physical bearing while also producing a representation that would be in some way recognizable, or at least acceptable, to anyone who approaches the book having already formed a strong mental image of Nahmanides.

We were very careful not to project onto Nahmanides or Friar Paul stereotypically Jewish or Semitic features. Although those characteristics occasionally found their way into depictions of Jews in late thirteenth-century Christian illuminated manuscripts, there is little evidence to support the notion that most European Jews looked any different from their Christian neighbors or appeared to Christians to be different. In *Debating Truth*, Nahmanides and Paul wear clothing and haircuts commensurate with other participants in the disputation: Paul wears the robes of his Dominican brothers, and Nahmanides dresses in simple but respectful attire, in keeping with the clothing worn by the respectable men who fill the hall as observers.

But considerations about the symbolism and politics of imaging—and imagining—medieval Jews also drove our thinking about whether to depict Nahmanides as clean-shaven or bearded. Though evidence suggests that facial hair was read as a marker for many Christians of Jewishness (or Muslim-ness, as the case may be), there is also substantial evidence that many Jews followed the same conventions of fashion as their Christian neighbors. Indeed, this was precisely the rationale offered for the many statutes, including the Fourth Lateran Council of 1215, legislating that Jews were required to wear beards or distinguishing clothing. But the beard also had religious cultural significance within Judaism. The Torah includes two very similar laws regarding the grooming of facial hair: the first in Leviticus 19:27, "You shall not round off the side-growth on your head, or destroy the side-growth of your beard"; and the second in Leviticus 21:5, "They shall not shave smooth any part of their heads, or cut the side growth of their beards." Both of these negative commandments related to personal grooming are grouped with injunctions related to physical disfigurement, and they express an anxiety that Israelite men would likely be drawn to participate in the rituals and fashions of surrounding societies.[27] As such, they aim to forestall such behavior through legal command. *Halakhic* or legal debates around this issue held to the same assumption, but also stretched to identify contingencies under which the punishment for certain kinds of beard trimming

27 A "negative commandment" forbids an action or behavior.

would be less severe.[28] In the late twelfth century, Maimonides argued explicitly that the biblical injunction exclusively prohibited shaving with a plane, but that cutting a beard with scissors, no matter how closely it was cut to the face, was permitted.[29]

Liz and I experimented with several styles of facial hair for Nahmanides, from clean-shaven to fully bearded [Illustrations 2, 3, and 4]. In the end,

Illustrations 2 and 3.

28 "If a man makes a baldness on his head or rounds the corner of his head, or mars the corner of his beard, or makes one cutting [in his flesh] for the dead, he is liable [to a flogging]. If he makes one cutting for five dead, or five cuttings for one, he is liable [severally] for each one. On [rounding] the head [he is liable] for the two corners, one for one side and one for the other; on [marring] the beard [he is liable] for two [corners] on one side, for two on the other and for one lower down; R. Eliezer says: If they were all taken off as one he is liable only on one count, and he is only liable on taking off with a razor; R. Eliezer says: even if he picks off the hairs with tweezers, or [removes then] with pincers, he is liable." *The Babylonian Talmud, Makkot,* trans. Rabbi Dayan H. M. Lazarus (London, Soncino Press, 1994), 20 a.

29 Maimonides, *Mishneh Torah*, Avodat Kokhavim, 12:7, 1 "So if one chopped the beard with scissors, he was not guilty. One who shaved [his beard] was not guilty unless he helped in the work." Moses Maimonides, *The Book of Knowledge: From the Mishneh Torah of Maimonides*, trans. H. M. Russell and J. Weinberg (New York: KTAV Publishing House, 1981), 106.

Illustration 4.

though, we settled for a relatively full beard. Throughout his writings, Nahmanides defaulted to modes of interpretation that acknowledged and accepted the legitimacy of shifting practices and traditions in response to local historical and cultural change. However, without challenging the legitimacy of other authorities, he consistently endorsed strict compliance with the spirit and letter of the 613 commandments contained in the Torah. Though it is certainly historically and halakhically possible that Nahmanides could have worn his beard clipped nearly to the skin, the decision to depict him with a full beard was intended to reflect his voice as an interpreter of Torah and halakhah. A man who chose a relatively loose understanding of traditions in order to subscribe to the fashion of the day did not mesh with the many biblical and Talmudic commentaries attributed to Nahmanides.

GRAPHIC DIFFERENCES

The documentary apparatus that supports a traditional work of history enables the author to linger on, even emphasize, complexity in many forms: differences of opinion between scholars, differences of perspective between sources, and minor, possibly tangential details that stand outside the purview of the central story. The graphic narrative, however, is by and large bound to a single perspective. The aesthetic and narrative of a sequential graphic place a distinctive stamp on the way the story unfolds. *Debating*

Truth is not the first effort to extract the disputation and its documentary record from the world of text and scholarship. In the 1980s, the late Hyam Maccoby, then a professor of history at University of Leeds in the UK, wrote a play based on the Hebrew disputation account. It was his view that Nahmanides' account was accurate and true and that he was punished for publicizing a version that made the friars appear foolish. He had some historical evidence to support his interpretation, but it was limited enough that he did not feel comfortable publishing it in an academic forum. Instead he wrote a stage play,[30] which presented an idealized account of the drama and drew attention to political and religious intrigue behind the scenes (specifically, the king's well-documented adultery) to explain the controversy that followed. Though Maccoby spruced up the theological bits to express modern orthodox views, much of the dialogue attributed to Nahmanides is true to the text. However, Maccoby revised nearly all of the dialogue and action of the king to accentuate Nahmanides' favorable position at court.

Fiction and history have very different objectives. In writing a stage play, Maccoby was intent on revealing a truth that cannot be extracted directly from sources or presented in academic discourse. However, as the author of a graphic history, I am obliged to ground my story in the documentary evidence. The project is most interesting at those points where the documentation does not produce evidence for an image, or where the aesthetic of the graphic is in tension with historical evidence. Graphic narrative certainly shares in some of the conventions of film. And, as in film, there are many ways to tell a story in the pictorial form. In each case, the conventions of sequential narrative assure that visual cues convey essential information about the perspective from which the story is being told. The relationship between graphics and text or story plays a decisive role in shaping the contours of the drama. Indeed, the relationship between the graphic and the script can vary widely depending on whether the images guide the story or the story guides the images.

I knew from the very outset that I wanted the graphic to tell Nahmanides' version of the disputation. This narrative strategy had a direct impact on the structure of the graphic, the temporality of the narrative, the pace at which the story unfolds, and, once again, portrayals

30 The play, staring Christopher Lee as King James, was staged as a television film and aired on the BBC. The DVD of that production is still available: H. Maccoby, *The Disputation: A Theological Debate between Christians and Jews*, directed by Geoffrey Sax (London: BBC, 1986). Productions of the play also traveled throughout England and America and played to sold-out crowds during the late 1990s and early 2000s. The house was packed when I saw the stage play in 1999 at the Coconut Grove Playhouse in Miami, Florida, with Theodore Bikel (perhaps best known for his portrayal of Tevye in the film version of *Fiddler on the Roof*) as Nahmanides. This film can be found on the syllabuses of many university courses in medieval Jewish history and Judaism.

of Nahmanides' interlocutors. The Hebrew account contains statements about Christian theology that likely would have drawn fierce and immediate punishment if he had uttered them in the presence of the king, the Dominicans, or other clergy. It was my hope that a graphic presentation of the text would help highlight the fact that Nahmanides' Hebrew Barcelona disputation account thus stands at the intersection between literature for literature's sake and the production of historical documentation in the service of posterity.

To alert the reader that Nahmanides was both the source of the story and its protagonist, Liz and I decided to use a flashback within a flashback. The first page introduces Nahmanides [Illustration 5]. In the first frame, a boat enters the harbor of Acre; a narrative box grounds this image in a specific time and place. In the second frame, the reader encounters a three-quarter view of Nahmanides leaning toward the approaching port and looking contemplative; the narrative box provides some biographical information about him. The third frame contains a full-face close-up with a narrative box explaining that his serious expression is the product of a painful memory. And the final frame is a flashback to Nahmanides writing his disputation account at his writing desk in Girona. The omniscient narrator's interventions in the narrative boxes are signaled by a standard comic-book font: all caps, tilting slightly to the right. On the second page, the reader encounters Nahmanides at his home in Girona reading a letter [Illustration 6]. The font in the narrative box is now different: it is the more rounded and stylized font of Nahmanides' composition on the previous page. Liz and I chose this rounded font to evoke Hebrew script. We wanted it to convey that the story underway is told from Nahmanides' distinctive perspective and also to make it very clear to the reader that changes in font represent changes in perspective. However, the very observant reader will note that Nahmanides is writing from left to right [Illustration 7], rather than from right to left, as he would were he composing in Hebrew. Here we wanted to be true to the chronology of events as depicted in the Latin sources, which indicate that he wrote an account that he gave to the bishop of Girona. The language of composition in that text was very likely Catalan, which, like English, is written from left to right. Although these Latin sources make no mention of Nahmanides writing a disputation account intended specifically for a Jewish audience, we wanted to make it perfectly clear that we relied on the Hebrew document for much of the content and dialogue of the graphic history and to alert the reader to the complications of documentation.

At some significant points, we emphasized Nahmanides' viewpoint by breaking away from strict historical realism. The second frame on the second page depicts Nahmanides as a solitary traveler [Illustration 8]. Roads were frequently very dangerous during the middle ages. A man traveling alone would be vulnerable to robbery or worse, so it is highly unlikely that a man of Nahmanides' age, fame, or stature would travel without companionship. However, we chose to represent him in this way to stress his sense of isolation and solitary responsibility that emerges in his narrative.

Illustration 5.

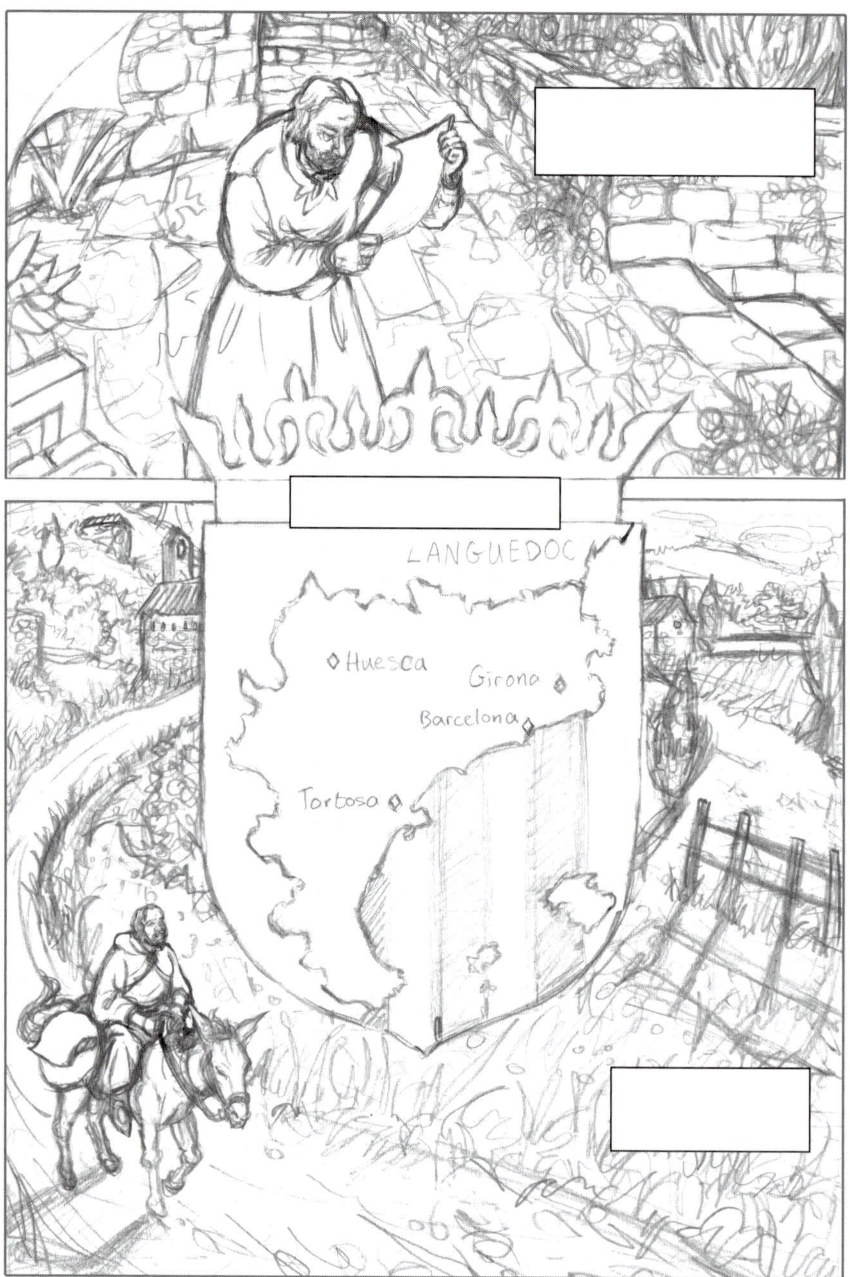

Illustration 6.

Finally, most of the graphic history depicts a drama that took place in Nahmanides' past. Liz highlighted the fact that the story unfolding here is based on a textual source by drawing the upper left hand corner of the cell as a page turning [Illustration 9]. To the narrative box, set in the

Illustration 7.

Illustration 8.

Hebrew font, Liz also affixed a sketch of Nahmanides' personal seal, which was discovered in Acre.[31] Because Nahmanides' account yields no information about the controversy that followed the disputation, we turn to the Latin sources to tell this part of the story. A change of font and

31 Isaiah Shachar, *The Seal of Nahmanides* (Jerusalem: Israel Museum, 1972).

Illustration 9.

seals based on royal and papal seals from the same period makes that clear as well [Illustrations 10 and 11].

We used these technical graphic markers of Nahmanides' perspective to draw the reader's attention to the varied and complex nature of the documentary evidence. This method works, we hope, both overtly and subtly. The switch in fonts when we turn to a different source is deliberately a bit jarring. We intended to jolt the reader to look twice and wonder if she missed something. The seals, on the other hand, are slightly less pronounced. Nevertheless, they put a distinct "signature" on each text.

In addition, it had been my intention to have Liz depict the other individuals who played a pivotal role in the disputation and the events that followed in a manner that would clearly reflect Nahmanides' personal feelings. In the Hebrew account, Nahmanides is unequivocally very hostile to Friar Paul, to the point of implausibility. In contrast, Nahmanides treats the king with great respect and honor. When Liz and I began discussing how to represent Friar Paul, I asked her to represent him as unattractive, bitter, and mean [Illustration 12]. My intention was to change his look subtly later in the text when we turn to Latin sources. However several of the reviewers of the proposal found this image distracting and offensive, especially in contrast with the almost regal depiction of Nahmanides. In response to their strong recommendation that we adopt a more neutral representation, Liz revised our characterization of Friar Paul [Illustration 13]. The reviewers may have been justified in their concern that this image could undermine the vitality and seriousness of the book, especially among readers with little background in medieval or Jewish history. But I can't help but feel that we missed an important opportunity unique to the graphic form.

Illustration 10.

A pictorial narrative opens a space in which deep and abiding ambiguities can find expression literally in the same frame. Nahmanides' high regard for the Christian king and, to a lesser degree, for Friar Ramon de Peñaforte, juxtaposed with his profound antipathy for Friar Paul, whom he considered to be a traitorous Jew who used his education as a weapon,

Illustration 11.

could have provided an emotionally and intellectually accessible lesson on the complexities of medieval interfaith relations. It may be that the emotional accessibility of this representative form as a mode of historical discourse is also a liability. Perhaps the power of graphic images to influence our mental images and interpretations necessitates that we mix representational and evidentiary narrative with caution.

Illustration 12.

Illustration 13.

PART V

RESOURCES FOR ADDITIONAL RESEARCH

QUESTIONS

Significant research has been conducted on the Barcelona disputation, and scholars contribute new work to the field every month. Still, there remain many avenues as yet underexplored, or even unexplored. The following section provides a series of research questions, grouped in thematic clusters ranging from very general to more specific, that may help you begin your own examination of the Barcelona disputation.

QUESTIONS TO GUIDE YOUR READING OF THE PRIMARY SOURCES

1. What were the central issues of debate during the Barcelona disputation? Where are the key points of agreement between the two versions, and the key points of difference?

2. Based on your assessment of the sources, what did each side hope to accomplish? To what degree was each side successful?

3. Why did Friar Paul turn to rabbinic literature for his polemical arguments? What did these sources offer him that biblical sources did not?

4. Based on your reading of the Hebrew and Latin accounts of the disputation, how would you describe the king's role in the disputation?

5. In what specific ways would your interpretation of the Hebrew account change if Nahmanides' authorship were conclusively challenged?

6. Based on your reading of the Hebrew and Latin accounts and the Latin documents, what do you think were the limits on Nahmanides' freedom of speech?

7. How do canons 1, 3, and 67–70 of the Fourth Lateran Council pertain to the disputation at Barcelona and the events that followed?

HISTORY OF POLEMICS AND INTERFAITH RELATIONS

8. What is the relationship between Nahmanides' Hebrew disputation account and other polemical works, including other disputation accounts?

9. What is the relationship between the Barcelona disputation and the Paris disputation of 1240? How does the Barcelona disputation fit on a spectrum with the Paris disputation? Are they comparable in any way?

10. What does this event teach us about the relationship between Christian and Jewish leaders locally, throughout the Crown of Aragon, and throughout Christendom?

11. What does the disputation and its aftermath show us about interfaith relations in Spain, and what are the implications for an understanding of *convivencia*?

HISTORY OF THE CROWN OF ARAGON

12. How might the study of this event contribute to an understanding of royal power and authority in the Crown of Aragon?

13. Did the king have pressing political or religious reasons for calling and participating in the disputation? What might he have gained from taking part? Might it have been in some way a political liability?

JEWISH HISTORY

14. How can the disputation help to shed light on dynamics within the Jewish community in Girona, Barcelona, and the Crown of Aragon?

15. How might you explain why Nahmanides wrote an account of this event in Hebrew and/or Catalan?

16. What does this text teach us about the patterns of communication and links between different Jewish communities?

17. Can there be a shared Jewish and Christian history of this event?

HISTORY OF THE CHURCH

18. What do the documents related to the disputation contribute to an understanding of the mendicant friars and their relationship with lay clergy and cloistered monks?

19. In what way did a public disputation serve the interests of the church as laid out in canons 1, 3, and 67–70 of the Fourth Lateran Council?

HISTORIOGRAPHIC ISSUES

20. What are the most appropriate contextual fields in which this event fits?

21. What story does the Barcelona disputation tell? Whose story is it?

22. What contextual frame does *Debating Truth* adopt? Do you think it is the appropriate context? What would you change and why?

23. The event was—and is—clearly significant to different people and communities in different ways. In your view, does the fact that it has captured the attention of scholars interested in Judaism and Jewish history far more than it has general medievalists or historians of Christianity change its relative significance?

24. How would you rewrite this graphic history entirely from the friars' perspective? What would be their great successes and failures in terms of religious and political outcome? From their perspective, was the disputation a success? What was their relationship with the king? What kind of power or authority might they have gained from this event?

25. Does Nahmanides' use of biblical passages to tell his story (outside of the interpretation of biblical passages as part of his debate with the friars) signal anything about the reliability or accuracy of his account?

SOURCES FOR ADDITIONAL READING

BIBLIOGRAPHY

Abulafia, David. "'Nam iudei servi regis sunt, et semper fisco regio deputati': The Jews in the Municipal 'Fuero' of Teruel (1176–7)." In *Jews, Muslims and Christians in and around the Crown of Aragon*, edited by Harvey Hames and Elena Lourie, 97–123. Leiden: Brill, 2004.

Assis, Yom Tov. *The Golden Age of Aragonese Jewry: Community and Society in the Crown of Aragon, 1213–1327.* London: The Littman Library of Jewish Civilization, 1997.

Baer, Yitzhak. *A History of the Jews in Christian Spain: From the Reconquest to the Fourteenth Century.* 2 vols. Philadelphia, PA: Jewish Publication Society of America, 1961.

Bisson, Thomas N. "The Fiscal Power of James the Conqueror (ca. 1230–1276): A Provisional Study." In *Jaume I: Commemoració del VIII centenari del naixement de Jaume I,* edited by Maria Teresa Ferrer i Mallol, 249–57. Barcelona: Institut d'Estudis Catalans, 2011.

———. *The Medieval Crown of Aragon, A Short History.* Oxford: Clarendon Press, 1986.

———. "Prelude to Power: Kingship and Constitution in the Realms of Aragon, 1175–1250." In *The Worlds of Alfonso the Learned and James the Conqueror: Intellect and Force in the Middle Ages*, edited by Robert I. Burns, 23–40. Princeton: Princeton University Press, 1985.

———. *Medieval France and Her Pyrenean Neighbours: Studies in Early Institutional History.* London: The Hambledon Press, 1989.

———. "The Problem of Feudal Monarchy: Aragon, Catalonia, and France." *Speculum: A Journal of Medieval Studies* 53, no. 3 (1978): 460–78.

———. "A General Court of Aragon (Daroca, February 1228)." *English Historical Review* 92, no. 362 (1977): 107–24.

Burke, Peter. "Context in Context." *Common Knowledge* 8, no. 1 (2002): 152–77.

Burns, R. I. "Castle of Intellect, Castle of Force: The Worlds of Alfonso the Learned and James the Conqueror." In *The Worlds of Alfonso the Learned and James the Conqueror: Intellect and Force in the Middle Ages*, edited by R. I. Burns, 3–22. Princeton: Princeton University Press, 1985.

———. "The Spiritual Life of James the Conqueror, King of Arago-Catalonia, 1208–1276: Portrait and Self-Portrait." *The Catholic Historical Review* 62, no. 1 (1976): 1–35.

———. *Medieval Colonialism: Postcrusade Exploitation of Islamic Valencia.* Princeton: Princeton University Press, 1975.

———. *Islam under the Crusaders: Colonial Survival in the Thirteenth-Century Kingdom of Valencia*. Princeton: Princeton University Press, 1973.

Caputo, Nina. *Nahmanides in Medieval Catalonia: History, Community, and Messianism*. Notre Dame, IN: University of Notre Dame Press, 2007.

Catlos, Brian A. *The Victors and the Vanquished: Christians and Muslims of Catalonia and Aragon, 1050–1300*. Cambridge Studies in Medieval Life and Thought, 4th ser., 59. Cambridge, UK: New York: Cambridge University Press, 2004.

Cawsey, Suzanne F. *Kingship and Propaganda: Royal Eloquence and the Crown of Aragon, c. 1200–1450*. Oxford Historical Monographs. Oxford, UK: Oxford University Press, 2002.

Chazan, Robert. *Fashioning Jewish Identity in Medieval Western Christendom*. Cambridge: Cambridge University Press, 2004.

———. "Joseph Kimhi's 'Sefer Ha-Berit': Pathbreaking Medieval Jewish Apologetics." *Harvard Theological Review* 85, no. 4 (1992): 417–32.

———. *Barcelona and Beyond: The Disputation of 1263 and Its Aftermath*. Berkeley: University of California Press, 1992.

———. *Daggers of Faith: Thirteenth-Century Christian Missionizing and Jewish Response*. Berkeley: University of California Press, 1989.

Cohen, Jeremy. *Living Letters of the Law: Ideas of the Jew in Medieval Christianity*. Berkeley: University of California Press, 1999.

———. "Medieval Jews on Christianity: Polemical Strategies and Theological Defense." In *Interwoven Destinies: Jews and Christians through the Ages*, edited by E. J. Fisher, 77–89. New York: Paulist Press, 1993.

———. *The Friars and the Jews: The Evolution of Medieval Anti-Judaism*. Ithaca: Cornell University Press, 1982.

———. "The Christian Adversary of Solomon Ibn Adret." *Jewish Quarterly Review* 71, no. 1 (1980): 48–55.

Cohen, Martin A. "Reflections on the Text and Context of the Disputation of Barcelona." *Hebrew Union College Annual* 35 (1964): 157–92.

Constable, Olivia Remie, ed. *Medieval Iberia: Readings from Christian, Muslim, and Jewish Sources*. 2nd ed. Philadelphia: University of Pennsylvania Press, 2012.

Denifle, D. P. H. "Quellen zur Disputation Pablos Christiani mit Mose Nachmani su Barcelona 1263." *Historisches Jahrbuch* 8 (1887): 225–44.

Fox, Marvin. "Nahmanides on the Status of Aggadot: Perspectives on the Disputation at Barcelona, 1263." *Journal of Jewish Studies* 40, no. 1 (1989): 95–109.

Graetz, H. "Die Disputation des Bonastruc mit Frai Pablo in Barcelona." *Monatsschrift für Geschichte und Wissenschaft des Judentums* 14 (1865): 428–33.

Gutwirth, Eleazar. "Habitat and Ideology : The Organization of Private Space in Late Medieval 'Juderías'." *Mediterranean Historical Review*, 1994.

Hames, Harvey J. "Reconstructing Thirteenth-Century Jewish-Christian Polemic: From Paris 1240 to Barcelona 1263 and Back Again." In *Medieval Exegesis and Religious Difference: Commentary, Conflict, and Community in the Premodern Mediterranean*, 115–27. New York: Fordham University Press, 2015.

———. "'Fear God, My Son, and King': Relations between Nahmanides and King Jaime I at the Barcelona Disputation." *Hispania Judaica Bulletin*, 2014.

Kagay, Donald J. "The Emergence of 'Parliament' in the Thirteenth-Century Crown of Aragon: A View from the Gallery." In *On the Social Origins of Medieval Institutions: Essays in Honor of Joseph F. O'Callaghan*, edited by Donald J. Kagay and Theresa M. Vann, 223–41. Leiden: Brill, 1998.

Kagay, Donald J., and Theresa M. Vann, eds. *On the Social Origins of Medieval Institutions: Essays in Honor of Joseph F. O'Callaghan*. Leiden: Brill, 1998.

Klein, Elka. *Jews, Christian Society, and Royal Power in Medieval Barcelona.* Ann Arbor: University of Michigan Press, 2006.

———. *Hebrew Deeds of Catalan Jews, 1117–1316.* Barcelona; Girona: Societal Catalana d'Estudis Hebraics; Patronat Municipal Call de Girona, 2004.

———. "Splitting Heirs: Patterns of Inheritance among Barcelona's Jews." *Jewish History* 16, no. 1 (2002): 49–71.

Kosto, Adam J. *Making Agreements in Medieval Catalonia: Power, Order, and the Written Word, 1000–1200.* Cambridge University Press, 2001.

Maccoby, H. *The Disputation: A Theological Debate between Christians and Jews.* Directed by Geoffrey Sax. London: BBC, 1986.

Menache, Sophia. *Communication in the Jewish Diaspora: The Pre-Modern World.* Leiden: Brill, 1996.

Novikoff, Alex J. *The Medieval Culture of Disputation: Pedagogy, Practice, and Performance.* Philadelphia: University of Pennsylvania Press, 2013.

Prawer, Joshua. *The History of the Jews in the Latin Kingdom of Jerusalem.* New York: Oxford University Press, 1988.

Prawer, Joshua, B. Z. Kedar, H. E. Mayer, and R. C. Smail, eds. *Outremer: Studies in the History of the Crusading Kingdom of Jerusalem Presented to Joshua Prawer.* Jerusalem: Yad Yitzhak Ben-Zvi Institute, 1982.

Ragacs, Ursula. "Edieren oder nicht edieren . . . ?: Überlegungen zu einer Neuedition des hebräischen Berichtes über die Disputation von Barcelona 1263." *Judaica* 62, no. 2 (2006): 157–70.

———. "Edieren oder nicht edieren . . . ?: Überlegungen zu einer Neuedition des hebräischen Berichtes über die Disputation von Barcelona 1263. Teil 2: Dei Hanschriften." *Judaica* 65, no. 3 (2009): 239–58.

Ray, Jonathan. *The Sephardic Frontier: The Reconquista and the Jewish Community in Medieval Iberia.* Conjunctions of Religion and Power in the Medieval Past. Ithaca, NY: Cornell University Press, 2006.

Régné, Jean. *History of the Jews in Aragon: Regesta and documents, 1213–1327.* Hispania Judaica 1. Jerusalem: Magnes Press, Hebrew University, 1978.

Riera Melis, Antoni. "James I and His Era. Brief Analysis of a Major Political and Cultural Inheritance." *Catalan Review: International Journal of Catalan Culture* 1 (2008): 9–16.

Shachar, Isaiah. *The Seal of Nahmanides.* Israel Museum, 1972.

Simonsohn, Shlomo, ed. *The Apostolic See and the Jews.* Vol. 1. 8 vols. Studies and texts 94–95, 99, 104–106, 109. Toronto: Pontifical Institute of Mediaeval Studies, 1988.

Smith, Damian J. *Innocent III and the Crown of Aragon: The Limits of Papal Authority.* Church, Faith, and Culture in the Medieval West. Burlington, VT: Ashgate, 2004.

Smith, D., and H. Buffery. *The Book of Deeds of James I of Aragon: A Translation of the Medieval Catalan Llibre Dels Fets.* Crusades Texts in Translation; 10. Aldershot: Ashgate, 2003.

Szpiech, Ryan, *Conversion and Narrative: Reading and Religious Authority in Medieval Polemic.* The Middle Ages. Philadelphia: University of Pennsylvania Press, 2012.

Thienhaus, Ole J. *Jewish-Christian Dialogue: The Example of Gilbert Crispin.* Baltimore: Publish America, 2006.

Vose, Robin J. E. *Dominicans, Muslims, and Jews in the Medieval Crown of Aragon.* Cambridge Studies in Medieval Life and Thought. Fourth Series. Cambridge, UK: Cambridge University Press, 2009.

Weber, Elka. "Sharing the Sites: Medieval Jewish Travellers to the Land of Israel." In *Eastward Bound: Travels and Travellers, 1050–1500*, edited by Allen Rosamund. 35–52. Manchester, UK: Manchester University Press, 2004.

Webster, J. R. "Patronage and Piety: Catalan Letters from Llull to March." In *The Worlds of Alfonso the Learned and James the Conqueror: Intellect and Force in the Middle Ages*, edited by R. I. Burns, 68–94. Princeton: Princeton University Press, 1985.

———. "Unlocking Lost Archives: Medieval Catalan Franciscan Communities." *The Catholic Historical Review* 66, no. 4 (1980): 537–50.

Weijers, Olga. *In Search of the Truth: A History of Disputation Techniques from Antiquity to Early Modern Times*. Turnhout, Belgium, 2014.

Whalen, Brett Edward. *Dominion of God: Christendom and Apocalypse in the Middle Ages*. Cambridge: Harvard University Press, 2009.

Wiersma, Syds. "The Dynamic of Religious Polemics: The Case of Raymond Martin (ca. 1220–ca. 1285)." In *Interaction between Judaism and Christianity in History, Religion, Art and Literature*, edited by Marcel Poorthuis, Joshua Schwartz, and Joseph Turner, 201–17. Leiden: Brill, 2009.

Yuval, Israel Jacob, and Ram Ben-Shalom, eds. *Conflict and Religious Conversation in Latin Christendom: Studies in Honour of Ora Limor*. Turnhout, Belgium: Brepols, 2014.

PRINTED EDITIONS OF NAHMANIDES' HEBREW ACCOUNT OF THE BARCELONA DISPUTATION

Braude, Morris. *Conscience on Trial; Three Public Religious Disputations between Christians and Jews in the Thirteenth and Fifteenth Centuries*. New York: Exposition Press, 1952.

Chavel, Charles B. *The Disputation at Barcelona*. New York: Shilo Publishing House, 1983.

Chavel, Hayim Dov. "Vikuah ha-Ramban." In *Kitvei Rabbenu Moshe ben Nahman*, 1:302–20. Jerusalem: Mosad Ha-Rav Kook, 1964.

Hyam, Maccoby, *Judaism on Trial: Jewish-Christian Disputations in the Middle Ages*, 102–46. Oxford: Littman Library of Jewish Civilization, 1982.

Tostado Martín, Alfonso. *La disputa de Barcelona de 1263: controversia judeocristiana*. Salamanca: Universidad Pontificia de Salamanca, Servicio de Publicaciones, 2009.

Trautner-Kromann, Hanne. *Shield and Sword: Jewish Polemics against Christianity and the Christians in France and Spain from 1100–1500*. Tübingen: Mohr, 1993.

GLOSSARY

AGGADAH (PL. AGGADOT; CAN ALSO BE SPELLED HAGGADAH AND HAGGADOT): One of the central components of rabbinic literature. An *aggadah* generally deals with questions of interpreting narrative. In contrast to the legal portions of the Talmud (*halakhah*), *aggadot* offer folklore about the rabbis and biblical figures, ethical and moral lessons, and homilies. As a general rule, *aggadot* are not prescriptive of specific actions, but rather offer models for proper behavior.

ALBIGENSIAN CRUSADE: A military action against the followers of the Albigensian or Cathar interpretation of Christianity in Languedoc, in southern France. Catharism had been labeled heretical by the church, largely because adherents rejected the authority and teachings of the Roman Church as departure from true apostolic Christianity. The Albigensian Crusade, named for one of the towns that was targeted in this effort, began in 1209. Those who fought and died in this effort were promised the typical indulgences offered to crusaders in the east, including absolution of sins and remission of debts.

ALJAMA: The vernacular term describing organized Jewish or Muslim communities throughout Spain. The term derives from the Arabic *al jama'a*, which means assembly. This term can refer to the governmental structure or to the physical space occupied by the community.

ALMOHAD: A traditionalist form of Islam that first developed among Berber Muslims and then spread from parts of North Africa to al-Andalus during the second half of the twelfth century. The Almohads adopted a strict literalist interpretation of Quran and Sunna, established a caliphate, and suppressed communities of Jews and Christians living among Muslims in al-Andalus. They also waged a fairly systematic war against Christians in Iberia.

ALMORAVID: A reformist interpretation of Islam that began playing an important role in al-Andalus in the late eleventh century, as Christian military advances drove beleaguered Muslim leaders to call for support. The Almoravids favored a highly legalistic reading of the Quran, which included a stricter interpretation of privileges offered to Jewish and Christian communities living under Muslim rule.

BET DIN (PL. BATTEI DIN): "House of judgment" or court of law. The *bet din* in medieval Jewish communities was a central component of Jewish self-governance. It oversaw practices related to marriage, divorce, business contracts, tort or property law, and inheritance in accordance with rabbinic tradition. The *battei din* made every effort to officially prohibit Jews from seeking justice in gentile courts.

CONTRA JUDAEOS (ALSO SPELLED IUDAEOS): A genre of polemical Christian literature that argued against the biblical interpretations and practices of Judaism. The earliest examples of this genre of literature date from the second century, but it remained a favored form of Christian–Jewish controversy through the early modern period.

DHIMMI: "Peoples of the book" (*ahl al-kitab*) who followed the theological practices and traditions of a monotheistic faith that was rooted in revealed scripture. Members of recognized *dhimmi* communities were granted a legal status (*dhimma*) as recognized religious minorities who were generally permitted to practice their religious traditions in exchange for clear signs of capitulation to Muslim rule.

HAGGADAH: The *Haggadah* is the text that contains the ritual, liturgy, and narrative for the Passover Seder. While the foundation of the Seder itself is contained in *Mishnah Pesahim*, 10, a *Haggadah* generally add songs, commentaries, or traditions. Many manuscripts of the *Haggadah* from the fourteenth century have been elaborately illustrated.

HALAKHAH: Jewish law, based on rabbinic interpretations of the biblical law. By the middle ages, an expert in *halakhah* would have been responsible for a mastery of Mishnah and Talmud, as well as more localized legal traditions that developed in the diaspora.

JIZYA: The *jizya* is a poll-tax levied on *dhimmi* populations living under Muslim rule. Payment of the *jizya* signaled to the Muslim leadership and populace that members of the *dhimmi* community acknowledged and accepted their status as a subjugated people.

KABBALAH: A form of mysticism that developed in northern Iberia during the thirteenth century. Kabbalists sought concealed meanings in biblical texts and wrote suitable commentaries. Several kabbalist schools emerged in different locations throughout Spain; Nahmanides was a leading figure in one of the early centers in Girona. The *Zohar*, the central text of the movement, was produced in the late thirteenth century in Castile.

KEHILLAH (PL. KEHILLOT): Hebrew term for community. During the middle ages, the *kehillah*, like the *aljama*, could refer to the organization that ran the community as well as a more abstract concept of community.

MISHNAH: A body of rabbinic teachings based on biblical legal formulas. Organized thematically in six orders, or *sederim*, the Mishnah was redacted by Rabbi Judah ha-Nasi at the beginning of the third century.

MUDÉJAR (PL. MUDÉJARES): Muslims living under Christian rule. In particular, this term refers to Muslims who were conquered and who capitulated to remaining under Christian rule. Communities of *Mudéjares* were generally self-governed according to the laws of Islam.

RESPONSA: Questions and answers (*she'elot u-tshuvot* in Hebrew) between rabbis concerning the interpretation of *halakhah*. This body of literature, which dates back to the rabbinic period, is very much the product of diaspora. When legal experts in far-flung communities encountered tricky legal questions, they sent the details of the case along with their inquiries to authorities at recognized academies. Findings in *responsa* often provide precedent for additional legal discussion.

SCHOLASTICISM: A pedagogical and discursive methodology based in rationalism and disputation. Medieval scholasticism is directly associated with the highly disciplined forms of argument that developed in university faculties of philosophy and theology.

TAIFA: Taifa kingdoms, or "Party kingdoms," were the political and military units that succeeded the Umayyad Caliphate in al-Andalus. Military and political leaders, many of whom had gained experience serving either the caliphate or insurgents, formed petty principalities that tended toward factionalization and local self-interest. Warfare among them was common, and they were known to make alliances with Christian rulers against other Muslim princes.

TALMUD: The bodies of literature discussing, elaborating, and commenting on the Mishnah. The Babylonian Talmud was the product of the Babylonian rabbinic academies (the main academies were in Sura and Pumbedita), while the Jerusalem Talmud came out of the Palestinian academies in the Galilee. Both bodies of literature are based on the thematic orders of the Mishnah. The Babylonian Talmud, which is considerably larger and more elaborate than the Palestinian Talmud, includes legal debates (*halakhah*) as well as narrative traditions, ethical and moral teaching, legends about the rabbis and biblical figures, and homilies (*aggada*). While local traditions emerged in individual Jewish communities, the Babylonian Talmud was the foundation of European Jewish life and practice by the twelfth century.

TANAKH: An acronym for the books in the Hebrew Bible: Torah, or the five books of Moses—Genesis, Exodus, Leviticus, Numbers, and Deuteronomy—that contain biblical law; Nevi'im, or prophets, and Ketuvim, writings.

YESHIVA (PL. YESHIVOT): An academy of rabbinic learning. During the middle ages *yeshivot* formed around individual teachers and interpreters of Torah and Talmud as well as around groups of teachers. Students were known to travel great distances to study with important rabbis at their *yeshivot*.